RELIGIOUS LIFE FOR OUR WORLD

RELIGIOUS LIFE FOR OUR WORLD

Creating Communities of Hope

MARIA CIMPERMAN, RSCJ

ORBIS BOOKS

Maryknoll, New York 10545

ORBIS BOOKS
Maryknoll, New York 10545

Fathers and Brothers
MARYKNOLL

Third Printing, July 2021

Founded in 1970, Orbis Books endeavors to publish works that enlighten the mind, nourish the spirit, and challenge the conscience. The publishing arm of the Maryknoll Fathers and Brothers, Orbis seeks to explore the global dimensions of the Christian faith and mission, to invite dialogue with diverse cultures and religious traditions, and to serve the cause of reconciliation and peace. The books published reflect the views of their authors and do not represent the official position of the Maryknoll Society. To learn more about Orbis Books, please visit our website at www.orbisbooks.com.

Library of Congress Cataloging-in-Publication Data

Names: Cimperman, Maria, author.
Title: Religious life for today's world : creating global communities of
     hope / Maria Cimperman, RSCJ.
Description: Maryknoll, NY : Orbis Books, [2020] | Includes bibliographical
     references and index. | Summary: "A valuable theological and pastoral
     resource for the conversion, transformation and revitalization needed in
     consecrated life today"—Provided by publisher.
Identifiers: LCCN 2020002334 (print) | LCCN 2020002335 (ebook) |
     ISBN 9781626983809 (trade paperback) | ISBN 9781608338443 (ebook)
Subjects: LCSH: Catholic Church--Clergy—Religious life. | Monastic and
     religious life.
Classification: LCC BX2385 .C48 2020 (print) | LCC BX2385 (ebook) |
     DDC 255—dc23
LC record available at https://lccn.loc.gov/2020002334
LC ebook record available at https://lccn.loc.gov/2020002335

To all the women and men in consecrated life around the globe

who in manifold ways pray, build community,

and minister at the peripheries.

Thank you for your witness to Love in action!

CONTENTS

Part Two
Mission, Love, and the Vowed Life

Acknowledgments

A book on religious life can be written only amid that wonderful combination of prayer, community, and ministry. Throughout this process I felt God's Spirit accompanying the pondering and writing. It has been a sacred space and time. Gratitude abounds for the spaces of solitude for writing, for community of all kinds, and for invitations to share and engage with conversation partners around the globe.

The conversations on religious life have been countless over the years, and I cannot possibly thank all those who helped bring this book to completion. Still, I begin with a few thanks for the accompaniment of many.

Aware of the pitfalls of saying something from one context that may not be relevant or even helpful in another, I have been consistently encouraged to write and to allow my sisters and brothers to decide what is helpful or not. For this I am particularly grateful to the wonderful women and men at the Institute for Consecrated Life in Asia (ICLA) in the Philippines, and the Association of Women Religious Leaders of Korea, who encouraged me to write this book. For calling and trusting me, *Salamat po! Kamsahamnida!*

I am grateful for our learning community at Catholic Theological Union (CTU). Whether in a classroom, faculty seminar, over coffee or a meal, I am always enriched and inspired by the mutual sharing and learning. Thank you!

Invitations from near and far to engage with newer members, leaders of congregations and institutes, and congregations both local and international have been graced spaces for learning, offering, and deepening in consecrated life as it continues to evolve and call us forth.

I am grateful for being called forth over the years by groups whose mission is to engage various facets of consecrated life, including the National Religious Vocation Conference, Leadership Conference of Women Religious, Giving Voice, and Religious Formation Conference (RFC). Opportunities in the past few years allowed me to probe many of the topics presented in this book. For the gift of such engagement, I particularly thank Maryknoll Mission Institute, UISG Formation Programme, Association of Women Religious Leaders of Korea, and ForMission program of RFC, ICLA, and Australian Conference of Leaders of Religious Institutes in New South Wales. Encounters among you moved many ideas here to completion. Thank you also for your commitment to consecrated life!

One of my earliest invitations, almost two decades ago, was to participate in a gathering of twelve women religious theologians held in Leuven, Belgium, sponsored by the Suenens Center (John Carroll University) and headed by Doris

Donnelly. The symposium was titled "Religious Life in the Postmodern World." It was there that I found myself, the youngest and newest member present, still in PhD studies, called to offer a contribution from my theologian lens and experience. From the women gathered there, I learned more deeply and widely what it means to be a woman religious and a theologian. I am particularly indebted to the challenging and encouraging conversations there with Margaret Brennan, IHM, and Sandra Schneiders, IHM.

Samuel Canilang, CM, a colleague and friend at ICLA, continues to challenge and teach me much by his example of scholarship and lived experience. Pat Murray, IBVM, an encouraging friend, colleague, and mentor, continually helps me see beyond what I can see.

Writing requires space, time, solitude, and community—all in different forms. For spaces to write, particular gratitude goes to the wonderful hospitality of the Sisters of St. Mary of Oregon, Susan Hickman, Feely family, and RSCJ at Encounter Point. I'm grateful to my Sacred Heart sisters in our Chicago local community and beyond who over the years offered support through conversation, prayer, and wondering alongside me. To the sisters at Oakwood and Albany who prayed this writing to completion, thank you!

Friends are a great gift and those who find in "the life" a compelling way to offer the whole of their lives and who passionately engage in depths of conversation on religious life, are a great treasure. I want to particularly thank Kristin Matthes, SNDdeN, Marcelle Stos, SSND, Katherine Feely, SND, Vicki Wuolle, CSA, Xiomara Méndez-Hernández, OP, Mary Sharon Riley, RC, Lisa Buscher, RSCJ, Annmarie Sanders, IHM, Mary Charlotte Chandler, RSCJ, Mary Bernstein, RSCJ, and Mely Vasquez, RSCJ. The sharing of our lives is an incarnation of God's love. To the many who engage in the conversations that matter when we have the opportunity for discussion, thank you!

For encouragement and staying in touch via emails, calls, and presence in the midst of writing, I want to especially mention Katie Klaus, IHM, Connie Schoen, OP, Charlene Herinckx, SSMO, Juliana Monti, SSMO, John Therese Miller, SSMO, and Ellen Dauwer, SC. I am very grateful for the editing expertise of Susan Hickman. For the love and friendship of my family, particularly Joe, Nora, Maeve, and Samuel, thank you!

Finally, I am grateful for the incredible community at Orbis Books! It is a privilege to work with you, one and all! I especially wish to thank Jill Brennan O'Brien, PhD, the editor for this book. You are gracious, insightful, and skilled, and this is a better book because of your wisdom.

My hope and prayer is that this offering contributes to the ongoing journey of consecrated life to respond to God's call in our world today. May our depth of sharing, discerning, and responding continue and grow ever more fully and deeply.

INTRODUCTION

In This Time of Grace

Thank you for opening this book and beginning a conversation on religious life and consecrated life.

This is an amazing time in religious life and in the world. Our context is that of massive shifting, including dying and rising to new life. It is a markedly paschal time. This is the case not only for religious life, since education, politics, economics, the environment, technology, social media, civil discourse, and a myriad of other areas are also navigating an era of massive uncertainty and transition.

In 2015, Pope Francis opened a Year of Consecrated Life, calling us to "Wake Up the World!" He announced this year on November 29, 2014, at a meeting with the Union of Superiors General.[1] He called us to "be witnesses of a different way of doing things, of acting, of living! It is possible to live differently in this world. We are speaking of an eschatological outlook, of the values of the Kingdom incarnated here, on this earth." In order to wake up the world, however, we in consecrated life must also wake up. Pope Francis gives us some direction for this, calling us again and again to live in a prophetic way that comes from a deep encounter and relationship with God. The pope at the same time entrusts us to look at our contexts to see what is being called for at this time.

In speaking of formation and how we are to respond to young people, Pope Francis acknowledges that we are in a new time, even saying that "we are living through an epochal change."[2] He spoke of many areas in consecrated life, from formation to leadership to relationships with bishops and more, where change and even transformation are needed. In this is an invitation to new life, though not without cost. Birthing new life is a painful, messy, and joyful transformation process.

---

[1]   Union of Superiors General (USG) is a forum for male leaders of religious orders to reflect on issues facing religious life today. The cited document is found at https://w2.vatican.va.

[2]   Antonio Spadaro, SJ, "'Wake Up the World!' Conversation with Pope Francis about the Religious Life," *La Civiltà Cattolica* (2014) I, 3–17, trans. Donald Maldari, SJ (revised, January 6, 2015), https://onlineministries.creighton.edu. The meeting with the members of Union of Superiors General (USG) occurred on November 29, 2013.

This is good news, for while there is massive shifting, there is much that is budding as well. Something is emerging that we cannot yet see, though more and more I meet people who sense this movement. Some places in the world of religious life are experiencing growth, and there is need for formation resources and other supports for religious. Other places in the world are experiencing a decline in numbers of religious as well as an increase of ministries that have a long history, which are now in the capable hands of partners in mission.

Yet the call to consecrated life is much deeper, inviting a conversion that will help us continue to participate in God's mission. We are asked for openness to personal and communal transformation. The Year of Consecrated Life in 2015 invited religious to look with gratitude upon the past, to live the present with zeal, and to look forward to the future by being joyful and brave men and women of communion.[3]

Consecrated life is being asked to look at its structures in order to see what is still helpful and what needs to change for the sake of mission. In November 2017, the Congregation for Institutes of Consecrated Life and Societies of Apostolic Life (CICLSAL) issued guidelines titled *New Wine in New Wineskins* to further encourage religious to the conversion, transformation, and revitalization needed for our time and our futuring.

The hope and goal of this little book on religious life is to provide a framework for analysis and reflection toward transformation. Personal conversion is needed in order to respond to the Spirit. Communal transformation is required if congregations are to make the changes needed to respond to the cries of this time through the gift of charism. External revitalization is also needed if we are to respond to the church and world today. We do all of this through spiritual, theological, pastoral, experiential, and practical lenses.

Title and Audiences

I offer a few words about the title, *Religious Life for Our World: Creating Communities of Hope*. Although neither I nor anyone else can speak to religious life in the *entire* twenty-first century, we live this life in and for this time. The context is intentionally present, and not simply for the next few years. The vision of religious life is to be expansive even as the details evolve in living in and responding to the times. Just as religious life has a storied history, this title presumes religious life will be part of this entire century—and beyond.

Though the changes in some places will be significant and costly, there is no indication that God is closing the chapter on religious life. Too much is in motion calling us to renewal and revitalization. There is no guarantee that each congregation will continue beyond this epoch, but it is certain that the Spirit is still calling people to religious life. We cannot know exactly what religious life will look like in

---

[3]   Pope Francis, Message for the Opening of the Year of Consecrated Life, November 30, 2014, https://w2.vatican.va.

the future. Religious life and consecrated life will continue and evolve, though the details will vary according to present congregations and those yet to come.

I use the term *religious life* in the title because it is a term accessible to many. I am aware, though, that *religious life* is a subheading under *consecrated life*. I speak to religious life and consecrated life similarly, though the terms are distinct. *Consecrated life* "refers to several ways of life in the Church, all of which presume a special dedication to God marked by the attempt to conform oneself to the life of Jesus Christ."[4] Within consecrated life, one way of life is religious life. In *religious life*, women and men "express their dedication through the profession of the public vows of poverty, chastity, and obedience within a canonically established religious institute. The charism and spirituality of each institute and the needs of its apostolate determine its particular practices regarding community, prayer, and ministry."[5] Many of the topics I discuss in this book have relevance to other areas of consecrated life. Ministry and prayer, while lived differently in different religious orders or movements, are key elements in every order and movement.[6]

Religious life as I discuss it here is *for* the twenty-first century. The call is to contribute to this time in which we live. The term "for" focuses us outward even as the revitalization will be both internal and external.

Creating speaks to engaging the religious imagination in religious life, in the church and in our world today. Creativity is a characteristic of the Spirit.

Creating Communities of Hope

Joan Chittister, OSB, famously said some years ago that this was not the time for prophetic individuals, but for prophetic communities. While the individual prophet must be acknowledged and encouraged, religious life is asking us to create *communities* of hope. The antidote for the challenges of this time must include persons and groups building inclusion rather than exclusion.

Hope is a transcendent virtue, pointing us to God and God's vision. Hope is also a communal virtue, for we hope together. Communities of hope create conditions for persons and communities to thrive. Hope connects us to the past and present, for we bring with us all those who have lived religious life before us. Hope, far from being a fantasy, is rooted in the real—yet it sees the vision of the Reign of God and works toward it. Communities of hope, in religious life and beyond, serve as a transformative witness of God's in-breaking in this time.

---

[4] This helpful definition is found in Mary Johnson, SNDdeN, Patricia Wittberg, SC, and Mary L. Gautier, eds., *New Generations of Catholic Sisters: The Challenge of Diversity* (Cambridge: Oxford University Press, 2014), 32.

[5] Ibid. In addition, it is to be noted that some congregations have four vows. Two examples are the Ursuline Sisters of Cleveland and the Sisters of Mercy.

[6] Contemplative orders would say that their prayer for the world is part of their ministry.

For Our World

Creating communities of hope for our world is not only for international congregations. Each of us is called to create communities of hope. We may be monastics living in the same place our entire religious lives, congregations connected to a city or region or country, or congregations with members in many countries. Each person and each community has something significant to contribute. Connecting these people and communities helps us offer what is required and builds a wider communion as witness in our divided, wounded world, hungering for belonging. As we create such communities of hope, we link our efforts together with others to the ends of the earth. We link with one another in religious life, but even more we are called to connect *all* persons and communities. When we are so linked, no one falls in the cracks. Everyone belongs. All is in God. All are in relationship in our common home. Our call to create communities of hope includes all people—not only "the poor," the marginalized, and the oppressed—because we are part of the whole, and thus we recognize that our individual selves are connected to every other self and to our planet. Even the fact that a book can be written with the title *Religious Life for Our World: Creating Communities of Hope* speaks to the shifting that has already begun in religious life.

I have written this book because I believe that when we engage in conversations of consequence and depth about religious life, the life moves. Intentional, reflective conversations reveal the roots of our call and give us the courage to go deeper in our response to God, to one another, and to all of creation.

This book is written for many readers: anyone interested in the transformation of religious life; women and men religious interested in delving into areas of revitalization in religious life today; persons serving in leadership; persons in various stages of formation and for those walking with them; and persons in partnership with religious, who wish to live out their calls as associates or colleagues/partners in mission.

My personal context is that of a North American woman religious (born in Slovenia) who is Caucasian, lives in an international community, and is part of an international congregation, Religious of the Sacred Heart of Jesus. I am a theologian, and I teach at Catholic Theological Union (CTU), a graduate school of theology and ministry in Chicago with an international student body and faculty. I am the director of CTU's Center for the Study of Consecrated Life (CSCL), created to engage contemporary issues in consecrated life today. Over the course of more than twenty-five years in religious life I have had the privilege of dialoguing with and learning from women and men religious on six continents. I have offered presentations on four continents, and it was these most recent experiences, together with my years of teaching courses on religious life, that have encouraged me and finally galvanized the writing of this book.

All can be one at the table, with our diverse gifts creating the emerging consecrated life. One of the calls of religious life is to peacebuilding and reconciliation.

We are called to offer space even for those who are missing so that we may build communities of hope on both a global and local scale.

Overview and Structure of the Book

Part One: Contexts, Call, Charism, and Contemplation

Chapter 1 considers some local and global snapshots of religious life today in light of the cries we hear.[7] These are simply meant to be broad strokes and starter images. Within each continent and country are many details that are not possible to encapsulate in this project. I instead offer some basic statistics from the Vatican's *Annuariam*[8] and some "state of the question" observations. I provide some broad observations about realities and questions concerning sisters, brothers, and religious priests, as well as five points of concern and movement in religious life in broad regional areas.

There are three parts to this chapter. I begin with a look at some of the calls from the world, listening to the cries of the people and the cries of the earth. These are not comprehensive but indicative of realities that God is seeing and that we must see as well, with heart, mind, and will. Second, as religious life is part of the heart of the church, I also look at the calls from the church in our time. Third, I look at the context of consecrated/religious life today. In all three sections, the call for interior conversion, internal transformation, and external revitalization is clear and inviting.

Chapter 2 looks at call and charism. Call begins with God, who longs for us and for relationship with us. This first call at some point brings us to Christian community, rooted in baptism. The call to consecrated life is a call within a call, beckoning us to a particular community whose way of lived discipleship attracts us. Within the larger charism of consecrated life, there is a charismatic attraction that brings us to one congregation rather than another. Living our Christian baptismal call is within the call to consecrated life, connected to both the charism of religious life and to a particular charism within religious life. I will delve into the role of the Spirit and of charism as a gift of the Spirit from which religious life flows. A renewed look at charism helps us see more clearly and deeply our participation in God's mission.

Chapter 3 explores how our religious life vocation can be sustained only through a life of prayer in relationship with God. While we have many names for our way of prayer (meditation, contemplation, faith reflection, and so on), in each of these God draws us to friendship and union. Religious life is, in essence, a call to contemplation. We will see in this call the oneness of the commandments of the

---

[7] The format of this book came from a fall 2017 lecture series I was invited to offer at Catholic Theological Union.

[8] The *Annuarium Statisticum Ecclesiae 2017*, published by the Vatican Press on June 3, 2019, https://press.vatican.va.

love of God and the love of neighbor. A religious life vocation is thus also a call to relationship.

I will particularly look at contemplation through the lenses of (1) missionary discipleship and Jesus's prayer and ministry, (2) mystical prophetic life. and (3) radical prophetic hope.

Part Two: Mission, Love, and the Vowed Life

Chapter 4 connects God's call to the cries of the world and discusses how the vows are to be lived in light of charisms. The vows are to be Good News for us, for one another, and for all the people of God and all of God's creation. The vows also have particular meanings in particular times, framed and reframed, with the essentials still intact.

In this chapter I briefly: (1) set the evangelical counsels in a historical context, (2) frame the vows as virtues, and (3) set the vows within the context of mission and charism. We will see how each of the vows must be lived out in prayer, community, and ministry. The vows have personal, communal, and congregational dimensions. I conclude with twelve keys to considering the vows.

Chapter 5 begins with a brief historical overview of the terms that often get bounced around with celibacy. I look at how consecrated celibacy is to be Good News for us, for those around us, particularly the most vulnerable, and for all God's creation. We approach consecrated celibacy as an invitation to love God and receive God's love, and through this primary Love to love others and all of God's gifts. Consecrated celibacy cannot be sustained without intimacy, so I look at elements of intimacy to be cultivated in religious life. We will see the gift of friendship as part of God's invitation to experience and grow in love.

The vow of celibacy also helps us go to vulnerable places—our own and that of others. It can be the space of healing. Because we come to vulnerable places we must be attentive to how we live this vow. A healthy human sexuality is crucial.

Chapter 6 focuses on community. There are so many ways in which the deepening of our love for others gets lived out in community (ad intra and ad extra). Community is a door we have to go through with our own self-knowledge, and a door through which we have to let others in. Community is also a destination because we are called to create and build community, within and outside of our own living situations and even congregations. We do this through our charism and in response to particular needs around us. In this chapter I look at some biblical foundations of community and then move to contemporary calls in building intercultural communities, gender justice, racial justice, and the role of religious brothers. I consider how both conflict and friendship offer opportunities for building community, locally and on a global scale.

Chapter 7 explores poverty as both an invitation and a challenging reality in the world today, asking how our vow of poverty is to be Good News for all the people of God. I begin with some contemporary challenges to living poverty and then move to a brief look at scripture, history, and virtue regarding how one might consider poverty today. The vow of poverty is to be a witness to the freedom of the people of God, the abundance that is possible. Religious life and the vow of poverty call us to a closeness to those who are poor. I offer some ways in which the vow of poverty lives in our prayer, community life, and ministry. The living of this vow flows, as do all the vows, into prayer, ministry, and community.

Chapter 8 reminds us that obedience is about deep listening that then moves one to action. I briefly look at the evolution of this vow and some of its challenges over the years, and I consider what the post-Resurrection narratives might offer toward an understanding of obedience. Foundational to obedience is radical dependence on God. A stance of openness that flows out of relationship with God moves one to *disponibilidad* (radical availability). Radical openness and availability pertain to personal as well as communal discernment. In the latter part of the chapter I look at leadership and authority as well as the abuse of power.

In Chapter 9, I consider ministry and what these times ask of us in ministry. Looking around the world, the needs can seem endless. Our call is to discern, through the lens of our charism, the cries around us. From there, the who, what, where, when, and how of ministry emerge. We are not called to do this alone. The call is to work together. Reading the signs of the times is essential; we do this together as well as personally, sensing where the call is. We also do so with Gospel light, with freedom and our creative religious imagination that sheds further light for each next step.

This chapter looks at four areas of great need, with examples of where religious are at the peripheries and where they are being called to engage further.

Finally, Chapter 10 explores the ways in which charism asks us to look more deeply and widely at the call of our collaborators or partners in mission. The call is to see what the Spirit is calling us to now—together. The invitation is to widen our work within the charism of religious life and to continue to work together on common cause projects. The invitation is also to encourage all the members of our charism families to participate more fully and for all to participate from wherever the compelling initiative emerges. This is a transformation whereby religious families are all changed by the calls of the Spirit. It will also mean that all will be present at the table of participation and discernment. This requires a new attitude, and perhaps a new virtue: *participatory solidarity*.

Throughout this book I invite readers to the conversations we must have if religious life is to continue living its mystical, prophetic call today. Each chapter includes questions for reflection and discussion.

Part One

Contexts, Call, Charism, and Contemplation

1

WAKE UP THE WORLD!

Religious life is continually being called. We know the way as we walk together, open-heartedly responsive to the convergence of cries and calls.

In 2014 Pope Francis asked consecrated life to "wake up the world," to witness to the world that there is another way of being, acting, and living: a prophetic way of life. In order to wake up the world, religious need to be awake to the joys and cries of the world around us and to God's call. Where we stand, what we see, and how we listen all matter. Context matters. A prophetic way calls because when we look at the world we will not only see incredible love, goodness, beauty, and generosity, we will also see people and the earth suffering needlessly, begging for a response. We are called to respond.

The Catholic social tradition reminds us to read the signs of the times. Religious life today, along with the whole church, sees life in God intimately and intricately connected to a life concerned for the world. Religious orders are born in response to God's call and in response to a particular context. Consecrated life can continue to live and evolve only in particular local and global contexts. The Holy Spirit's gift of charism to each congregation serves not only as a founding impulse but continually moves a congregation to respond to the calls and cries of God in the world. Love of God and love of neighbor link our responses as the Spirit's work in us continues.

This chapter (1) names five cries and calls of the world around us and three cries within the church, (2) examines some key realities of apostolic religious/consecrated life today, and (3) offers three movements necessary for religious life to continue to respond to the Spirit's call to wake up the world today.

Cries from the World around Us

I name here five cries that have a global resonance, not limited to any one region and often part of multiple regions: (1) violence, (2) migration, (3) poverty, (4) earth sustainability, and (5) hunger for meaning and belonging—a "holy longing"[1] in the words of Ron Rolheiser, OMI. Each cry is linked to other cries.

---

[1]   Ronald Rolheiser, *The Holy Longing: The Search for a Christian Spirituality* (New York: Doubleday, 1999).

In *Laudato Si'*, Pope Francis made it very clear that the cries of the people and the cries of the earth are interconnected: "We are not faced with two separate crises, one environmental and the other social, but rather one complex crisis which is both social and environmental."[2] Because the cries are interconnected, we can all find some connection and shape a response. Again, this is not an exhaustive account but points to some key global cries.

Violence

Suffering created by violence cries out all over the world. Abuse, particularly against women, whether by an intimate partner, an acquaintance, or a stranger, is pandemic. The #MeToo movement has grown across continents, and women are speaking up and out, particularly to power.

The United Nations continues to highlight the number of women and girls affected by sexual and physical violence, child marriage, and female genital mutilation.[3] As UN reports remind us, "The numbers are shocking: at least one in three women on the planet has suffered physical or sexual violence, usually at the hands of a family member or intimate partner. More than 700 million women alive today were married as children. Up to 250 million women and girls have undergone female genital mutilation."[4]

The interconnection of the cries is found in this poignant description:

> We recognize that violence against women and girls is a complex phenomenon deeply embedded in unequal power relations between men and women, and persistent social norms, practices and behaviours that discriminate against women at home, in the workplace, and in society at large. Several factors can further heighten the risk of women and girls facing violence, such as their ethnicity, religion, age, income, immigrant status, disability, and sexual orientation. Those who are most vulnerable to violence are very often those whose lives are under threat in other ways, through poverty or lack of access to healthcare or education.[5]

---

[2]   Pope Francis, *Laudato Si' (On Care for Our Common Home)* (2015), 139, http://w2.vatican.va. Hereinafter referred to as *LS*.

[3]   See "The Spotlight Initiative: Eliminating Violence & Harmful Practices against Women & Girls," written by Natalia Kanem, Phumzile Mlambo-Ngcuka, and Achim Steiner, United Nations (Inter Press Service news agency, June 6, 2018), http://www.ipsnews.net. Natalia Kanem is UN Under-Secretary-General and Executive Director, UN Population Fund; Phumzile Mlambo-Ngcuka is UN Under-Secretary-General and Executive Director, UN Women; and Achim Steiner is Administrator, UN Development Programme.

[4]   Ibid.

[5]   Ibid.

The forms of violence are numerous and multifaceted. Rape is employed as a weapon of war. Human trafficking, particularly of women and children, is a global, multi-billion-dollar industry. Bullying, in person or on social media, continues. The same is true for gun violence, whether in schools, workplaces, on the streets, inflicted on others, or self-inflicted. According to the Centers for Disease Control and Prevention (CDC), in 2017 the United States had more deaths from firearms (39,773) than in the past fifty years. Of those, nearly two-thirds were suicides.

Armed conflict from a variety of sources continues to ravage countries and local communities that are already vulnerable, from Syria to Honduras and to Yemen and the Democratic Republic of Congo and beyond. Violence is on the city streets of Port-au-Prince, Haiti, as well as parts of Chicago's South Side. Gang violence in El Salvador and cartels in Mexico are the impetus for the extremes to which parents will go to keep their children safe. Every day mothers and fathers are risking their own lives and the lives of their children as they employ any means possible to enter the United States, hoping for the opportunity for a new life. Extremist violence continues: ideological, religious, and political. Too often we hear horrific accounts of violence in the Philippines, Myanmar, India, the United States, New Zealand, and elsewhere, and our responses continue to be sorrow, thoughts and prayers, and ineffectual murmurs of "never again," without sufficient practical responses.[6] Our Christian tradition reminds us that we lament because we hope—and hope requires deeper responses.[7] While Steven Pinker argued in 2011 that we are much less violent than we once were,[8] in many places there is still too much killing. The Catholic tradition does not end its concern when the numbers decrease, but only when violence ends. The people whose lives are affected and threatened by violence cry out for the violence to end. Violence prevention and peacebuilding are crucial needs.

The call to wake up the world includes us. In March 2019, Sr. Norma Pimentel, MJ, speaking to thousands at the Los Angeles Religious Education Congress, declared: "It's time that we wake up," explaining that this means recognizing one's responsibility to

---

[6] Jacinda Ardern, current prime minister of New Zealand, is an exception to this. In response to the Christchurch mosque terrorist attack of March 2019, which killed fifty people and injured fifty more, she led her government to ban the type of assault weapons that were used. See Barbara Campbell, "New Zealand Banning Weapons Like Those Used in Mosque Attacks in Christchurch," NPR, March 20, 2019; and Matthew S. Schwartz, "New Zealand Passes Law Banning Most Semi-Automatic Weapons," NPR, April 10, 2019; both at www.npr.org.

[7] I will describe and reflect about the hope needed in later sections of this book.

[8] Steven Pinker, *The Better Angels of Our Nature: Why Violence Has Declined* (New York: Viking Press, 2011). Some have criticized who Pinker is including when he refers to "Our Nature." See, for example, the Frequently Asked Questions section of Pinker's website and Elizabeth Kolbert's review in the *New York Times*, which Pinker references, both at https://stevenpinker.com.

go and do something, be a voice to those things we see that are wrong and be a voice and act and help others who are close to me to do that as well. It's not okay to just complain, it's not okay to just be silent, it's not okay to just be afraid. We have to put all that aside.

She noted that she is witness on a daily basis to the suffering of the people who walk into the center she runs, suffering that she says is "being caused by governments who do not put a stop to criminals destroying the lives of families and destroying innocent victims."[9]

We are all called.

Migration

According to the United Nations High Commissioner for Refugees (UNHCR), by the end of 2017 there were more than 68.5 million persons across the globe forcibly displaced because of persecution, conflict, or generalized violence. This is an increase of 2.9 million from 2016, making 2017 another record high.[10]

The UNHCR further documents that of the 68.5 million displaced persons, 16.2 million were newly displaced in 2017 (11.8 million within the borders of their own countries and 4.4 million newly displaced refugees and new asylum-seekers). This is equivalent to an average of 44,400 being forced to flee their homes each day in 2017. Fifty-two percent of the total refugee population in 2017 were children under the age of eighteen. There were 3.1 million persons awaiting a decision on their applications for asylum, about half of these in developing regions, and 1.7 million new claims were submitted with the largest numbers submitted to the United States (331,700), Germany (198,300), Italy (126,500), and Turkey (126,100). Five million displaced persons returned to their areas or countries of origin, including 4.2 million internally displaced persons and 667,400 refugees.

In looking at where refugees are coming from, UNHCR states that in 2017 "more than two-thirds (68 percent) of all refugees worldwide came from just five countries: Syrian Arab Republic (6.3 million), Afghanistan (2.6 million), South Sudan (2.4 million), Myanmar (1.2 million), Somalia (986,400)."[11]

Important to note here is that "developing regions hosted 85 percent of the world's refugees under UNHCR's mandate, about 16.9 million people. The least developed countries provided asylum to a growing proportion, amounting to one-third of the global total (6.7 million refugees.)."[12] This asks countries that do not have great economic or other resources to bear a vastly disproportionate burden.

---

[9] Elise Harris, "America's Most Prominent Nun Says Women Should Seize the Moment," *Crux*, March 26, 2019, https://cruxnow.com.

[10] United Nations High Commissioner for Refugees, Global Trends: Forced Displacement in 2017, https://www.unhcr.org.

[11] Ibid.

[12] Ibid.

Bangladesh, for example, accepted 655,500 refugees from Myanmar (predominantly the Rohingya people), most of whom arrived within a 100-day period. It is clear that the international community is needed to support countries who are hosting, accepting, and integrating persons in need.

Migration is a global phenomenon, though not a new one. Elizabeth W. Collier and Charles R. Strain of Catholic Relief Services write:

> At the latest count, 244 million people reside in a nation in which they were not born. While some are concerned about the level of migration to the United States, the reality is that while the United States is host to the largest number of foreign-born people (46.6 million), numerous other countries have welcomed a greater percentage of immigrants relative to their overall population (e.g., Canada's 22 percent to the United States' 15.2 percent).[13]

Many are economic migrants, those who move to another country to find employment when there are insufficient opportunities in one's own country, and many economic migrants send remittances to their families. The International Organization for Migration (IOM) reports:

> Remittances continue to climb globally while remittance-sending costs remain relatively high. The sum of financial remittances sent by international migrants back to their families in origin countries amounted to an estimated $581 billion in 2015—over three-quarters of which were sent to low and middle income economies. Remittance transfer costs are particularly high in Sub-Saharan Africa—now standing at 9.5% on average.[14]

Climate change migrants, persons who migrate because of extreme conditions in their home countries due to extreme weather events and natural disasters, are another group. According to the IOM such migrants are classified as follows.

- "Environmental migrants are defined as 'persons or groups of persons who, predominantly for reasons of sudden or progressive change in the environment that adversely affects their lives or living conditions, are obliged to leave their habitual homes, or choose to do so, either temporarily or permanently, and who move either within their country or abroad' (IOM, 2011:33 in IOM, 2014:13)."[15]

---

[13] Elizabeth W. Collier and Charles R. Strain with Catholic Relief Services, *Global Migration: What's Happening, Why and a Just Response* (Winona, MN: Anselm Academic, 2017), 8. The statistics are from UNHCR, "Global Trends," 2015.

[14] International Organization for Migration, "Global Migration Trends Factsheet" (for 2015), https://gmdac.iom.int.

[15] IOM's Glossary on Migration, Environment and Climate Change: Evidence for Policy (MECLEP), 2014, https://migrationdataportal.org.

- "Environmentally displaced person refers to 'persons who are displaced within their country of habitual residence or who have crossed an international border and for whom environmental degradation, deterioration or destruction is a major cause of their displacement, although not necessarily the sole one. This term is used as a less controversial alternative to environmental refugee or climate refugee [in the case of those displaced across an international border] that have no legal basis or raison d'être in international law, to refer to a category of environmental migrants whose movement is of a clearly forced nature' (IOM, 2011:34 in IOM, 2014:13)."[16]

Whatever the circumstances of migration, we need to be aware of the link between forced migration and human trafficking. Men, women, and children are made vulnerable to human trafficking by the mass displacements caused by violence, extreme poverty, humanitarian crises, natural disasters, and conflict.

Refugees, migrants, and asylum seekers are looking for life in the face of death. No continent can be excluded from receiving people, even as there is a need to address the systemic realities in the countries people are leaving. The challenge is not to build walls but opportunities—new opportunities for people to find life in their home countries or the opportunity to be welcomed as sisters and brothers in a new country. The Gospels remind us that our God is extravagantly generous, desirous of building friendships and communion. Solidarity, justice, and hospitality are needed, and consecrated life must contribute to this effort.

Poverty

The World Bank defines persons as living in "extreme poverty" if they live on less than the equivalent of $1.90 USD per day. About 35 percent of the world's population (1.8 billion) lived in extreme poverty in 1990. It is good news that today the number of people living in extreme poverty worldwide has decreased to about 10 percent. While all regions have made progress, the most significant was in the East Asian region, which recorded an extreme poverty rate of just 3.5 percent in 2013, a dramatic fall driven largely by China. In South Asia extreme poverty also fell sharply, to a third of its 1990 level (from 45 percent to 15 percent). But even with substantial progress, considerable challenges remain. Despite a decline in the extreme poverty rate in Sub-Saharan Africa, to 41 percent, the region's population growth means that 389 million people lived on less than $1.90 a day in 2013, 113 million more than in 1990. Sub-Saharan Africa now accounts for half the world's extreme poor.[17] While there is some good news here, the number of persons living in extreme poverty and poverty is still staggering. These are our neighbors. Pope Francis considers all the people of God our neighbors and reminds us that we are called to do so as well.

---

16   Ibid.
17   The World Bank, "SDG Atlas 2017: No Poverty," http://datatopics.worldbank.org.

The impact of poverty has particularly deadly effects on children.[18] The United Nations Children's Fund (UNICEF) reports that every day 18,000 children under age five die from hunger and diseases related to poor nutrition. Bread for the World reports that the child mortality rate is 13 times higher in low-income countries than high-income countries. Six million children under age five die each year, and half of those deaths are attributed to undernutrition. Approximately 165 million children in our world younger than five years old are stunted because of chronic malnutrition, which also causes brain damage.

The United States Census Bureau showed an increase in median household income in 2017: "The real median income of households maintained by non-Hispanic Whites ($68,145) and Hispanics ($50,486) increased 2.6 percent and 3.7 percent, respectively, between 2016 and 2017. This is the third annual increase in median household income for these two groups. Among the race groups, households maintained by Asians had the highest median income in 2017: $81,331." The bureau also notes that in 2017, there were 39.7 million people in the United States living in poverty.[19]

Everywhere in the world, including the United States, poverty remains an issue for far too many persons. The inequalities intertwined with poverty speak to the structural injustices that must be countered along with a deeper connection with our brothers and sisters so that all have what is needed for a life of human dignity.

Violence and migration are linked to poverty. Around the world we find youth who leave their home countries because of lack of employment, underemployment, or lack of access to skills for employment. Corruption continues to burden the hard working, many of whom struggle for even subsistence living. Lack of access to basic necessities is a critical factor. Lack of access to food results in hunger and malnutrition. Lack of access to education, particularly for girls, who often are among the least educated, minimizes or eliminates opportunities for jobs and entrepreneurial possibilities. Access to basic health care, particularly in the areas of prevention, immunization, and prenatal care is essential; poverty contributes to many illnesses, both in the short and the long term. The need for access to mental health care is being recognized in ever more countries, and poverty limits or makes access to care impossible for many.

Human dignity requires that we respond to the cries of those who are living in poverty and on the margins. According to the Ellis Island Foundation, between 1880 and 1930, 27 million people migrated to the United States in order to

---

[18]   The data that follows is collected from the Social Justice Resource Center April 2019 newsletter. https://socialjusticeresourcecenter.org.

[19]   The document that contains this information is: Kayla Fontenot, Jessica Semega, and Melissa Kollar, *Income and Poverty in the United States: 2017*, United States Census Bureau, September 12, 2018, https://www.census.gov. The data in it is found in *How the US Census Measures Poverty, US Census Bureau; Income, Poverty, and Health Insurance Coverage in the United States: 2016, US Census Bureau* (p. 17). See https://povertyusa.org for a breakdown by such factors as age, gender, and ethnic group.

leave poverty or persecution.[20] What did they find when they arrived? For some, a welcome with many opportunities, and for others, a mentality of scarcity and resulting perceptions that migrants are a threat. To this day, a theology of abundance is needed in the midst of such an appalling lack of basic resources for so many.

Earth Sustainability

The Earth itself is crying out. Water, soil, and air, which keep humans alive, are being despoiled and polluted. The Earth is God's creation, in which we are called to live with respect and care. As we acknowledge that all is interconnected, we realize that every facet of creation that is thriving or struggling is also our own thriving and struggling. We have begun to address significant areas of what Pope Francis reminds us is our common home,[21] but much more must be done. We will look at various important ecological and planetary issues throughout the book, but as a way to simply begin to see the calls and challenges, I focus here on some realities connected to water.

In the United States, although we know so much more now about toxins and pollutants, often, as is the case in Flint, Michigan, it took too long for the people crying out to be taken seriously about the brown water they were supposed to drink.[22] The efforts to find the truth had to be sustained and outside groups had to intervene with data before the responsible parties in the city, state, health care system, and construction industry would finally recognize that children and adults were exposed to dangerous levels of lead and other toxins in the water they were drinking.

Potable water is a limited resource, and droughts in various parts of the world cry out that water is a human right, not a commodity to be sold. Gary L. Chamberlain's book *Because Water Is Life* brings to the fore many of the implications that go with water challenges of all kinds, from privatization of water to the impacts of mining and fracking on water, the earth, and people.[23]

The United Nations 2019 World Water Development report, *Leaving No One Behind*, describes how "improvements in water resources management and access to water supply and sanitation services are essential to addressing various social and economic inequities, such that 'no one is left behind' when it comes to enjoying the multiple benefits and opportunities that water provides." The report states:

---

[20]   Immigration Timeline, The Statue of Liberty—Ellis Island Foundation, Inc., www.libertyellisfoundation.org. I am grateful to Collier and Strain's *Global Migration: What's Happening, Why, and a Just Response* for this reference.

[21]   See *LS*.

[22]   CNN, Flint Water Crisis: Fast Facts, CNN Library (December 6, 2018), https://www.cnn.com.

[23]   Gary L. Chamberlain, *Because Water Is Life: Catholic Social Teaching Confronts Earth's Water Crises* (Winona, MN: Anselm Academic, 2018).

Water use has been increasing worldwide by about 1% per year since the 1980s, driven by a combination of population growth, socio-economic development and changing consumption patterns. Global water demand is expected to continue increasing at a similar rate until 2050, accounting for an increase of 20 to 30% above the current level of water use, mainly due to rising demand in the industrial and domestic sectors. Over 2 billion people live in countries experiencing high water stress, and about 4 billion people experience severe water scarcity during at least one month of the year. Stress levels will continue to increase as demand for water grows and the effects of climate change intensify.

The report also notes that "safe drinking water and sanitation are recognized as basic human rights, as they are indispensable to sustaining healthy livelihoods and fundamental in maintaining the dignity of all human beings," and points out that

International human rights law obliges states to work towards achieving universal access to water and sanitation for all, without discrimination, while prioritizing those most in need. Fulfilment of the human rights to water and sanitation requires that the services be available, physically accessible, equitably affordable, safe and culturally acceptable. "Leaving no one behind" is at the heart of the commitment of the 2030 Agenda for Sustainable Development, which aims to allow all people in all countries to benefit from socio-economic development and to achieve the full realization of human rights.[24]

Stating that access to potable water is a human right is a hopeful sign that international efforts can change access. We know that those on the margins struggle disproportionately. Indigenous peoples, whose connection to the earth is deeply relational yet whose basic rights have been stripped in many countries, also struggle with access to basics.[25] Care for the earth includes care for those who still need these basics from the earth and its people.

Plastics, while making a positive difference in some areas such as medical equipment, are overwhelming our oceans and landfills.[26] And recycling cannot

---

[24]   United Nations, World Water Development Report 2019, "Leaving No One Behind," March 28, 2019, http://www.unwater.org.

[25]   Ibid. The report states: "Indigenous peoples number about 370 million, accounting for about 5% of the global population. They are over-represented among the poor (15% of the total and one-third of the world's 900 million extremely poor rural people), the illiterate and the unemployed. Even in developed countries, indigenous peoples consistently lag behind the non-indigenous population in terms of most indicators of well-being, including access to water supply and sanitation services."

[26]   Speaking ahead of World Ocean Day (June 8, 2018), UN Secretary-General António Guterres spoke of the necessity of reducing all manner of marine pollution,

keep up if we do not increase efforts to reduce our consumption of disposable products. Consumerism plays a significant part in the increasing burden of waste in the world's water. The use of minerals (e.g., copper, gold, silver) in cell phones should make us think twice before listening to ads that tell us we should upgrade to the next level of phone. We also forget that violence is linked to resources.[27]

Caring for earth as our mother who cares for us in a relationship of a mutuality of respect is needed. An ecological conversion will require a deeply contemplative spirit to envision and move into different practices and structures. From the depths of our beings, the call of religious life has an offering to make in this area.

Hunger for Meaning and Belonging

People are longing for meaning and belonging. This longing for connection, to each other and to something beyond ourselves, intersects with all the areas I identify and discuss in this chapter. There is a deep thirst in our world today that goes to the very depths of identity. People are asking: Where do I belong? To whom do I belong? How do I belong? Am I an object or a subject in a relationship? While manifested differently in various regions, these challenging questions can be heard around the globe.

This longing is particularly found in youth and young adults, including the self-identified "nones" and the "spiritual but not religious." Pope Francis's recent post-synodal apostolic exhortation, *Christus Vivit*, is addressed to "young people and the entire people of God"[28] in response to the youths he listened to at the Synod on Young People. He is reaching out after listening, acknowledging the challenging realities of this time in the world as well as the challenges of crises in the Catholic Church. He frames meaning and belonging. He spends a good deal of his writing encouraging the gifts that young people bring and inviting them to bring their gifts ever more to the church and world. He is not only asking them to do more. Pope Francis is first and foremost inviting them to an encounter with Jesus. He made a similar invitation in 2013's *Evangelii Gaudium*. In response to the calls and cries of the world today, he invites and asks young people to

---

including plastics: "Eighty per cent of all pollution in the sea comes from land, including some 8 million tons of plastic waste each year. It chokes waterways, harms communities that depend on fishing and tourism, kills turtles and birds, whales and dolphins, and finds its way to the most remote areas of the planet and throughout the food chain on which we ultimately rely." See "Effort needed to reduce marine pollution" UN (June 7, 2018) http://www.ansamed.info.

27   Consider, for example, that some of the world's illicit diamond mine production also financed civil wars, torture, violent working conditions, and environmental degradation. See the documentary "Blood Diamonds," at https://topdocumentaryfilms.com. See also https://www.amnestyusa.org.

28   Pope Francis, Apostolic Exhortation *Christus Vivit,* March 25, 2019, http://w2.vatican.va.

offer their gifts both as members of the Catholic Church and the wider human community.

The longings for meaning and belonging are real, and religious traditions have the challenge of bringing spiritual resources forth in a way that is easily communicable and accessible to more people in all walks of life. Institutional structures will need to address this as well. There can be a tendency among some to think that those seeking meaning and belonging will always come to them. Not so. The call is to be among the people and respond to them in their realities. We must invite people and build community in the midst of the daily lives of the people of God. Outreach and welcoming are needed. New spaces will also need to be created.

These cries are coming from the secular world as well as from people who have been connected to religious traditions. In the United States, for example, the number of people who name themselves as "none of the above," or as unaffiliated, is growing. In 2017 the Pew Research Center reported that about 27 percent of US adults now identify as spiritual but not religious, which was up eight points from the previous year.[29] When a 2018 study asked the unaffiliated why they chose not to identify with a religion, the most common reason was that they question many religious teachings. Becka A. Alper's article in the "Pew Research Center Fact Tank" offers this further detail:

> Six-in-ten religiously unaffiliated Americans—adults who describe their religious identity as atheist, agnostic or "nothing in particular"—say the questioning of religious teachings is a very important reason for their lack of affiliation. The second-most-common reason is opposition to the positions taken by churches on social and political issues, cited by 49% of respondents (the survey asked about each of the six options separately). Smaller, but still substantial, shares say they dislike religious organizations (41%), don't believe in God (37%), consider religion irrelevant to them (36%) or dislike religious leaders (34%).[30]

In the next section I look at realities in the Catholic Church that call for a response, but clearly the sexual abuse scandal in the Catholic Church will continue to affect people who are seeking God but questioning institutions or institutional structures. In the final document of the Synod on Youth, the Vatican acknowledges that a substantial number of young people, for a variety of reasons, do not ask the church for anything because they do not see it as significant for their lives. Some even ask to be left alone, as they find the presence of the church a nuisance, even an irritant. There are serious and understandable reasons for this:

---

[29] Michael Lipka and Claire Gecewicz, "More Americans Now Say They're Spiritual But Not Religious," Pew Research Center, September 6, 2017, https://www.pewresearch.org.

[30] Becka A. Alper, "Why America's 'Nones' Don't Identify with a Religion," Pew Research Center Fact Tank, August 8, 2018, https://www.pewresearch.org.

sexual and financial scandals; a clergy ill-prepared to engage effectively with the sensitivities of young people; lack of care in homily preparation and the presentation of the word of God; the passive role assigned to young people within the Christian community; and the Church's difficulty in explaining its doctrine and ethical positions to contemporary society.[31]

What becomes clear is that people are thoughtfully engaging in their search, desiring a spirituality that connects to the situations and issues around them. People often simply choose to leave a tradition or institution if it lacks integrity, honesty, and humility. And the longing for spirituality continues but not necessarily within an institution. These are important realities.

The longing for belonging is a key area connected not only to religion but also to the human condition. Studies show that a sense of belonging is crucial for a person's health, happiness, and well-being.[32] Cries for connection, meaning, and belonging are everywhere in the wider society. People look to many different places to find their way.

One interesting example comes from care.coach, an online platform that was formed to create virtual connections for vulnerable persons. Consider the story of Bill Langlois, a retired machine operator who is home alone while his wife works.[33] An on-screen avatar in the form of a cat speaks to him, encourages him, and reminds him about the positives in his life, at times flashing pictures of happy occasions. Persons around the globe are watching him from the camera on his tablet and offering responses that come forth in slow, consistent robotic format. Bill, who lives in a low-income senior housing complex in Lowell, Massachusetts, knows this cat is computer created, yet he credits her with bringing him back to life: "I found something so reliable and someone so caring, and it's allowed me to go into my deep soul and remember how caring the Lord was. . . . She's brought my life back to life."[34] Although social media can of course cause a great deal of harm, this program has actually made interventions when some persons contemplated suicide. The successful application of this type of program challenges us to ask what is missing in our attempts at connecting today. The article offers an important observation: "There is also the reality that in our culture of increasing isolation, in which many of the traditional gathering spaces and social structures have disappeared, screens are filling a crucial void. Many who have enrolled in the avatar program and Element Care were failed by the humans around them or never had a community in the first place, and they became isolated," said Cely Rosario, the occupational therapist who

---

[31]   Final Document of the Fifteenth Ordinary General Assembly of the Synod of Bishops, 50, http://www.vatican.va.

[32]   See, for example, Marianna Pogosyan, PhD, "On Belonging: What Is Behind Our Psychological Need to Belong?" *Psychology Today*, April 11, 2017, https://www.psychologytoday.com.

[33]   As told in Nellie Bowles, "Human Contact as a Luxury Good," *New York Times*, March 24, 2019, www.nytimes.com.

[34]   Ibid.

frequently checks in on the participants. She added, "Poor communities have seen their social fabric fray the most."[35]

The number of people who are connected via the internet and social media is large, and yet a question remains about how people find belonging and connection. Again citing from *Christus Vivit* and the *Final Document of the Synod on Youth*, we see the complex realities:

> The digital environment is characteristic of the contemporary world. Broad swathes of humanity are immersed in it in an ordinary and continuous manner. It is no longer merely a question of "using" instruments of communication, but of living in a highly digitalized culture that has had a profound impact on ideas of time and space, on our self-understanding, our understanding of others and the world, and our ability to communicate, learn, be informed and enter into relationship with others.[36]

In many parts of the world, digital technology (in some form) is a reality. There are good things about some of the networks that abound. As Pope Francis notes, some of these offer

> an extraordinary opportunity for dialogue, encounter and exchange between persons, as well as access to information and knowledge. Moreover, the digital world is one of social and political engagement and active citizenship, and it can facilitate the circulation of independent information providing effective protection for the most vulnerable and publicizing violations of their rights. In many countries, the internet and social networks already represent a firmly established forum for reaching and involving young people, not least in pastoral initiatives and activities.[37]

As with all realities, however, technological realities should be considered in light of the Gospel's Good News. There are challenges that must be attended to in social media, as Pope Francis writes:

> It is not healthy to confuse communication with mere virtual contact. Indeed, "the digital environment is also one of loneliness, manipulation, exploitation and violence, even to the extreme case of the 'dark web'. Digital media can expose people to the risk of addiction, isolation and gradual loss of contact with concrete reality, blocking the development of authentic interpersonal relationships. New forms of violence are spreading

---

[35] Ibid.

[36] Final Document of the Fifteenth Ordinary General Assembly of the Synod of Bishops, 21. Also in *Christus Vivit*, 86.

[37] Final Document of the Fifteenth Ordinary General Assembly of the Synod of Bishops, 22; Also in *Christus Vivit*, 87.

through social media, for example cyberbullying. The internet is also a channel for spreading pornography and the exploitation of persons for sexual purposes or through gambling."[38]

These realities are not unknown to young people or to many who utilize digital technology. This is evidenced by a touching quote from a document prepared by three hundred young people around the world before the Synod: "Online relationships can become inhuman. Digital spaces blind us to the vulnerability of another human being and prevent us from our own self-reflection. Problems like pornography distort a young person's perception of human sexuality. Technology used in this way creates a delusional parallel reality that ignores human dignity."[39] Pope Francis cites this and also the challenges of both "digital migration" and the new areas that young people must walk as "they must find ways to pass from virtual contact to good and healthy communication."[40]

In all of this we must walk together as church so that no one is alone. No one in the world. Consecrated life must see this as a yet unmet need calling us to do this together. Consecrated life, built on longing and encounter with God, has something essential to offer and much to learn in the midst of these realities and the cries they evoke.

Needs and Calls in the Roman Catholic Church

I briefly offer three calls and cries within the Catholic Church today. The Spirit is also calling consecrated life to respond to these internally and externally. They are not exhaustive, although each connects to other elements.

Catholic Church Abuse Crisis

The sexual abuse crisis continues to unfold around the world. Although some thought that sufficient protective structures were put in place after the 2001 revelations in Boston, the roots of the scandal continue to require humility, justice, and mercy.[41] Humility is necessary to name all the areas that contribute to the ongoing scandals, which are not limited to sexual abuse but also include finances and power. Abuse and violence are found across all traditions and institutions, including

---

[38]   *Christus Vivit*, 88. The part in quotations is also in the Final Document of the Fifteenth Ordinary General Assembly of the Synod of Bishops, 23.

[39]   Document of the Pre-Synodal Meeting in Preparation for the XV Ordinary General Assembly of the Synod of Bishops, Rome (March 24, 2018), I, 4.

[40]   *Christus Vivit*, 90.

[41]   See, for example, Brian Flanagan's challenging book, *Stumbling in Holiness: Sin and Sanctity in the Church* (Collegeville, MN: Liturgical Press, 2018), in which he reminds all that only a humble church can dialogue.

families. Yet we must continue to hear and acknowledge the cries of victims and survivors of various forms of abuse by some bishops, priests, religious, and laypersons in the church, and we must respond in ways that promote healing and demand prevention. The 2018 Synod Document strongly states:

> Abuse exists in various forms: the abuse of power, the abuse of conscience, sexual and financial abuse. Clearly, the ways of exercising authority that make all this possible have to be eradicated, and the irresponsibility and lack of transparency with which so many cases have been handled have to be challenged. The desire to dominate, lack of dialogue and transparency, forms of double life, spiritual emptiness, as well as psychological weaknesses, are the terrain on which corruption thrives.[42]

When the institutional church leaders forget that sin as well as grace is part of our human condition, hubris can build up and create the space for abuse and corruption. Young and old alike are asking for honesty and accountability. A response to these requests is imperative and no one is exempt from this responsibility, neither clergy nor laity. Until an honest, full account is given to the people of God, there will be mistrust of church ministers. Truth-telling is an essential first step in response to the cry to end the scandals. Justice, a covenant we owe one another, requires this. Mercy, a willingness to enter into the chaos of another's life, requires that we listen, listen, listen, to the narratives all around us. The listening must happen as long as the people need, and especially as needed by those wounded by the crimes and cover-ups. Healing and reconciliation require this. It will be onerous work, and it will take a long time. Yet much is possible once we enter the process.

Pope Francis points to an essential need for the church at this time that goes beneath the scandals to the attitudes that can create the atmosphere for scandal:

> Although many young people are happy to see a Church that is humble yet confident in her gifts and capable of offering fair and fraternal criticism, others want a Church that listens more, that does more than simply condemn the world. They do not want to see a Church that is silent and afraid to speak, but neither one that is always battling obsessively over two or three issues. To be credible to young people, there are times when she needs to regain her humility and simply listen, recognizing that what others have to say can provide some light to help her better understand the Gospel. A Church always on the defensive, which loses her humility and stops listening to others, which leaves no room for questions, loses her youth and turns into a museum. How, then, will she be able to respond to

---

[42]   Final Document of the Fifteenth Ordinary General Assembly of the Synod of Bishops, 40. Also in *Christus Vivit*, 98.

the dreams of young people? Even if she possesses the truth of the Gospel, this does not mean that she has completely understood it; rather, she is called to keep growing in her grasp of that inexhaustible treasure.[43]

Consecrated life must take ownership and responsibility for its sins, wounds, and efforts in this crisis. It must also look at its own practices of listening with openness and humility.

Greater Leadership and Responsibility from Lay Catholics

The call is clear that the baptismal commitments of all people are necessary. The need for greater mutuality, synodality, and processes that include rather than exclude is also clear. And an ecclesiology of communion is essential—this does not eliminate or sideline those ordained but brings all vocations forth. Greater collaboration reminds us all that our Christian call is that of faithfulness and service. At the Opening of the Fifteenth Synod of Bishops on October 5, 2018, Pope Francis reminded those present that all must resist the temptation to see "the ministry they have received as a power to be exercised, rather than a free and generous service to be offered. It makes us think that we belong to a group that has all the answers and no longer needs to listen or has anything to learn."[44] The costs of such thinking are high—the basic sacredness, dignity, and freedom of each person is lost.[45]

New structures and systems are needed, and there are enough models around that can assist with this. Sufficient formation for both clergy and laity is required. In addition, new language is needed so that the word "laity" is not simply a broad term to mean those not ordained.

Consecrated life in all its forms is also being asked to see itself in communion with all. While sisters and religious brothers are, canonically, laity, the religious life structures need to see that while each call is distinct, we are all missionary disciples working toward God's mission.

Listening and Participation

The voices of those on the margins of society and of the church must be actively sought. We hear often, from Pope Francis as well as others, that the participation of women is urgently needed. We are also beginning to listen to the voices of indigenous people too often silenced and colonized. The voices of persons most often silenced are in vulnerable situations due to economics, politics, culture, sexuality, geography, health, religion, or relationships. A Catholic Church that follows Jesus

---

[43]   Final Document of the Fifteenth Ordinary General Assembly of the Synod of Bishops, 41.

[44]   Final Document of the Fifteenth Ordinary General Assembly of the Synod of Bishops, 30. Also in *Christus Vivit*, 98.

[45]   *Christus Vivit*, 98.

must find itself in the midst of the people of God everywhere, employing new ways of listening and responding to the cries around us. A church that preaches love of the poor must seek out those on the margins and peripheries and ask for the privilege of listening. It is then that the people of God may together be able to respond to the movements of the Spirit.

Consecrated life, which has often responded to the persons on the margins, is again being asked to look at the cries today of the people and the earth, and to respond once again. This will require new energy and life to infuse the good work already happening, and very likely a letting-go in order to hear and respond to the voices still unheard by many.

The needs and cries are myriad. Much is being done, yet more is needed. Consecrated life, as part of the church, is also being urged to consider its realities interiorly, internally, and externally in order to respond by creating the communities of hope that are longed for locally and globally. In preparation for this, let us look briefly at some of the external realities in which consecrated life finds itself today.

Realities of Consecrated Life Today

Consecrated life, including apostolic religious life, is a response to a call from God into the particular realities of the time, and the Spirit offers the particular gifts or charisms to be lived in response to the calls of God and needs of creation. I go into more detail about call and charism in Chapter 2, but it is important to note both call and response as part of consecrated life today, no matter the form of consecrated life. As mentioned in the Introduction, the term "consecrated life" "refers to several ways of life in the Church, all of which presume a special dedication to God marked by attempting to conform oneself to the life of Jesus Christ."[46] The focus in this book is on religious life. In religious life men and women make public professions of the vows of chastity, poverty, and obedience within a canonical religious institute. The prayer, ministry, and community life are lived in accordance with each institute's particular charism, spirituality, and context.[47] All of these are living and evolving areas that require attentiveness and attunement.

Sometimes people see religious life only through the lens of ministry. Even the descriptions of contexts might give one the impression that religious life is only about ministry. That would be deeply wrong. All areas of religious life, while distinct, are interconnected. Prayer, community, and ministry each affect and are affected by contexts, calls, and lived expressions of the call to a religious institute. Thus, while ministerial and engaged in the world, religious life is not a nongovernmental organization (NGO) but a way of life that includes community, prayer, and

---

[46]   This helpful definition is found in Mary Johnson, SNDdeN, Patricia Wittberg, SC, and Mary L. Gautier, eds., *New Generations of Catholic Sisters: The Challenge of Diversity* (Cambridge: Oxford University Press, 2014), 32.

[47]   Ibid. In addition, as mentioned in the introduction, some congregations have four vows. Two examples are the Ursuline Sisters of Cleveland and the Sisters of Mercy.

ministry. What each looks like is determined by the needs, spirituality, and charism of a particular institute, which evolve over time. The essentials remain—prayer, ministry, and community are lived responsively to the ongoing calls of the Spirit.

Responses are personal as well as systemic. Religious also know that they can do nothing alone. With the Spirit's direction, religious are to work together and with all people of good will. This participation in responding to the calls is with an awareness of the interconnection with all of life. As Pope Francis reminds us, "Strategies for a solution demand an integrated approach to combating poverty, restoring dignity to the underprivileged, and at the same time protecting nature."[48] Just as Pope Francis is calling all to an integral ecology, realizing all is interconnected, women and men religious are called to a religious life that is fully integrated as well.

News of the declining numbers in religious life could make one think that religious life is dying, but that would be naïve. Globally, by the end of 2017 there were 648,910 women religious (nuns and sisters), down from 659,445 sisters the previous year; 51,535 religious brothers, down from 52,625 brothers; and 233,138 religious priests, a slight decrease from 2016.[49] Continentally, the numbers of religious in Europe and the Americas are decreasing; some institutes are now sending members to these continents for presence and service. In contrast, the number of religious professing vows in Africa continues to increase, though not at the same rate as a decade earlier. Asia also continues to have a slight increase in numbers.[50]

In the United States, there were 179,954 sisters in 1965; at the end of 2017 there were 45,605. In 1965 there were 12,271 brothers; in 2017 there were 4,007. In 1965 there were 22,797 religious order priests; in 2017 there were 11,424.[51] The movement of these demographics in religious life signals both changes and a kind of dying; this is not, however, an end to religious life. Some congregations will cease to exist in the next few decades, but others will continue as they respond to the calls of this time. All religious are called to evolve according to the calling of the signs of the times and the leading of the Spirit.

The diversity of newer members continues to be one of the ongoing gifts in religious life today. That religious life is found across all continents is a gift to be explored even as membership in particular places decreases numerically. A different vision is needed. Ministries in which religious have engaged for long periods of time are inviting examination to discern whether such ministries are still needed. More specifically, community life in areas where the numbers have changed must be examined with the goal of discerning the mission's direction for this time. Where

---

[48]   *LS* 139.

[49]   See the Center for the Applied Research of the Apostolate (CARA), https://cara. georgetown.edu. The *Annuarium Statisticum Ecclesiae*, upon which the world data above is based, is released two years after the most current year measured.

[50]   See Pontifical Yearbook 2019 *Annuarium Statisticum Ecclesiae* 2017 for further details (Stampa Ufficiale Romana, *Annuario Romano per l'anno 2019* and CARA).

[51]   See CARA.georgetown.edu.

there are spiritual families or groups of religious and married and single persons who share a common spirituality and charism, the needed communities, ministries, and prayers can be determined together.

A great transformation is being asked of religious life, but not without the lead and accompaniment of the Spirit. Religious must use their religious imagination, guided by the Spirit, to see beyond numbers. Religious life is being asked to connect more globally and is being given numerous opportunities for global connections. Agility, adaptability, openness, clear communication, collaboration, and a deep, contemplative, reflective spirit are essential.

Religious life is also being asked to respond to evolving charisms and the movements of the Spirit. To do so, religious must learn to adapt and to practice greater agility for the sake of the Reign of God. In order to move in these times in a way that reflects religious life *for* the twenty-first century and to create communities of hope on a global scale, religious must open themselves to three essential calls: interior conversion, internal or communal transformation, and external revitalization. I offer a brief explanation of each here; the rest of the book will further explore these areas.

Three Essential Calls for Religious Life

Interior Conversion

For some years there has been a realization that much is shifting in religious life and that each of us will be asked to shift, adapt, change, and live into a future that will not look the same as we see it now. This is true on every continent, though what this looks like differs according to context. What is needed? A conversion that only God can give us, and to which we must be open. I suggest we begin with these four areas: (1) openness to be led deeper in prayer, (2) learning and practicing discernment and moving toward communal discernment, (3) disposition (and practices) of radical availability (*disponibilidad*), and (4) listening to how our charisms are being called today so we may offer our lives where the needs and our gifts converge. I offer a few explanatory words about these here, though much more will be said in the chapters that follow.

The deep change that God is creating (evolving) requires our depths, where we are opened and formed into this time. While we are beginning to see some directions forward, we will need to sense from our depths, rather than simply from external signs, what God is asking of us. This is not magic but the slow, intentional process of making of our lives congruent with God's mission and vision.

The process of discernment asked of us is deeper than decision-making, for it will be transformative at its very core. Those who do this well will be asked to assist the wider church.[52] Pope Francis has asked that the church help young people

---

52   I think, perhaps, of the Sisters of the Cenacle, whose ministry has included discernment in the style of the Ignatian Spiritual Exercises. Certainly Ignatian discernment is very

with discernment.[53] He has also asked every seminary and school of theology to teach discernment. This is crucial learning. Knowing how to practice individual discernment brings us to communal discernment with some requisite skills and dispositions. Although religious life holds a stance of availability and desire to respond to God's calls, in moments of honesty we can acknowledge that parts of religious life right now are struggling with entropy, apathy, or lethargy. At times we are in a rut. Some storytellers remind us that a rut is just a shallow grave. In such times, people and groups tend to hold on to what is known more than staying open to what is calling. The call is to listen to how and what the Spirit is moving in our charism of religious life and in our particular charisms. Our identity will flow from this movement. The overarching call is to a radical availability, to our surrender to God's movements in our lives.

Internal/Communal Transformation

Realizing that God acts and that God asks our participation in the living of our call to God through a religious community, we look now at some areas needing internal transformation. Note that transformation is deeper than change. I can change but not be transformed. This is equally true for individuals, communities, and structures.

Four areas that need internal transformation in religious life today are (1) the quality of community life, (2) movement toward living interculturally, (3) structural changes in religious life, and (4) communal discernment. These will flow from our communal engagement of our charism amid the cries we hear.

In many congregations the quality of community life is challenged by circumstances. In some parts of the world, institutes are trying to adapt to many external changes, such as fewer sisters or brothers in local communities as elders move to retirement centers. In some places fewer people available for particular ministries means that the size of a local community or area decreases. In other parts of the world, there are more people in the formation process than persons who have completed initial formation. Congregations are trying to make external changes, but the internal growth of community living is not keeping up. The stresses in society also exist in religious life, and so there is unevenness in acknowledging or responding to these challenges. We are, at times, simultaneously grieving the increasing losses of our eldest members. We also find ourselves explaining why there are no more religious in a given parish, school, organization, or city. There are already a number of ministries carried out in collaboration with partners in mission.

---

important. I look at this further in Chapter 8 on obedience and communal discernment, and I suggest that there are other spiritual traditions that can and need to offer a way of discernment. This is not simply for religious life but also for the wider church and world.

[53]   See "Young People, the Faith and Vocational Discernment," Pre-Synodal Meeting Final Document, March 2018, http://www.synod.va.

The moment asks us what the creative Spirit and the cries around us are calling forth for the sake of God's mission going forward.

Determining what will be life-giving and life-generating for a community requires honest, revelatory conversations, lest we withdraw into our own individual pods of life. Our world is in need of living models of the Risen Christ's message of love, forgiveness, nonviolence, reconciliation, and dialogue. The call is to live not perfectly, but with authenticity and love.

In a world that struggles with the other who is not like us, religious life has the gift of many such "others" who are part of us. We still have work to do in this. The diversity of membership in our congregations and communities makes the call to creating intercultural community essential for religious life and the world. We are called to witness the Good News of all creation. This interculturality must be felt in our vowed life, including in prayer, in community, and in ministry.

In order to respond to the call of God in this time, a transformation of structures is needed for the sake of mission. Many congregations are discerning this or are already in this process. In November 2017 the Congregation for Institutes of Consecrated Life and Apostolic Life issued a document called *New Wine in New Wineskins: The Consecrated Life and Its Ongoing Challenges since Vatican II*. It is an honest, hopeful, and helpful document that urges congregations toward the transformation needed in this time, which is not only structural but interior as well.[54] Both leadership and membership must be involved.

Congregations often use a process of communal discernment in General Chapters. The call now is to use it for other significant decisions in the life of a community or congregation. Our evolving charism calls us forth in this. One challenge will be to give the necessary time to this effort. Another is that there is often a gap between desire and skill in this—people with expertise are needed. Internal transformation will serve not only religious life but also all those with whom we minister. There are groups outside religious life already doing some of these processes and we have much to learn from them.

External Revitalization

Perhaps most obvious to many religious is a call to listen and respond to what God is asking of us in our outreach. I mention four areas briefly: (1) ministry realignment, (2) proximity to the peripheries and margins according to our charisms, (3) widening charisms, and (4) collaboration across the charism of religious life and consecrated life. I develop these further in subsequent chapters.

Ministry is in flux. We are walking with Jesus among our current commitments and compelling calls to our charism. Some congregations serve in areas that are part

---

[54]   See Congregation for Institutes of Consecrated Life and Societies of Apostolic Life, *New Wine in New Wineskins: The Consecrated Life and Its Ongoing Challenges since Vatican II* (Guidelines), 2017.

of an emerging call to religious life. Revitalization here will include offering the needed education, training, and mentoring.

Our religious histories all include responding to unmet needs. It is where the charism given to our founders moved us. In some areas religious continue to be at the growing edges of need or in the centers of great challenge. The martyrs of each age attest to this. Some communities have ministries in places where they can influence those who have power, or they may have positions of influence themselves. The positions of influence are for the sake of the margins. This is a delicate and dangerous place to be, for it takes skill and centeredness in God's mission not to succumb to the real temptations of power, privilege, and wealth.

A critical question for religious life today is whether we are still at the margins and peripheries. Are our places of ministry where we are wanted, or are they where we are still needed? There is an old Maryknoll adage: "They came where they were needed but not wanted and stayed until they were wanted but not needed." External revitalization calls for responding to the needs of today that are not met and to which our charisms call us.

The widening of charisms speaks to the call to consider what colleagues, collaborators, and others living in the same charism family yet in different life commitments and calls, invite us to at this time. We speak easily enough of people ministering with us but there is still room for growth in terms of inviting our "family" to the tables of discussion and discernment in various areas of ministry. While different members have different roles, working together more in common cause could help create a beautiful tapestry, a weaving that could keep more people from falling into the cracks of despair, poverty, and unrealized potential. There is much unrealized potential to be invited and explored—and religious, and perhaps all people, will be revitalized as a result.

In some places we see the need but don't have the structural, financial, or personal resources to serve on our own. This is a great gift! It means we have to work with others, with all that this entails in terms of collaboration and mutuality.

The Call for Creativity in Religious Life

What are our God and this time asking of us? Everything. And our response is worth everything, for we want to follow God's desires for a world at peace, living justly and tenderly. The direction of this book will be to look both at the edges and from the edges. We will see religious life as yeast,[55] present where the Spirit asks us to serve, encouraging the life already there, and constantly being created in our prayer, community, and ministry. We are called to a particular mystical-prophetic witness in this time.[56] This is a call to each of us that has no age limit or end to its creativity. The vulnerability and incompleteness of religious life at this time is a gift, for it means we will need to continue together to look to God and to the calls for

---

55   Both Pope Francis and John Paul Lederach use the image of yeast.

56   This idea is developed in Chapter 3.

our direction. Ultimately this is a book about living our sacred Paschal time—the living, dying, and rising, wounds and all, with the Risen Christ. The Resurrection stories will accompany us.

Questions for Reflection and Discussion

1. What cries do you hear from the world?
2. What cries are calling in the church?
3. What is the reality of religious life in your region?
4. What is the reality of religious life in your congregation or institute?
5. What do you sense is the call to your congregation, community, or institute toward:
   a. Interior conversion?
   b. Internal/communal transformation?
   c. External revitalization?

2

CALL AND CHARISM

"Come, Holy Spirit"

The relationships among us and with others can be a clear expression of the charism, and they are a way of making it visible. The quality of our relationships reveals the presence of the love of God among us.

— Patricia Garcia de Quevedo, RSCJ
Feast of the Sacred Heart, 1996

In the Name of Love
Jennifer Corlett, OSU (sung with Mark Hobson)

Do you remember the call?
When did you hear your name out loud?
Can you remember the word that you heard
When the story began in you?
Listen, remember, catch glimpses of Springtime
And roots sinking deep in the heart of our God
And you were carried
Green and stretching to light
In the name of love.

Do you remember the call?
The call into full red rose of day?
Can you remember the vision, the dream
And the courage to love for life?
Listen, remember, catch glimpses of Summer
And all blossom gentleness radiant with light
And you were dancing

Full and given to life
In the name of love.

Do you remember the call?
And you letting go golden to grace
Trusting the journey and all it would be
Full of love and fidelity.
Listen remember catch glimpses of Autumn
Of all that's surrendered in wisdom and hope
For it is given
Full and yet to become
In the name of love.

Do you remember the call
Sung in the silent depths of you?
Know that its power is deep in your heart
As a fire, a song, a dream.
Listen, remember, catch glimpses of Winter
Touch new life in hiding and set it ablaze
And let it grow into fullness of life
In the name of love.[1]

Every story begins with a call. Each one of us has a personal story of God's call. Whether in a large crowd, in the quiet of one's room, or anywhere in between, each person hears a call, an invitation, to come and see, to come and follow in consecrated life. This call flows from our baptismal call that has already joined us to a community. The Trinity reminds us that our God is "essentially relationship,"[2] and we are invited into the relationship of the Trinity. God shows us, through the Son, Jesus, how to be community in the world around us, and the Spirit befriends us on this journey.

Even in community, the call is personal, from a God who deeply desires us, is passionately in love with us, longs for us, and is alluring us into the future. The gift of faith is that as we open ourselves, we too find ourselves longing for God. We thirst. As we thirst and find God in myriad ways in our lives we find that our thirst for God, rather than being satiated, only grows. This is Love. God's passion for us is found in every vocation. For some the thirst for God calls them to religious life, in one of myriad forms.

Sandra Schneiders's description speaks profoundly to the whole gift of self and permanence of religious life: "Religious life is a life, a total self-gift, all that I am,

---

[1]   "In the Name of Love," by Jennifer Corlett, OSU (sung with Rev. Mark Hobson), 1989. Used with permission. The music may be found by contacting Ursuline Sisters of Cleveland, 2600 Lander Road, Pepper Pike, Ohio 44124.

[2]   See the work of theologian Catherine Mowry LaCugna in *God for Us: Trinity & the Christian Life* (San Francisco: Harper, 1993).

with nothing held back, from the moment of my profession to my last breath."[3] The call is to the totality of our lives—not eight hours or even twelve hours a day. All of me, twenty-four hours a day, seven days a week. This life must be worth everything and all of me or it is not worth it. It IS worth ALL.

We live our call in a particular congregation or institute, yet the vow formula makes clear that our vows are to God and God alone. Canon law dictates that before someone professes perpetual vows the person must confirm that this permanent commitment is made with complete freedom. One must be free to love. It is also important that perpetual vows are public, in the midst of God's people, the *ekklesia*. Our commitments are the way religious participate in God's mission among the whole of God's people and creation. This journey, both for individuals and congregations, is ongoing to the last breath. Conversion, transformation, and revitalization are the continuous processes of our lives.

Holy Spirit

Speaking to the National Directors of the Pontifical Mission Societies, Pope Francis reminded them (and us) that "things must always be renewed: renew the heart, renew the works, renew the organizations, because otherwise, we would all end up in a museum."[4] Just as Pope Francis is calling the entire church to missionary renewal, he is also inviting the Pontifical Mission Societies to renewal. Each part affects the other parts. So too with consecrated life. As Francis notes, this was also Pope Benedict XV's message in his Apostolic Letter *Maximum illud*, "to evangelically renew the Church's mission in the world."[5]

What does such renewal mean? Note the dispositions and practices (virtues) involved and the role of the Holy Spirit emphasized by Pope Francis:

> This common goal can and must help the Pontifical Mission Societies to live a communion of spirit, reciprocal collaboration, and mutual support. If renewal is to be authentic, creative and effective, the reform of your Societies will consist of a re-foundation, a redevelopment according to the needs of the Gospel. It is not simply a matter of rethinking the motivations to do better what you already do. The missionary conversion of the structures of the Church (cf. Apostolic Exhortation *Evangelii Gaudium*, 27) requires personal holiness and spiritual creativity. So not only to renew the old but to

---

3   Sandra M. Schneiders, IHM, Giving Voice Conference, June 2002. Author's notes.

4   Pope Francis, Audience with the National Directors of the Pontifical Mission Societies, June 1, 2018. Found at: https://zenit.org. Pontifical Mission Societies, also known as Missio, is a group of Catholic missionary societies under the authority of the pope. Included in these organizations are the Society for the Propagation of the Faith, the Society of St. Peter the Apostle, the Holy Childhood Association, and Missionary Union of Priests and Religious.

5   Ibid.

allow the Holy Spirit to create the new. Not us: the Holy Spirit. Make room for the Holy Spirit, allow the Holy Spirit to create the new, make all things new. . . . Do not be afraid of the newness that comes from the Crucified and Risen Lord: these changes are beautiful. . . . Be bold and courageous in the mission, collaborating with the Holy Spirit, always in communion with Christ's Church. . . . And this boldness means going with courage, with the fervor of the first who proclaimed the Gospel. Your habitual book of prayer and meditation is the Acts of the Apostles. Go there to find inspiration. And the protagonist of that book is the Holy Spirit.[6]

What will renewal do for the mission societies? Build communion of spirit, reciprocal collaboration, and mutual support. To what will reform and renewal respond? To the needs of the Gospel *today*. What are markers of the process? Authenticity, creativity, and effectiveness. What is needed for persons to participate in this process? Personal holiness and spiritual creativity! What will happen if we do so? Beyond renewal the Spirit will be creating something new, through and with us. Is there a timeline? The Spirit will lead the timeline. Is this a Paschal journey? Yes. Birth, life, death, and resurrection are the Spirit's timeline.

Even as we remember the story that began in us, we are linked with the story that began all of this, God's story, and for Christians, the Risen Christ promising to send the Spirit. This is the Spirit that brought forth the church and consecrated life. The Spirit moves us to live the mission as we are being called today. It is the Holy Spirit that today continues to move and inspire religious life. We are being invited to renewal and to being re-created through interior conversion, internal transformation, and external revitalization. God is trying to create something new in religious life as well as in the church. The befriending, inviting, and challenging Spirit leads in the midst of life in this world. Religious life is a gift of the Spirit in each time, and the Spirit's gifts never atrophy but are continually evolving.

Let us first consider some signs of the Spirit.[7] Scholar Kirsteen Kim reminds us: "Biblically, the terms 'Holy Spirit' and 'Spirit of God' are ways of talking about God's presence and activity in the world."[8] The Holy Spirit is a messenger of Good News, although Good News is not always easy to hear and is usually challenging.

Four attributes of the Spirit are particularly relevant to this moment. The Spirit is (1) prophetic, (2) creative, creating, (3) focused in Jesus Christ, and (4) free. I offer a few words about each of these attributes, as they give a sense of where and how the Spirit is leading us.

---

[6]   Ibid.

[7]   I take sections about encounter from my presentation and subsequent publication at the Institute of Consecrated Life in Asia on January 20, 2018. See Maria Cimperman, RSCJ, "*Missio Spiritus*: Deepening and Widening Our Charisms for the Sake of the World," *Religious Life Asia* 20, no. 1 (January–March 2018): 21–48. (Used with permission.)

[8]   Kirsteen Kim, *The Holy Spirit in the World: A Global Conversation* (Maryknoll, NY: Orbis Books, 2007), 2.

The Spirit Is Prophetic

The Spirit enters into our humanity to name where we need to change, where we have lost our way. The Spirit comes at times of crisis and endows women and men with her prophetic spirit. Theologian Leonardo Boff reminds us:

> We see another great manifestation of the spirit in the prophets. These men and women are seized and driven by the Spirit. Their power is in the word that denounces the injustice perpetrated by the powerful on the weak and vulnerable. They attack unjust wages (Jeremiah 22:13), fraudulent business dealings (Amos 8:5, Hosea 12:8), the venality of judges (Micah 3:11, Isaiah 3:15, Amos 2:6–8 and 8:4–5), cruelty to debtors (Amos 2:8), economic exploitation (Isaiah 3:15, Amos 2:6–8 and 8:4–5), lives of ostentation and dissipation (Isaiah 3:16–23, Amos 6:5). They accuse kings of being bad shepherds (Ezekiel 34, Jeremiah 23:1–4).[9]

In her prophetic nature the Spirit not only names where we have lost our way; she shows us a new way. Again, Boff's words speak boldly of the prophetic nature of the Spirit: "They [prophets] also proclaim a new world, a new humanity and a new heart (Jeremiah 31:33–34), and a different spirit (Ezekiel 36:26). They comfort and encourage the people (all of Second Isaiah, Ezekiel 37), in order to strengthen their faith and hope (Sirach 49:10)."[10] This is today's call. The Spirit encourages us to fortify and also to galvanize. Boff continues:

> Prophets innovate; they seek to renew God's eternal covenant with God's people (Micah 6:1–8), and to transform a perverse reality with a right spirit and a new heart (Ezekiel 36:16–38). This is why prophets are always mixed up in politics: that is where injustice occurs and the needed transformations are possible.... Wherever crises leave the people stunned and disoriented, prophetic voices are raised to point out new paths and build courage and hope. This is where we see clearly the transforming energy of the Spirit.[11]

The Spirit Creates and Transforms

The Spirit is creative, innovating, and purifying. Images of Spirit in scripture include, among others, fire and water, "both in their constructive sense of peace and well-being, and also in the sense of purification, purging and destruction (e.g., Isa 30:27–28)."[12] The important work of Carmelite Constance FitzGerald, OCD,

---

9   Leonardo Boff, *Come, Holy Spirit: Inner Fire, Giver of Life, and Comforter of the Poor*, trans. Margaret Wilde (Maryknoll, NY: Orbis Books, 2015), 44.

10   Ibid., 44–45.

11   Ibid., 45.

12   Kim, *Holy Spirit*, 13–14.

speaks of a Spirit that transforms, first by helping us de-link or hold lightly both the gifts received and challenges and pains suffered, and then to leave contemplative space open for God's movements in our present.[13] Note the *creativity* that is the nature of Spirit; new creation is part of her very nature.

The prophetic nature of consecrated life to which Pope Francis and the Spirit call us is to witness to a new way of living, speaking, and doing. In this, our lives witness both what is contrary to the Spirit of God and what goodness is calling us to in all aspects of life around us. What we see and hear compels us, and so where we are matters.

For Christians, the Spirit Is Focused on Jesus Christ

Kim writes, "The Spirit comes in a new way in the New Testament and is sent from Jesus Christ as well as from God. In this respect, the Holy Spirit in the Christian Testament becomes clearly defined by the character, life and spirit of Christ."[14]

Our way is the way of Jesus Christ. We encounter Jesus who teaches us by his life—his relationships, ministry, suffering, death, and resurrection—about the Reign of God and our identity as God's beloved. The Spirit leads us toward living into the Reign of God in our time.

We participate as members of the church in this effort. We are reminded how to be church in "The Pastoral Constitution on the Church in the Modern World" (*Gaudium et Spes*): "The Church seeks but a solitary goal: to carry forward the work of Christ under the lead of the befriending Spirit. And Christ entered this world to give witness to the truth, to rescue and not to sit in judgment, to serve and not to be served."[15] In religious life, witnessing, loving, rescuing, and serving are components of all areas of our lives—ministry, prayer, and community. Yet the Spirit is not limited to our church and congregations.

The Spirit Is Free

The Spirit goes where the Spirit will. Spirit is not bound by any religious tradition but goes anywhere and everywhere. No one has a monopoly on the Spirit, and this, too, is great news! God's Spirit blows where the Spirit wills (Jn 3:8) and is given to Jew and Gentile (Acts 11:15–17), and none of the gifts of the Spirit are the exclusive possession of Christians.[16] Our call as Christians is to attune ourselves to the Spirit, to discern the Spirit calling us, and to follow the lead of the befriending Spirit in our own Christian and collaborative contexts.

---

[13]   Constance FitzGerald, OCD, "From Impasse to Prophetic Hope: Crisis of Memory," *CTSA Proceedings* 64 (2009): 21–42.

[14]   Kim, *Holy Spirit*, 20–21.

[15]   Vatican Council II, *Gaudium et Spes* (*The Constitution of the Church in the Modern World*) (1965), 3, http://www.vatican.va.

[16]   Kim, *Holy Spirit*, 20.

The Spirit is dynamic; she moves and flows without limit, pervading all. Looking back, for over two millennia we can see the Spirit's prophetic nature in various persons and groups. The *creativity* of the Spirit is found in the manifold ways that people have encountered God. Each baptism reminds us of the Spirit building the beloved community. When we see groups working across religious traditions for the good of all, the Spirit is at work. When a pope kisses the feet of the leaders of South Sudan in a plea for peace, the Spirit is at work.[17] With the Spirit we can go where the needs are. There is no place the Spirit cannot go, no person the Spirit cannot invite to encounter. No group holds the Spirit exclusively, so the creative possibilities are limitless, for peace and all manner of relationships and structures. And there is so much more!

This is the Spirit at work in our world, our Christian tradition, and our lives.

One of the gifts of the Spirit, which flows from its *prophetic, creative,* and *free* nature, *which is focused in Jesus Christ,* and from which consecrated life was created, is charism.

Charism

The Spirit is the source of all charisms. We begin with a few words about charism generally. Theologian Wilfrid Harrington, OP, explains:

> The Greek word *charisma* means free gift, favor. It is Paul who introduced the term into religious language: the word means a free gift of grace. To be more precise, it is a supernatural gift bestowed by the Holy Spirit for building up the body of Christ. A charism is a gift which has its source in the *charis*—grace or favor—of God and which is destined for "the common good" (1 Cor 12:7). This being so, charisms are many and are related to various services and functions.[18]

In considering St. Paul's treatment of charism, Harrington powerfully links love, service, and the common good. He reminds us that because "the characteristic of Christian life is (or ought to be) *agapē,* one would expect to find charisms in the service of love. . . . We may sum up the New Testament data as follows: because a charism is a gift of the Spirit for the building up of the church, it is always meant for the common good; it has upon it the stamp of service."[19]

Pope Francis has also noted: "All charisms are gifts that the Holy Spirit gives us. Gifts given not to remain hidden but to participate in them with others. They

---

17   Andrea Tornielli, "The Gesture of the Servant of the Servants of God," *Vatican News,* April 12, 2019, https://www.vaticannews.va.

18   Wilfrid Harrington, OP, "Charism," in *The New Dictionary of Theology,* ed. Joseph A. Komonchak, Mary Collins, and Dermot A. Lane (Wilmington, DE.: Michael Glazier, 1987), 180.

19   Harrington, 180.

are not given for the benefit of those who receive them but for the usefulness of the people of God." He continues, "If on the other hand, a charism serves to affirm oneself, it is doubtful whether this is an authentic charism or that it is faithfully lived. Charisms are special graces given to some to do good to many others."[20]

The gift of charism is not static; it doesn't appear one way and remain the same through time. If it is to build up the Christian community, this gift or service in love will take many forms, depending on our contexts and the calls and the cries around us. Creativity and adaptability flow through these gifts of the Spirit.

In speaking with religious from the Order of St. Camillus, Pope Francis encouraged them to remember that their charism of mercy toward the sick is a gift from the Holy Spirit, meant to be shared with others. He reminded them that "charisms always have a transitive character: they are orientated towards others. Over the years, you have made efforts to incarnate your charism faithfully, translating it into a multitude of apostolic works and in pastoral service to the benefit of suffering humanity throughout the world."[21] He also encouraged them to be open to new apostolates if the Spirit so leads them. The Spirit's prompting is key.

Listening to the Spirit calling through one's charism is not new. During the Second Vatican Council all religious institutes were asked to go more deeply into their foundations and their charisms. A few years later Pope Paul VI, in his Apostolic Exhortation *Evangelica Testificatio* on the ongoing renewal of religious life according to the teaching of Vatican Council II, continued to call on religious to delve into their charisms, stating that religious life "is the fruit of the Holy Spirit, who is always at work within the Church."[22]

We move now to considering the charism of religious life and that of particular congregations. Religious life and scripture scholar Sandra Schneiders, IHM, helpfully connects charism with charisms of religious life and then with particular charisms. Based on religious life as a gift of the Spirit to the church, she writes that religious life is the "single-minded quest for God to the exclusion of any other

---

20   Pope Francis remarks to the Camillian Family, Vatican, March 18, 2019, https:// aaog.blogspot.com. His reference to charism in his catechism talk at St. Peter's Square on November 6, 2013, is: "The Holy Spirit distributes to the faithful a multitude of spiritual gifts and graces; the 'imaginative' wealth, let us say, of gifts of the Holy Spirit is ordered to building up the Church. The charisms—that word is a little difficult—are gifts that the Holy Spirit gives us, talents, possibilities. . . . The charisms are special graces, given to some for the good of many others. They are attitudes, inspirations, and interior promptings that are born in the consciences and experiences of certain people, who are called to put themselves at the service of the community. In particular, these spiritual gifts further the sanctity of the Church and her mission. We are all called to respect them in ourselves and in others, to receive them as serving the Church's fruitful presence and work. St. Paul warns: 'Do not quench the Holy Spirit' (1 Thess 5:19). Let us not quench the Spirit who gives us these gifts, these abilities, these very beautiful virtues that make the Church grow." http://w2.vatican.va.

21   Pope Francis's remarks to the Camillian Family, Vatican, March 18, 2019.

22   Pope Paul VI, Apostolic Exhortation *Evangelica Testificatio* (1971), 11, http:// w2.vatican.va.

primary life commitment."[23] This means that the way religious life is lived must support this "single-minded quest for God." The way of life integrates this not only in prayer but also in ministry and in community. All must proclaim this fully embodied quest.

Within the charism of the different forms of religious life, there are also charisms of particular religious congregations or religious families. Particular charisms or gifts of the Spirit are given to various persons in time so they may respond to God and the cries around them. The Redemptorists' charism, for example, is preaching the good news of plentiful redemption: that Jesus loves us and knows us by name.[24] What this meant in 1749, when Alphonsus Maria de Liguori founded the Congregation of the Most Holy Redeemer, has evolved over the years and as the Redemptorists have served in eighty countries. Today one can see the great need for reconciliation in the world and can hear the Spirit calling Redemptorists through their charism to respond to that need. The Redemptorist website communicates that the call of their congregation is to constantly be available to mission: "The Redemptorist mission calls for different types of apostolic work in different settings and the Redemptorist Constitutions remind the missionaries that they are not to settle into structures that would prevent them from being truly missionary (Constitution 15). In this spirit, the Congregation has taken on many apostolates during its history."[25]

The reminder that mission, rather than structures, is the call is particularly appropriate to this time in which we live. Choices are to be for the sake of mission rather than for what we have always done. As congregations partner for mission with many others in common ministry, the charism may well live differently yet just as profoundly in an institution when a religious order no longer can serve in a particular place or field of endeavor due to other compelling calls or because there are no others available from the congregation. We are all being asked to engage our thinking and imagining with charism and collaboration as we widen our focus. Reminding ourselves that we are yeast, not the majority ingredient, is a humble and liberating truth if we are willing to hear it.

In some cases a spirituality emerges from a charism, helping people see how the gospel can be lived through this particular lens. Richard Gula describes Christian spirituality as "a way of discipleship involving a personal relationship with Jesus under the power of the Holy Spirit working in and through the community of believers to bring about a world marked by justice and peace."[26] The particular spiritualities of religious orders such as Benedictine, Ignatian, or Franciscan, for example, flow from their particular foundations, and then continue to develop as a

---

23   Sandra M. Schneiders, *Finding the Treasure: Locating Catholic Religious Life in a New Ecclesial and Cultural Context* (New York: Paulist Press, 2000), 303–4.

24   See website of Liguori Publications, a Redemptorist ministry: http://www.liguori.org.

25   Found on Redemptorist vocations website at http://www.redemptoristvocations.com.

26   Richard M Gula, *The Call to Holiness: Embracing a Fully Christian Life* (New York: Paulist Press, 2003), 21.

lived experience. In time the spirituality is articulated and engaged through popular and scholarly writing.

Persons find an attraction to a particular spirituality (e.g., Vincentian, Salesian, Carmelite) that invites a deeper experience and exploration with those who live this spirituality in their everyday lives. Sometimes this moves one to so identify with the attraction that one feels called to live the God-quest through this spiritual discipline in religious life. Something in the person's being resonates with the charism. Sometimes a person feels the call to live the gospel through this spirituality in other life callings. In addition, some find an attraction to the charism and spirituality and make ministry choices to be in places grounded in the spirituality (e.g., Holy Cross institutions, Mercy ministries) or even bring that spirituality to a ministry that does not name a particular spirituality. So much is possible!

An attraction to a particular religious congregation must at some level connect with a way of offering the whole of our lives. Charisms are not limited to any one ministry, though some institutes saw that a particular ministry (education, health care, social work) was at a particular moment the best way to offer their gifts to the world. A congregational charism will be gospel-based—some particular aspect of the gospel needed and heeded when the congregation was founded. The gift for the church and world, however, is lived in all aspects of one's religious life: prayer, community, and ministry. The Spirit's creativity knows no bounds.

Sometimes congregations identify with the gospel as a whole rather than a particular spirituality or even a charism. Schneiders describes the charisms of such particular ministerial congregations as "the deep narrative of the community which includes its own particular history and traditions, its myths and symbols, leaders and saints, struggles and triumphs, and spirituality, which give it its own unique identity among other congregations with which it shares the charism of ministerial Religious Life."[27] I would call this a description of the deep story of a particular congregation among other similarly named congregations. While the Dominican charism would be the same, what distinguishes each group of Dominican women and men would be how each would name their deep narrative.

Among religious orders there are often commonalities, in ministry, in general ways of living community, or in types of prayer. It is in looking at the totality—all the stories, histories, and current life—that one can see the unique personality of the different religious orders.

Sometimes we see the similarities even amid the distinctions. In my early years in the Religious of the Sacred Heart of Jesus, I was looking at some volunteer possibilities in San Diego. Immigration challenges and realities were of interest and I heard about the Casa Cornelia Law Center that provided pro bono legal services to victims of human and civil rights violations.[28] Upon further research I found that

---

[27]   Schneiders, *Finding the Treasure*, 300. I would not limit this to ministerial religious life but include all consecrated life.

[28]   The Casa Cornelia Law Center website is: http://www.casacornelia.org.

it was a ministry of the sisters in the Society of the Holy Child Jesus.[29] They are an international religious order founded by Cornelia Connelly in 1846. I was shocked, however, when I read that they too used the phrase that I had, until that moment, thought was distinctly Sacred Heart: "called to discover and reveal God's love!" It was fascinating to learn a little later that at various points in her journey Cornelia Connelly not only taught at a school of the Sacred Heart but at one point shared in the life of the RSCJ. This was my introduction to the intersection of the many characteristics and charisms in religious life, and I find even more today. This is a gift, for connecting across similar charisms can serve groups working together on common cause projects.

Among orders within the same family there is commonality and a distinctiveness. There are different congregations of Dominican and Franciscan women's orders, for example, but while there is a common Franciscan or Dominican spirituality, original founder, and charism, the congregations see their "deep story"[30] as distinct within their family tradition. Each congregation had distinct beginnings, ministries, and geographical locations. The narratives that helped form each group's identity are different. The struggles that helped shape the group are part of the identity of its present congregation.

Sometimes provinces within the same family come together to create a new province for the sake of mission. Or congregations with great commonality join groups together to create a new religious institute for the sake of the mission. The question has come forth in the past twenty years about whether, for the sake of mission, individual provinces and their cultures (deep stories/deep narratives) would be willing to come together. There is both loss and new life in this process. For some there are issues of identity. In the case of provinces joining, the focus of each particular province must be thanked and let go so that a new way, in response to the calls around them and the new common province vision, is to be lived for the sake of the gospel. For new life to emerge a dying must happen. Sometimes it is the newest members whose formation was already with other provinces who help create bridges. Sometimes joint projects, committees, and spiritual gatherings have already helped with bridge building and can help the rest move forward. In any case, it is certainly an experience of entering other cultures to create the new life that the Spirit is longing to create. I look at interculturality more in ensuing chapters. It is also the case that for some provinces or congregations to join together at this time for common projects is what is most possible and desirable at this moment in consecrated life.

In all of these configurations and movements, the essentials remain. What distinguishes and unites consecrated life is the gospel. Religious life scholar

---

[29] See their American province website at https://www.shcj.org.

[30] For more on deep story, see the work of Bernard J. Lee, SM, particularly *The Beating of Great Wings: A Worldly Spirituality for Active, Apostolic Communities*. (Mystic, CT: Twenty-Third Publications, 2004).

Samuel H. Canilang, CMF, exhorts us to "Always start from the Gospel," and goes on to remind us that "the particular charism of an Institute of Consecrated life is a concentration of the whole Gospel through a specific aspect of Jesus' life and ministry. In this way, the charism is a *living exegesis* of the Gospel. Hence, the Gospel is the Institute's fundamental and highest rule."[31]

Our gospel living of consecrated life is rooted in love and flows out of love. Schneiders wisely reminds us that

> the writings of founders and later leaders of virtually all Religious congregations make clear that the motivation for the foundation of these congregations and for entering them was always primarily and basically the desire of these women to give themselves wholly to God in and through service of Christ in the neighbor. In other words, *what is characteristic of this form of Religious Life is a powerful sense of the absolute oneness of the great commandments of love of God and love of neighbor—that these are not two but one command. Service of the neighbor is not simply the overflow, or even the expression, much less a substitute for, or in competition with, the love of God. It is the love of God in action.* The experiential, contemplative grasp of this truth is what gave rise to apostolic Religious Life and is what sustains it to this day.[32]

This is an important point, particularly for apostolic religious life. Often people outside religious life see what religious *do*. The relationship underneath the doing, which undergirds/underlines/underscores the doing and gives life to the community, can get lost. Doing good works, including in the name of God, is part of our call as Christians, but one does not need to be in religious life to do good works. Catholic Worker communities, Sant'Egidio, Society of St. Vincent de Paul, and many other groups, along with faith-based and non-faith-based NGOs,[33] do good works. The call to religious life is first and foremost a call rooted in a relationship with God.

This interconnected way of life, one that includes all of creation as our neighbor, is the lens from which we see, love, and live. It is integral consecrated life, lived according to the ever-evolving charism that calls us to new frontiers of gospel calls as we hear the cries of the people and the cries of the earth. The Spirit— prophetic, creative, focused in Jesus, and free—calls us to an interior conversion, internal/communal transformation, and external revitalization. Our charisms, gifts

---

[31]   Samuel H. Canilang, CMF, *Wake Up the World: Religious Life as a Prophetic Presence in the Church and in the World*, ICLA Monographs no. 16, 44). He cites *Perfectae Caritatis*, 2, which states: "The ultimate norm of religious life is the following of Christ set forth in the Gospels."

[32]   Schneiders, "The Charism of Religious Life," Part I: Religious Formation Conference, 11; emphasis added.

[33]   NGOs are nonprofit and nongovernment organizations.

of the Spirit who knows no limits, are dynamic, and the Spirit is constantly communicating with us in our specific realities about where and how to offer these gifts. The Spirit is quite practical!

The Spirit Is Not Static

It is essential to realize that the Spirit's gift or charism to a religious institute is not static; it doesn't show up one way and need to remain the same through time. If it is to build up the Christian community, this gift or service in love will take many forms, depending on our contexts and the calls around us. Charism also evolves in response to the ways the gift is needed, so the iteration will adapt to the needs. In this way our understanding of charism also evolves.

A wonderful example comes from a congregation that recently held its general chapter. The Medical Mission Sisters congregation knew its charism to be healing in the manner of Jesus of Nazareth. For many decades the ministry of many in the congregation was of medical or psychological healing. This was their participation in the Gospel and Jesus's healing ministry. Over the years an awareness of the needs of the physical earth moved the group to see the Spirit's invitation to their charism calling them to participate in God's healing of earth. Since their Chapter they have begun integrating care for the earth in their ministries of healing among the people. In many places they are also learning from the people who are connected to the land as they are responding to the Spirit's lead. New ministries, ways of prayer, and ways of living in community with the earth are emerging. Yes, the Spirit is quite practical, even if often beyond our initial imaginings!

What is possible with the Spirit? Everything, including joy! Throughout these pages we will look at what the Spirit is inviting us to as prophetic, creative, focused on Jesus Christ, and free. In his 2018 Pentecost address, Pope Francis reminded us that the Spirit both changes hearts and changes situations.

As we look at different topics and areas of religious life we will ask whether we are heeding this Spirit.

Come Holy Spirit, Come!

Questions for Reflection and Discussion

1. In one sentence: What is your charism?
2. What is the Spirit, who enters into critical moments with prophecy, creativity, and freedom, asking of your charism today?
3. How is your charism reflected in your prayer? In your community life? In ministry?
4. What must awaken us if we are to awaken the world?

3

Friendship with God

Encounters and Peripheries

God created us out of love and for love. Jesus invites us to ongoing encounter. Spirit is our companion in building/creating community everywhere. All three persons of the Trinity equally call the whole of our religious congregations for the sake of sharing God's mission with all. In this time of dramatic change, enormous need, and great possibility, three particular calls open us up to necessary interior conversion, internal transformation, and external revitalization.

What are these calls of the befriending Spirit? Where is the Spirit leading us more deeply? Three areas of call invite us personally and communally. We are called to (1) missionary discipleship, (2) mystical-prophetic life, and (3) radical prophetic hope. If we say yes to these calls, we and our congregations open ourselves to conversion, transformation, and revitalization.

Called to Be Missionary Disciples

All baptized persons are called to be missionary disciples. In his apostolic exhortation *Evangelii Gaudium*, Pope Francis states this clearly:

In virtue of their baptism, all the members of the People of God have become missionary disciples (cf. Mt 28:19). All the baptized, whatever their position in the Church or their level of instruction in the faith, are agents of evangelization, and it would be insufficient to envisage a plan of evangelization to be carried out by professionals while the rest of the faithful would simply be passive recipients. The new evangelization calls for personal involvement on the part of each of the baptized. Every Christian is challenged, here and now, to be actively engaged in evangelization; indeed, anyone who has truly experienced God's saving love does not need much time or lengthy training to go out and proclaim that love. Every Christian is a missionary to the extent that he or she has encountered the love of God in Christ Jesus: we no longer say that we are "disciples" and "missionaries," but rather that we are always "missionary disciples."[1]

Where does consecrated life fit into this? Francis writes that "the Church is herself a missionary disciple; she needs to grow in her interpretation of the revealed word and her understanding of truth."[2] The same is true for persons in consecrated life, for we also need to grow in understanding of the gospel and the truth calling us through our charisms. How might we do so?

While Pope Francis has made the phrase "missionary disciple" a key in our lexicon, the term has deep biblical roots, particularly in the Gospels and in the New Testament. The biblical roots of the two words help us understand our call as members of consecrated life. Missionary discipleship is an invitation to encounter and an invitation to inclusivity, responsibility, and community. Missionary discipleship calls us to proclaim the Reign of God, which is marked by justice, peace, and joy. We are called to be disciples and then sent out to proclaim the good news to all and participate in the mission of the Reign of God. Let us look at this more closely.

Discipleship is an invitation *to encounter*.[3] The new life calling consecrated life today happens when we, again and again, open ourselves to encounter with Jesus Christ. Our deepest longings, which God longs to fill, open us to the transformation needed for this time. We hear, with the psalmists, "deep calls to deep in the torrent at the thunder of your cataracts; all your billows and waves have gone over me."[4] The call is to the interior life, to be opened more deeply and widely. Pope Francis offers an essential call: "I invite all Christians, everywhere, at this very moment, to a renewed personal encounter with Jesus Christ, or at least an openness to letting him encounter them."[5] An encounter is the foundation of each of our vocations, and we know that relationships require continual encounters of depth. Silent listening and depth of conversation are both crucial to knowing our God. It is our call again and again and again.

---

[1]   Pope Francis, *Evangelii Gaudium* (*The Joy of the Gospel*), 20, http://w2.vatican.va. Hereinafter *EG*.

[2]   *EG* 40.

[3]   I take sections about encounter from my presentation and subsequent publication at the Institute of Consecrated Life in Asia on January 20, 2018. See Maria Cimperman, RSCJ, "*Missio Spiritus*: Deepening and Widening Our Charisms for the Sake of the World," *Religious Life Asia* 20, no. 1 (January–March 2018): 21–48. (Used with permission.)

[4]   Psalm 42:7. A cataract is a large waterfall.

[5]   *EG* 2, 3. Pope Francis writes of the encounter after naming one of the big challenges of our time: "The great danger in today's world, pervaded as it is by consumerism, is the desolation and anguish born of a complacent yet covetous heart, the feverish pursuit of frivolous pleasures, and a blunted conscience. Whenever our interior life becomes caught up in its own interests and concerns, there is no longer room for others, no place for the poor. God's voice is no longer heard, the quiet joy of his love is no longer felt, and the desire to do good fades. . . . That is no way to live a dignified and fulfilled life; it is not God's will for us, nor is it the life in the Spirit which has its source in the heart of the risen Christ" (*EG* 2).

As it is in scripture, it is Jesus who calls us. Scripture scholar vanThanh Nguyen, SVD, reminds us that the term "disciple" comes from the Greek word *mathētēs*, which is defined as "one who learns," and comes from the verb *manthanō*, "to learn."[6] In Latin, "disciple" comes from the word *discipulus*, meaning, "pupil, student, follower," and from the verb *discere*, which means "to learn." There is clear evidence here that Jesus calls people to follow him, to be his disciples. Nguyen notes that the term "disciple" is found 257 times in the New Testament.

An important reality of Jesus's call is that it was, and is, inclusive. Unlike the Rabbinic Judaism of his time, Jesus called women as well as men to be his disciples. Nguyen notes that Jesus's radical inclusivity extended to those on the margins who were otherwise considered unacceptable. He writes, "There is definitely an inclusive feature in Jesus' call that is quite radical, extending not only to female disciples but also to those who are normally considered unclean, for example, 'tax collectors and sinners' (Mk 2:15)."[7] Quoting from Hans Weder, Nguyen notes, "The gospels provide enough evidence to support that 'Jesus called people into fellowship regardless of social, religious, and ethnic background or gender.'"[8] Furthermore, Nguyen reminds us that Jesus did not just gather them to be around him but to send them out as apostles or missionaries to preach about the arrival of the Reign of God (Mk 3:13–15; 6:7–13).[9] Jesus's call to us is personal and inclusive, reminding us that he longs for each of us, for *all* persons. This is a message we are to carry in all the manifestations of our lives.

Jesus's life, words, and ministry show us all the dimensions of love. He knew himself as the beloved of God and he offered the same love to all. Everything in Jesus's life and death revolved around his message of love. As John the Gospel writer tells us, *"For God so loved the world that he gave his only Son, so that everyone who believes in him may not perish but may have eternal life"* (Jn 3:16). This reminds us that Jesus came among us out of love and to show us love. His life, death, resurrection, and encounters with the disciples and with us are to enfold us in our belovedness and our call to love God, one another, and all creation. Our responsibility as disciples is to live and share this good news everywhere. As disciples, we are loved, taught, and trained and then sent out to share the message of our teacher. Nguyen writes, "In the Gospel of John Jesus' entire life is about sending and being sent."[10]

Scripture scholar Raymond Brown also shows us how in John we see Jesus's call continuing into our call to God's mission: "The special Johannine contribution to the

---

[6]   vanThanh Nguyen, SVD, "A Biblical Foundation of Missionary Discipleship," in *Missionary Discipleship in Global Contexts*, ed. Lazar T. Stanislaus, SVD and vanThanh Nguyen, SVD (Siegburg: Franz Schmitt Verlag, Studia Instituti Missiologici Societatis Verbi Divini NR. 112, 2018), 121–35.

[7]   Ibid., 123.

[8]   Ibid.; and Hans Weder, "Disciple, Discipleship," in *Anchor Bible Dictionary*, vol. 2 (New Haven, CT: Yale University Press, 1992), 208.

[9]   Nguyen, "Biblical Foundation," 123.

[10]   Ibid., 124.

theology of mission is that the Father's sending of the Son serves both as the model and the ground for the Son's sending of the disciples. Their mission is to continue the Son's mission; and this requires that the Son must be present to them during this mission, just as the Father had to be present to the Son during His mission."[11]

In Jesus's call to announce the mission of God, we see the disciples' call and our calls—each in our own time and context. It is critical to remember that the mission is God's mission, not our mission.

We announce and further God's mission through our particular congregation and members, and together with others. This is part of the communal nature of missionary discipleship. Scripture scholar Charles Talbert reminds us that "In Luke-Acts, the disciple who is shaped by the tradition of Jesus and enabled by an ongoing experience of the Lord is no solitary individual but a participant in a community. The communal dimension of discipleship is seen both in the way one is called to walk and in the mission he or she is commissioned to fulfil."[12] We participate in mission together.

What is this mission of the Reign of God that Jesus came to bring about in the here and now? What does love look like? Luke's Gospel offers a key to understanding Jesus's mission:

> The Spirit of the Lord is upon me,
> because he has anointed me:
> To bring good news to the poor.
> He has sent me to proclaim release to the captives
> And recovery of sight to the blind,
> And to let the oppressed go free,
> To proclaim the year of the Lord's favor.[13]

Luke's Jesus says, "I came to bring fire to the earth and how I wish it were already kindled."[14] Nguyen powerfully offers:

> What is this fire that was apparently burning within him and that he wanted to cast into this world? The answer to that question is succinctly expressed in his statement: "To the other towns also I must proclaim the good news of the reign of God, because for this purpose I have been sent"

---

[11]   Raymond E. Brown, *The Gospel according to John*, vol. 2 (New York: Doubleday, 1970), 1036. I am grateful to vanThanh Nguyen for this reference. See Nguyen, "Biblical Foundation," 125.

[12]   Charles H. Talbert, "Discipleship in Luke-Acts," in *Discipleship in the New Testament*, ed. Fernando F. Segovia (Philadelphia: Fortress Press, 1985), 73. Again, I am grateful to Nguyen for this reference, "Biblical Foundation," 129.

[13]   This is a compilation of Is 61:1–2 and 58:6. See Nguyen, "Biblical Foundation," 129. The beatitudes in Matthew (5:3–12) also speak to God's mission.

[14]   Lk 7:22.

(4:43). His vision is the arrival of the reign of God. It is a vision that will radically transform the world and will turn everything upside down. It is a vision in which the poor and the rich will joyfully dine at the same table, where enemies begin to peacefully embrace each other, where sinners are reconciled, where the outcasts of society are sheltered, and where the poor, the lame and the blind are treated justly (Lk 7:22). Indeed, the reign of God is the key. It is everything for which he stands. It is the meaning of his life and the focus of his ministry. . . . It is this fiery vision of the reign of God that Jesus preaches and for which he suffers and dies.[15]

The Good News changes everything, including us. What will this look like? In the passages we have considered above, we see the elements of justice, peace, radical inclusion, and joy. Throughout the four Gospels we see these virtues (dispositions and practices) in Jesus's words and actions. He is modeling what the Reign of God looks like as he announces it. So must we. Our lives are to be Good News for all: for us, for our communities, for all those with whom we interact, and to all places that are in need of this good news. The great commission in Acts is ours as well: "You will receive power when the Holy Spirit comes upon you, and you will be my witnesses in Jerusalem, throughout Judea and Samaria, and to the ends of the earth."[16] The call is clear and the invitation is ours. What does this require? We again see in Jesus a direction, an example to follow.

Jesus of Nazareth was close to God. We read many times in the gospels that Jesus went off to pray, either in the evenings or early in the morning. I find this pattern a profound example of prayer-ministry balance. One such image is from the end of the first chapter of Mark. After Jesus healed Peter's mother-in-law and she then in thanksgiving served them, we read that on that evening: "the whole town gathered at the door."[17] They brought many who needed healing; yet I can imagine the entire town needed healing. Jesus cured many people. Afterwards, Jesus went off to pray. It is a beautiful image and example from one who took on all the wounds of those he encountered and then at prayer gave these to his God. He gave it all to God,[18] as an oblation, from one who heard upon his baptism in the Jordan, "This is my beloved Son."[19] This would be repeated again and again from a God who is Love. This was an affirmation of Jesus's call. Jesus's relationship with God is one of intimacy. He invites us to the same intimacy.[20] In this space we are opened.

---

[15]   Nguyen, "Biblical Foundation," 130.

[16]   See ibid., 127–28.

[17]   Mk 1:33.

[18]   Jesus gave all back to God, daily. The cross was the epitome of giving all to God, with love triumphing over all evil of all time, but Jesus learned this practice on a daily basis. So too must we. All belongs to God. It always has.

[19]   Mk 1:11; Mt 3:17; Lk 3:22.

[20]   For example, see Jn 3:16; Mt 10:30.

Another step in the interior spiritual life happens when we allow ourselves to be opened and also *emptied*, fully reliant on God. Just after his baptism, Jesus was led by the Spirit to the wilderness for forty days and forty nights.[21] Jesus teaches us about *kenosis*, self-emptying. In the spiritual traditions deserts and wilderness are deeply spiritual places. These are also spaces of training, trial, and testing. St. Paul writes about the self-emptying that came with the Incarnation: "His state was divine, yet he did not cling to his equality with God, but emptied himself, being born in human likeness."[22]

Much happens in this space of openness. Listening in silence attunes our ears and hearts to the Spirit. We can learn much from a variety of traditions about this call to silence. Some years ago, one of my Korean sisters shared a photo with me of a child Buddhist monk sitting on the floor and leaning forward to hear the sound of a seashell. The image itself invited silence. What draws you into silence?

Listening to experiences of persons at the peripheries helps us hear deep truths and calls that will ultimately move our actions. In *Gaudete et Exsultate (On the Call to Holiness)* Pope Francis reminds us that "everything can be accepted and integrated into our life in this world, and become a part of our path to holiness. We are called to be contemplatives even in the midst of action, and to grow in holiness by responsibly and generously carrying out our proper mission."[23]

We create spaces for listening and responding to the Spirit in our lives and through our charisms. This is a journey, and we hear in *New Wine in New Wineskins* that "at the basis of every journey, we find it important to underline the need for consecrated men and women to have a new aspiration to holiness, which is unthinkable without a jolt of renewed passion for the Gospel at the service of the Kingdom. We are moved to this journey by the Spirit of the Risen One who continues to speak to the Church through his inspirations."[24] Patricia Murray, IBVM, Secretary General of the International Union of Superiors General (UISG), reminds us of the essential place of the interior life for consecrated persons. We go inward and ask God to effect an inner transformation that will propel us into the needs of the world.[25] "Allow yourself to be loved and liberated by God. Do not be afraid to let yourself be guided by the Holy Spirit,"[26] encourages Pope Francis. The result will be outward, for God "depends on us to love the world and to show how much he loves it."[27]

---

[21]   See Mt 4:1; Lk 4:2.

[22]   Phil 2:6.

[23]   Pope Francis, *Gaudete et Exsultate (On the Call to Holiness in Today's World)*, 26, http://w2.vatican.va. Hereinafter *GE*.

[24]   Congregation for Institutes of Consecrated Life and Societies of Apostolic Life (CICLSAL), *New Wine in New Wineskins: The Consecrated Life and Its Ongoing Challenges since Vatican II* (Nairobi, Kenya: Paulines Publications Africa, 2017), no. 10.

[25]   Patricia Murray, IBVM, "Religious Life: Called to Undertake a Journey of Transformation," http://www.ctuconsecratedlife.org.

[26]   *GE* 34.

[27]   *GE* 107.

Our encounters move us simultaneously deeper into the life of God and into the life of the world. Pope Francis writes:

> May you come to realize what that word is, the message of Jesus that God wants to speak to the world by your life. Let yourself be transformed. Let yourself be renewed by the Spirit, so that this can happen, lest you fail in your precious mission. The Lord will bring it to fulfillment despite your mistakes and missteps, provided that you do not abandon the path of love but remain ever open to his supernatural grace, which purifies and enlightens.[28]

These passages speak to a deep longing. In consecrated life we long to live the message of Jesus that God wants to speak to the world by our lives and that of our congregations. And we need and want to give the whole of our lives, for it is worth it all. We find in all this that it is a contemplative, prayerful attitude that grounds our ministries and activities—we see that the attitudes that go with this include silence and offering one's self without condition. The call is to *follow* the Risen Christ. The Reign of God is not going to happen *my* way. We must listen and be faithful to the One in, through, and around us.

Our encounter with Jesus Christ brings us to a dimension that bridges our love of God and love of neighbor, particularly our neighbors in greatest need. Living this daily call of missionary discipleship prepares us for another movement to which women and men religious are also called, the mystical-prophetic life. Let us look at this clarion call a bit more closely.

Call to Be Mystics and Prophets

Sometimes we separate mystics and prophets, thinking that mystics have a particular call that is separate from the calls of the prophets. And we don't necessarily think of prophets as mystics. Yet it is a linking of the two that gives authenticity to both mystics and prophets. Our lives, in depth, flow outward to the world in which we live, whether we are contemplative, monastic or apostolic religious, or any follower of Jesus.[29] Our world today is in need of mystics and prophets; thus consecrated life is called to be mystical and prophetic. Pope Francis, in his Apostolic Letter to all Consecrated People on the Occasion of the Year of Consecrated Life, offered some core dimensions of the mystical-prophetic life:

> Prophets receive from God the ability to scrutinize the times in which they live and to interpret events; they are like sentinels who keep watch in the night and sense the coming of the dawn. Prophets know God and they

---

28   *GE* 24.

29   This is not to deny that across religious traditions persons can be mystics and prophets. They are. I am simply limiting my comments here to Catholic consecrated life.

know the men and women who are their brothers and sisters. They are able to discern and denounce the evil of sin and injustice. Because they are free, they are beholden to no one but God, and they have no interest other than God. Prophets tend to be on the side of the poor and powerless, for they know that God himself is on their side.[30]

Pope Francis writes this to us! It's a gospel call to all believers, yet he is particularly calling upon the mystical-prophetic gifts of our charisms. These gifts are meant to be used for the times in which we live. As missionary disciples, this is our particular participation in building the Reign of God.

Five signs that a religious/consecrated life is mystical and prophetic are that individuals and congregations: (1) know God, (2) cultivate interior freedom, (3) read the signs of their times with a critical and creative fidelity to the gospel vision of the Reign of God, denouncing injustice and announcing the gospel vision, (4) live in closeness to and solidarity with the powerless, oppressed, and marginalized, and (5) invite all to bring their gifts to participate in the vision of the Reign of God. As the Risen Christ reminds us not to fear and promises that the Spirit will be with us, in his 2018 Pentecost address, Pope Francis reminded us that the Spirit changes both hearts and situations:

> *The Holy Spirit changes hearts.* Jesus had told his disciples: "You will receive power when the Holy Spirit has come upon you; and you will be my witnesses" (*Acts* 1:8). That is exactly what happened. Those disciples, at first fearful, huddled behind closed doors even after the Master's resurrection, are transformed by the Spirit and, as Jesus says in today's Gospel, "they bear witness to him" (cf. *Jn* 15:27). No longer hesitant, they are courageous and starting from Jerusalem, they go forth to the ends of the earth. Timid while Jesus was still among them, they are bold when he is gone, because the Spirit changed their hearts.
>
> The Spirit . . . does not revolutionize life around us, but changes our hearts. It does not free us from the weight of our problems, but liberates us *within* so that we can face them. It does not give us everything at once, but makes us press on confidently, never growing weary of life. . . .
>
> The Spirit does not only change hearts; he *changes situations.* Like the wind that blows everywhere, he penetrates to the most unimaginable situations. In the Acts of the Apostles—a book we need to pick up and read, whose main character is the Holy Spirit—we are caught up in an amazing series of events. When the disciples least expect it, the Holy Spirit sends them out to the pagans. He opens up new paths, as in the episode of the deacon Philip. The Spirit drives Philip to a desert road from Jerusalem to Gaza. . . . Along the way, Philip preaches to an Ethiopian court official and

---

[30]   Pope Francis, *Apostolic Letter to All Consecrated People on the Occasion of the Year of Consecrated Life*, November 21, 2014, 2.

baptizes him. . . . Then too, there is Paul, "compelled by the Spirit" (*Acts* 20:22), who travels far and wide, bringing the Gospel to peoples he had never seen. Where the Spirit is, something is always happening; where he blows, things are never calm. . . .

The Spirit will bring his power of change, a unique power that is, so to say, both *centripetal and centrifugal*. It is centripetal, that is, it seeks the center, because it works deep within our hearts. It brings unity amid division, peace amid affliction, strength amid temptations. Paul reminds us of this in the second reading, when he writes that the fruits of the Spirit are joy, peace, faithfulness, and self-control (cf. *Gal* 5:22). The Spirit grants intimacy with God, the inner strength to keep going. Yet, at the same time, the Spirit is a centrifugal force, that is, one pushing outward. The one who centers us is also the one who drives us to the peripheries, to every human periphery. The one who reveals God also opens our hearts to our brothers and sisters. The Spirit sends us, makes us witnesses, and so pours out on us—again in the words of Paul—love, kindness, generosity, and gentleness. Only in the Consoler Spirit do we speak words of life and truly encourage others. Those who live by the Spirit live in this constant spiritual tension: they find themselves pulled both *towards God and towards the world*.[31]

These five signs that a congregation is mystical-prophetic should be integrated in our lives. I will discuss a few points about each and then speak a bit more to the calls of religious life today.

Mystical-Prophetic Individuals and Communities Know God

The mystical dimension reminds us that the passion in our lives must be a passion for God, first and foremost, or we will not be able to sustain fidelity in the midst of the great needs of our world, or the woundedness in us and around us. Mysticism speaks of an intimate union with God. It is not correct that famous saints such as Teresa of Ávila and John of the Cross are the only ones who can experience this. There is a mysticism of everyday life in which we can open ourselves to encountering God in all. Spirituality scholar Mary Frohlich, RSCJ, writes about mysticism as the "radical surrender of self into participation into the mystery of Christ."[32] Others might look at mystical experience as an experience of the presence of God and to feel God's transformative presence and action in our lives.[33]

---

31   Pope Francis, Pentecost Homily, May 20, 2018, http://w2.vatican.va.

32   Mary Frohlich, RSCJ, "Drinking Living Water: Mysticism in the Midst of Life," *Religious Life Asia* 16, no. 1 (2014): 7–25.

33   Samuel H. Canilang, CMF, *Mysticism and Prophecy: Religious Life's Distinctive Contribution to the New Evangelization*, ICLA Monograph no. 14 (Quezon City, Philippines: Institute of Consecrated Life in Asia, 2013), 15.

God offers not only relationship but friendship. Mystical-prophetic persons and communities are friends of God. Scripture reminds us that "in every generation she [Wisdom] passes into holy souls, and makes them friends of God, and prophets."[34] In John's Gospel we hear from Jesus that "I have called you friends, because I have made known to you everything that I have heard from my Father."[35] Friendship with God changes us. Our sense of belovedness, loved as we are and called to be our best selves, through our gifts and vulnerabilities, opens us to neighbor and world. Josep Abella reminds us that "the experience of God is the only force capable of arousing that hope that never dies, in spite of the many difficulties and of giving impetus to our commitment towards life."[36]

Freedom Is Another Quality of the Mystical-Prophetic Life

Mystical-prophetic persons have God as their primary relationship and are ultimately beholden only to God; this provides a vision that sees all else in freedom. Acknowledging that Vatican II called forth the prophetic character of consecrated life, Pope John Paul II, in the Apostolic Exhortation *Vita Consecrata*, reminds us that consecrated life "takes the shape of *a special form of sharing in Christ's prophetic office*, which the Holy Spirit communicates to the whole People of God. There is a prophetic dimension which belongs to the consecrated life as such, resulting from the radical nature of the following of Christ and of the subsequent dedication to the mission characteristic of the consecrated life." He continues, "The sign value, which the Second Vatican Council acknowledges in the consecrated life, is expressed in prophetic witness to the primacy which God and the truths of the Gospel have in the Christian life."[37] It is this primacy of relationship that frees religious to discern the calls of the Gospel in daily life.

Mystical-Prophetic Life Reads the Signs of the Times

Intellectual and emotional intelligence are used to see realities with open eyes and to read them in light of the gospel. Pat Farrell, OSF, reminds us that "our rootedness in God needs to be deep enough and our read on reality clear enough for us to be a voice of conscience."[38] Reading the signs of the times requires the capacity

---

[34] Wis 7:7.

[35] Jn 15:15.

[36] Josep Abella, "New Horizons for the Mission of Consecrated Life," USG 77th Semi-Annual Assembly, Rome, May 2011, in *Identity and Prophecy: The Theology of Consecrated Life Today* (Rome: USG, 2011), 104.

[37] Pope John Paul II, Apostolic Exhortation *Vita Consecrata* (1996), 84, http://w2.vatican.va. Hereinafter *VC*.

[38] Pat Farrell, OSF, "Navigating the Shifts," Presidential Address, Leadership Conference of Women Religious, 2012 Assembly, https://lcwr.org.

to read in the midst of dark influences and evil in the world without getting caught in fear, mistrust, or hopelessness. Prayer and community are essential here. Our responses will be born of prayer, closeness to suffering, and an abiding sense that another way is possible. We hear in *Vita Consecrata*:

> *True prophecy is born of God*, from friendship with him, from attentive listening to his word in the different circumstances of history. Prophets feel in their hearts a burning desire for the holiness of God and, having heard his word in the dialogue of prayer, they proclaim that word with their lives, with their lips and with their actions, becoming people who speak for God against evil and sin. Prophetic witness . . . is also expressed through the denunciation of all that is contrary to the divine will and through the exploration of new ways to apply the Gospel in history, in expectation of the coming of God's Kingdom.[39]

For those of us in consecrated life there is always a sense that another way is possible that more closely resembles a vision for the good of all people. This must be announced as clearly as the evil and wrongs are denounced.

Mystics and Prophets Are Close to the Suffering People and the Earth

Vita Consecrata reminds us that "nothing can come before personal love of Christ and of the poor in whom he lives."[40] Our lives must welcome and are privileged by the presence of persons who are challenged, oppressed, or marginalized. Here we hear the cries of God among the people. We cannot simply read about people and situations; we must have a closeness and relationship to people and realities. Congolese Liliane Sweko, SNDdeN, stresses: "If we are to be mystics and prophets in the world today, we are called to involve ourselves in a world where men and women, bruised by violence, famine, poverty, wars and so many other attacks on their dignity, cry out and appeal for help."[41] This may feel overwhelming, yet it also flows from relationship.

A few years ago I had the privilege of traveling through a part of the Philippines with Samuel Canilang, CM, whose task was to introduce me to prophets. He did! I reference this more in succeeding chapters, but suffice it to say that every one of the prophets I met was close to the people and to the earth. We see the same closeness when we consider the life of Jesus. Our relationship with God opens up our relationship with God's creation. As Abella reminds us, "The experience of

---

[39]   *VC* 84.

[40]   Ibid.

[41]   Liliane Sweko, SNDdeN, "Called to Illuminate with Prophetic Light the World of Darkness," Plenary Assembly of Union of International Superiors General (UISG), Rome, May 8, 2010, 4.

God awakens in us a new ecologic and cosmic awareness that leads us to feel solidarity with all Creation and respectful of the dynamism that the Creator himself has established."[42]

The Mystical-Prophetic Life Builds Community

We come to see ourselves ever more united to Christ and to the world, in a communion that desires to unite us in the Reign of God. Gathering, welcoming, and building bridges are signs of the Reign of God among us. Desiring that we all may be one in God in the midst of our diversity, our vision of ourselves as part of the whole of creation helps us work toward a proper relationship with all people and all of creation. We see our health, well-being, and wholeness connected to that of each and all. In the mystical-prophetic life, God breaks through in us to share God's vision of love and unity with the world. This brings us to see possible partnerships in all kinds of places, through religious, geographic, cultural, and other diversities. All can be put to the service of Jesus's mission, which is ours here and now.

Canilang writes encouragingly that "an authentic mysticism, as an encounter with the living God, lover of life, cannot but nourish and express itself in bold and liberating prophetic action."[43]

The invitation here is to ask God for continual conversion, transformation, and revitalization, personally and communally, so that we and our religious institutes may be open to the calls of this time. Jesus is our model and image of the unity of mystical-prophetic life. To live this today takes great faith, hope, and love. We must remember that we do nothing alone. Because we have seen the Spirit changing us and changing situations, we cling to this "dangerous memory" from scripture, our experiences and the experiences of our congregations.[44] Sharing narratives is important. That sharing is part of the mystical-prophetic call and response.

Where is this to take us? Ever more deeply into the God of hope.

Radical Prophetic Hope

As we have seen, missionary discipleship calls us to live the Good News and serve God's mission. A mystical-prophetic life leads us and our congregations to the depth and breadth of our life in God and God's creation. The current realities in religious life, church, and world require another movement and capacity, that is, of surrendering, or holding lightly our own visions of how the future is to be so that

---

[42]   Abella, "New Horizons," 104.

[43]   Canilang, *Mysticism and Prophecy*, 17.

[44]   Dangerous memory here is connected to Johann Baptist Metz's work in which memories of the past (such as that of Jesus's suffering and resurrection) can transform the present because they remind us (even subversively) of both other such histories and an eschatological future.

we can open ourselves to the evolving future God longs to create with us. Our desire to see as God sees *frees* us and helps us look toward the future with hope. This hope is a contemplative hope, not derived from external successes but by the experience and conviction of accompaniment by a God who so loves us that God entered our humanity to show us the way of love on this earth.

On this journey we benefit from the works of St. John of the Cross and the writing of Constance FitzGerald, OCD. This is a great example of how the different charisms or gifts in consecrated life serve all in the church.

I first met Connie when I visited the Carmelite Monastery of Baltimore in 2006. Before this I had heard of her from another one of the giants of US Catholic sisters in religious life, Margaret Brennan, IHM. I had read Connie's 1984 essay "Impasse and Dark Night."[45] It was given to me as a "must read" in 2003 and so I read it. However, I have to admit that it didn't grab me. It helped me understand the context in which my sisters in their sixties and older were living, but it didn't touch my life. I couldn't relate to it.

When I finally met Connie, we spoke a lot about religious life and what we were seeing. At one point I mentioned I had read her 1984 essay and that I was wondering if there was something more. I admitted that while impasse was still a challenge in different areas of church and society, this wasn't how this moment felt for me or for many of my age-group peers. Her response was refreshing: "Well of course not. That was over twenty years ago." "What moment is this?" I asked. "Well," she explained, "using John of the Cross, I would go to his next point, and that is of purification of memory. This is how I would describe our time." As she explained purification of memory toward the dawn of hope, I immediately knew the wisdom, truth, challenge, and hope in her words. A few years later she offered a plenary address on this topic at the Catholic Theological Society of America's 2009 Conference, titled "From Impasse to Prophetic Hope: Crisis of Memory."[46]

That was over ten years ago, and we are now beginning to move on from this point as well. However, because we are in the midst of immense change in consecrated life, especially in North America and Europe, John of the Cross and FitzGerald offer a way to move through this time. Because we can cling to ourselves and our way of life with all the life force that is in us, I offer this reflection as part of how to discern what this time asks, invites, and demands of us. We can learn from John of the Cross and FitzGerald how we might navigate this time asking for interior conversion, internal transformation, and external revitalization.

"How are we to move and respond to where the Spirit is calling?" Through the lens of her Carmelite tradition, FitzGerald would say purification of memory

---

[45]   Constance FitzGerald, OCD, "Impasse and Dark Night," online at http://www.baltimorecarmel.org. The article originally appeared in *Living with Apocalypse, Spiritual Resources for Social Compassion* (San Francisco: Harper & Row, 1984), 93–116.

[46]   Constance FitzGerald, OCD, "From Impasse to Prophetic Hope: Crisis of Memory," Catholic Theological Society of America (June 2009), *CTSA Proceedings* 64(2009): 21–42, https://ejournals.bc.edu.

will lead us to the dawn of prophetic hope. Another way to answer is to speak of surrender into the heart of Christ. FitzGerald looks through the lenses of the mystical tradition and hope in John of the Cross. I offer now by way of introduction and summary four main points from her 2009 address that are salient to our topic and translate to religious life.[47] Wherever possible, I allow her words to speak.

Purification of Memory to the Dawn of Hope

Constance FitzGerald, using John of the Cross's writings on purification of memory, tells us that if we wish to get to the dawn of prophetic hope we will have to hold lightly, or even de-link, all our accolades as well as our painful experiences. Only when we can do this, so that we are not held back from the future by using the compass of the past, can we open ourselves to where God is leading. When God is the horizon we seek, then the future can emerge. De-linking from both the goods we've experienced and the wrongs we've suffered is not easy. Such an open stance both requires contemplation and is a result of contemplation.

De-linking and Holding Lightly in Our Lives and Congregations

We all know how to hold lightly, the way one would hold something with open hands. Successes, our own and that of our congregations, are part of the goods experienced, including personal accolades, degrees, positions, and honors. They include our congregations' successes and good experiences in ministries, outreach, service to church and society, and respect from church and society. Success also includes the goods we have experienced: good community experiences, friendships, and opportunities. All is to be acknowledged. We are not asked to forget them or dismiss them. We hold them all lightly so they do not impede us from moving toward what God draws us to now, in this new moment.

We also hold lightly wrongs suffered, whether from church, society, or within our congregations. These include our memories of misunderstandings or unjust treatment from segments of the church and segments of society or wrongs suffered within our congregations. Here too we include painful realities of sexual and emotional abuse by members of our congregations and of religious men and women. Here we see the entire church and wide society of humanity suffering greatly. Again, we do not forget these realities or the need for healing of painful memories. This certainly may mean we must do our work in these areas. Such work may include counselling, spiritual direction, having courageous conversations, silent contemplative sitting, working to transform unjust structures, and more. Yet we are asked to hold these in a manner that does not hold us back from where we are being

---

[47] I don't, however, see her points as limited to religious life. In fact, her plenary address was to Catholic theologians from all walks of life. In addition, I think her work could be helpful across religious traditions and also in civic and secular contexts. The wisdom here is great.

called today, beyond and perhaps through both our goods experienced and wrongs suffered, to the future God longs to create through and in us.

An image opposite to openness is that of someone whose hands are in fists, with arms crossed. This posture prevents the person (or congregation) from offering what each can and from receiving what is being offered. In such a posture there is no room for the Spirit to move—but the movement of the Spirit is exactly what is needed.

Holding lightly acknowledges the past but does not allow it to hold us back from the future God is trying to create right now. The Spirit will move into any of our realities, but we must be open. We must pray to be opened.

Emptiness Is Filled by God

When we do de-link and open ourselves, we will experience an emptiness. There is space now for God to move, yet our challenge is to allow the emptiness to be filled by God. Caution: Do not use filler! If we leave space for God, we have to hold that space and not attempt to fill it, as we are naturally apt to. Our temptation will be to fill the emptiness any way we can. Think of the times we avoid something by checking email, surfing the web, or getting up for something to drink or eat, for example.

Even our good activity and activism will only dry up if we do not allow the deeper movements of God to lead us. Redemptorist and bishop of Rustenberg, South Africa, Kevin Dowling knows this well. He works continually at the margins among the people most in need, and he knows the deep call to contemplation as necessity: "I have known the feeling of drying up inside because the tasks are just too demanding on my spiritual resources above all. Contemplation, silent reflection, prayer, holistic living, and responding consciously in God's presence—my responses and engagement must 'breathe' with a contemplative spirit. And I need to take time out for this, which I don't do enough."[48]

Speaking about what is possible when we de-link and allow ourselves to be open, FitzGerald writes, "When the emptiness of the memory on the level of affectivity and imagination becomes a deep void of yearning, it is hope that opens up the possibility of being possessed by the infinite, unimaginable, incomprehensible Mystery of love that is so close." She then quotes from John of the Cross:

Hope empties and withdraws the memory from all creature possessions, for as St. Paul says, hope is for what is not possessed. It withdraws the memory from what can be possessed and fixes it on what it hopes for. Hence only hope in God prepares the memory perfectly for union with [God].

---

[48]   Bishop Kevin Dowling, "Revisioning Religious Life for the 21st Century in a Global Context," (second talk) Conference of Religious, Ireland, June 2015, p. 17. Unpublished text, obtained from Kevin Dowling.

FitzGerald explains:

> Before memory is purified, we can thwart our encounter with the future, without even realizing it, by relying on the images which memory has saved for us—images of our past, joyful or sad, pleasant or unpleasant, fulfilling or detrimental. [When] we project these images onto our vision of the future, we block the limitless possibilities of God by living according to an expectation shaped, not by hope, by our own desires, needs and past experiences.[49]

When we allow ourselves to be open, silent spaces emerge. She notes, "This is the ultimate silence, the ultimate empty space and may very well be one kind of ecstatic experience of union." And, she adds, "Karl Rahner understood this: 'There is no such thing either in the world or in the heart, as literal vacancy, as a vacuum. And *whenever space is really left*—by death, by renunciation, by parting, by apparent emptiness, provided the emptiness that cannot remain empty is not filled by the world, or activity, or chatter, or the deadly grief of the world—there is God.'"[50]

The Posture of Hope as Prophecy

When we let God fill the space, a horizon opens up that allows us to both see the future and to invite others into it as well. This is a prophetic posture; we point to a horizon toward which we also walk. Our contemplation serves not only the direction of religious life but a broader community.

When we can allow this emptiness to be filled by God, we find hope. FitzGerald writes: "This dynamic of being able to yield unconditionally to God's future is what John of the Cross calls hope, a hope that exists without the signature of our life and works, a hope independent of us and our accomplishments (spiritual gifts or ordinary human achievements), a hope that can even embrace and work for a future without us." She continues, "This theological hope is completely free from the past, fully liberated from our need to recognize ourselves in the future, to survive, to be someone."[51] She iterates this further, citing David F. Ford's description: "Hope does not desire anything for itself. It does not return to itself but rather remains with that which is hoped for."[52] This is God. Our hope remains only in God.

Most important, FitzGerald reminds us: "You can see what a *radical call* this is. Those who answer it must be prepared to leave so much behind, to stop clinging to

---

    49   FitzGerald, "From Impasse to Prophetic Hope," 32.
    50   Ibid., 37. Emphasis added. Quoted by Daniel O'Leary in "Space for Grace," *The Tablet*, November 18, 2006.
    51   FitzGerald, "From Impasse to Prophetic Hope," 34.
    52   David F. Ford, *Self and Salvation: Being Transformed* (Cambridge: Cambridge University Press, 1998), 64.

a security that has been taken away." She suggests that perhaps those who accept the "gift of hope eschew keeping a death grip on what has given them assurance of their value and place in the Church."[53] This radical call is to give all to this relationship and mission of love. It is to depend on God and let go of all else. This is the radical call to which we give our whole selves, and it asks for ongoing conversion. Scripture scholar Donald Senior, CP, points out: "One has to be attentive to God's call, ready to leave something or someone behind in order to be free to follow Jesus: damp nets, a confused father, a tax collector's booth, memories of failure, a tired body, competing obligations, the tug of family and possessions, fear of the unknown and untried. Sometimes the burden to be shed is massive."[54]

FitzGerald helps us see beyond our fear of the unknown and what we must de-link from, as she assures us that

> obsession with the past gives way to a new undefinable sense of related-ness or intimacy, an experience of ultimate assurance, and this conversion releases creativity and most importantly freedom for the limitless possi-bilities of God, for hope. This freedom, this posture of hope, is really prophecy, for it enables a person to reveal the vision of a different kind of future than the one we want to construct from our limited capacities. Such a person becomes a prophet when she shows the way; when she is willing to stand on the horizon so that all can see this future, God's future.[55]

Hope becomes prophecy. FitzGerald concludes: "Be prophets of hope!"[56]

Creating Communities of Hope

Missionary discipleship asks us to also be mystics and prophets. We do so through the charismatic gifts we have been given for the sake of the church and world. If we can de-link and hold on only to what is essentially God and of God, we will be free to live radical hope in and for the world. In doing so, the dynamic nature of our charisms affects every area of our religious lives, including our vows, for the sake of the mission of God today. We will create communities of hope on a global scale as we open ourselves to this future God is already creating in our midst.

Friendship with God gives us what we need for the next steps. We shall now look at calls of the Spirit in and through our vows, lived from the depths of our charisms and in response to the cries around us.

---

53   FitzGerald, "From Impasse to Prophetic Hope," 35.

54   Donald Senior, CP, "Answering the Call: Biblical Perspectives," in *Catholics on Call: Discerning a Life of Service in the Church*, ed. Robin Ryan (Collegeville, MN: Litur-gical Press, 2010), 22. I am grateful to vanThanh Nyugen for this reference from his essay, "Biblical Foundation," 129–30.

55   FitzGerald, "From Impasse to Prophetic Hope," 35.

56   Ibid., 42.

Questions for Reflection and Discussion

1. What dimension of missionary discipleship draws you at this time?
2. What dimensions of religious life as a mystical-prophetic life do you sense calling you and your congregation?
3. What are you being invited to de-link from in order to listen, hear, and respond to God's alluring future? From what is your congregation being invited to de-link?

Part Two

Mission, Love, and the Vowed Life

4

Introduction to the Vows

Having looked at call, charism, context, and contemplation, I take a deeper look at how each of these has an essential role in how the vows are enfleshed. In this chapter I briefly situate the vows[1] in contemporary and historical contexts, frame the vows as virtues, and situate the vows within the context of mission and charism. I conclude with keys to considering the vows.

Setting Vows and Evangelical Counsels in Context

All people are called to holiness. In his Apostolic Exhortation, *Gaudete et Exsultate*, Pope Francis reminds all Christians, in all walks of life, that they are called to live a life of holiness.[2] The Dogmatic Constitution on the Church, *Lumen Gentium*, spoke of the universal call to holiness through a relationship with Christ, and proclaimed that the way to holiness is love.[3] This is further emphasized in Pope Francis's first major writing, *The Joy of the Gospel* (2013).[4] *All* are invited to an encounter with Jesus, and this changes everything, moves everything, and frames everything.

The initiative is God's. The initiative is Love, for love. All Christians are initiated into this experience through baptism, our common first consecration. Included in the sacraments of initiation and our way of living in love are Eucharist, communion, and confirmation, a commitment and sending forth in mission.[5]

As stated in Chapter 3, the call to discipleship, to follow in the way of love and service to God and all creation, belongs to all Christians. Pope Francis has several

---

[1]   The vows are also often called "evangelical counsels."

[2]   Pope Francis, Apostolic Exhortation *Gaudete et Exsultate* (*On the Call to Holiness in Today's World*) (2018), http://w2.vatican.va.

[3]   *Lumen Gentium* (*Dogmatic Constitution of the Church*) (1964), http://www. vatican.va, l. Hereinafter *LG*.

[4]   Pope Francis, Apostolic Exhortation *Evangelii Gaudium* (*Joy of the Gospel*) (2013), http://w2.vatican.va.

[5]   I am indebted to the work of José Rovira Arumí, CMF, in framing our calls in this way. See *Evangelical Counsels and Consecrated Life: Three Charismatic Ways to Follow Christ* (Quezon City, Philippines: Institute of Consecrated Life in Asia [ICLA], 2015). Here, the call to consecration, communion, and commitment comes from *Vita Consecrata*, 30, 31b.

times spoken of Pope Benedict XVI's reminder that it is our witness that attracts others to God, the source of love and service, and to Christianity:

> He [Pope Benedict XVI] said that the Church grows through witness, not by proselytism. The witness that can really attract is that associated with attitudes which are uncommon: generosity, detachment, sacrifice, self-forgetfulness in order to care for others. This is the witness, the "martyrdom" of religious life. It "sounds an alarm" for people. Religious say to people with their life: "What's happening?" These people are telling me something! These people go beyond a mundane horizon.[6]

Citing Pope Benedict's call that "religious life ought to promote growth in the Church by way of attraction,"[7] Pope Francis has called forth religious and the church as a whole:

> "The Church," therefore, "must be attractive. Wake up the world! Be witnesses of a different way of doing things, of acting, of living! It is possible to live differently in this world. We are speaking of an eschatological outlook, of the values of the Kingdom incarnated here, on this earth. It is a question of leaving everything to follow the Lord. No, I do not want to say 'radical.' Evangelical radicalness is not only for religious: it is demanded of all. But religious follow the Lord in a special way, in a prophetic way. It is this witness that I expect of you. Religious should be men and women who are able to wake the world up."[8]

Persons in consecrated life, as all persons, are called to holiness and living out this holiness in daily life. And there are many ways of living out our calls and charism in love and service.

Evangelical or gospel radicalness is not unique to religious. All are called to live and follow the radicalism of Jesus of Nazareth who came to love, to connect to the margins, to free all who were bound, to show what service for the Reign of God looks like in word and action.[9] However, Pope Francis reminds us that religious have a particular call to prophecy, to be prophetic in word and witness. In Chapter 2 I reflected on the prophetic characteristic of the Spirit. Pope Francis invokes this

---

    [6]   The reference is to a homily from Pope Benedict XVI at the inaugural Mass of the General Episcopal Conference of Latin America and the Caribbean at the Shrine of Aparecida, May 13, 2007. See Antonio Spadaro, SJ, "'Wake Up the World!' Conversation with Pope Francis about the Religious Life," *La Civiltà Cattolica* (2014) I, 3–17, trans. Donald Maldari, SJ (revised January 6, 2015), https://onlineministries.creighton.edu.

    [7]   See Benedict XVI, homily at inaugural Mass, Shrine of Aparecida, May 13, 2007. See also Spadaro, "Wake Up the World!" 3.

    8   See Spadaro, "'Wake Up the World!'" 3.

    9   See Mt 22:34–40.

spirit of naming sin and grace in the world today. We do this by our lived witness, which means we must be close enough to sin and grace, pain and new life, to hear the cries and joys in order to both denounce and announce. Our way of life wakes up the world around us only if we are awakened.

Our lives are to be Good News—in the most radical, that is, rooted in God, way, and grounded in realities around us. Religious life is the way that some Christians, after encountering and following him, point to Jesus and his message by their very lives. Religious life is one way of incarnating, albeit imperfectly, the radical message of the Reign of God. This is our call. This is our way. It is our way of loving God and loving God's world and all within it.

The call to consecrated life is God's initiative to the person who, desiring to follow Jesus, follows the lead of the befriending Spirit to a particular congregation or institute, with its particular charism within the gospel call. Members live their call through vows[10] made to God and lived through a congregation/institute. However, the vows are not exhaustive of one's religious life or its important dimensions. Claretian theologian José Rovira Arumí summarizes this well:

> Nevertheless, the three counsels (celibacy, poverty and obedience) have a special importance, because these evangelical counsels represent: "The threefold expression of a single 'yes' of our consecration" (EE II 14, FLC 44b); three ways to commit ourselves to live as Christ lived His whole life: possession of goods, love and autonomy (cf. EE II 15; VC 19bc, 22c): "The counsels are, as it were, the main support of the religious life, since they express in a significant and complete way the evangelical radicalism which characterizes it. . . . These touch the human person at the level of the three essential spheres of his [her] existence and relationship: affectivity, possession, and power" (PI 12).[11]

Clearly religious life entails the whole of one's life. The vows are a critical expression of the dimensions of one's life. The vows are each lived in prayer, community, and ministry. They do encompass all areas of our lives. Yet it is important to remember that even the evangelical counsels we call vows of poverty and obedience are not exclusive to religious but are gospel values meant for all Christians. It is only celibacy that is not meant for all, though certainly chastity is to be lived by everyone. Now a few words about the vows in their historical context.[12]

---

10   The terminology differs for some forms of consecrated life. Some institutes, for example, make promises or take oaths, depending on the group.

11   Arumí, *Evangelical Counsels*, 4.

12   I am indebted to Arumí for the historical dimensions offered in the following section. See ibid., 27.

Historical Context of the Vows

Although from Vatican II onward theologians have considered the "evangelical counsels of poverty and obedience as *the* characteristic of every kind of Consecrated life . . . this is a doctrine that was commonly accepted only little by little from the 12th century onwards."

Interestingly, beginning in the twelfth century, the traditional order placed poverty first, followed by celibacy and obedience. Vatican II placed celibacy first, followed by poverty and obedience. Most documents now follow that order. Celibacy, and the reason it is listed first, is discussed in the next chapter. The priority given to celibacy does not diminish the great importance of the other vows. All of the vows are to help us live the fullness of love and charity. This is our sharing in God's life and our way to love the world around us. Although today we tend to see the three vows as the norm, this was not always so; in the period of early monasticism, there was no limit to the characteristics describing their life:

They spoke of leaving one's homeland, of penance, constant prayer, poverty, fasting, meekness, continence, etc. Why? For them, every word of the Lord Jesus was important; and hence it was impossible to limit oneself to any single element. . . . In the treatises of the monastic renunciation, both the renunciation of one's family and of goods appear constantly together (cf. Pachomius, Basil, Evagrius, Cassian, etc.). The meaning was that the monk renounced everything: goods (poverty) and family (celibacy).[13]

It seems that the number three was a preference for some ancient writers, though which three varied.[14] Apparently the triad became established only in the Middle Ages, and then quickly became the traditional form for consecrated life. Arumí explains:

In a formula of profession, made in Paris in the year 1148, we find in fact: (1) chastity, (2) communion of goods and (3) obedience. In 1198 it had been included in the Rule of the Trinitarians. In the early 13th c., St. Francis of Assisi inserted it in his Rules (1221, 1223). In 1232, the triad together with stability appears in the Constitutions of the Dominican Sisters of St. Sixtus in Rome. In 1244, Pope Innocent IV wrote to the Clarists that these three elements "constitute the essential values of every

---

[13]   Ibid., 27–28.

[14]   Ibid., 28. "For example, Andrew, a desert monk, spoke of the characteristics of the monastic life as (1) leaving one's homeland, (2) poverty and (3) silence. . . . St. Augustine once spoke of (1) virginity, (2) poverty and (3) fasting, and another time of (1) virginity, (2) poverty and (3) community life. . . . St. Benedict spoke of (1) stability, (2) conversion and (3) obedience to the abbot" (28).

form of religious life." A few years later, St. Thomas Aquinas included it in his theology of religious life. However, it seems that the formula received its definitive character only in 1405, under Pope Innocent VII.[15]

This formula became the norm and spread widely, though even today various groups have their own combination from their tradition.[16] The vows will be covered in more detail in subsequent chapters. For now let us look at the vows through the lens of virtue and virtue ethics.

Vows and Virtues

Looking at the vows through the lens of virtue allows us to live the dynamic and evolving nature of vows. Virtues are practices and dispositions for becoming a particular kind of moral person. Virtues ask: Who am I? Who do I wish to become? How shall I get there?[17] Clearly this is a process that requires knowing ourselves, setting forth some goals, and intentionally choosing practices to live so as to become more of what the essence of celibate chastity, obedience, and poverty mean.

When we see vows as virtues we realize that it takes practice to live the vows. How I live the vow of celibate chastity has certainly evolved since I was in the novitiate and continues to evolve. This is a good thing! Virtues remind us of our ultimate horizon or *telos*, which is God, oneness with love of God, and the ongoing journey is never completed while we are alive. Virtues are practices. This means that we do indeed practice them. It is only in living the calls of our vows that we grow. Grace meets us at every step, but practice is our part in this effort of opening ourselves more and more fully to the grace and gift that is each vow.

Looking at vows as virtues that require dispositions reminds us that we must enter into this way of life with our whole selves: mind, heart, and will. Our vows must be lived as both acts and attitudes.

Seeing vows as virtues allows us to see our growing edges as gifts, our mistakes as part of the learning to live. Seen as virtues, the vows help us see many more dimensions than simply acts of commission or omission. This focus on virtues is not only for persons but also for congregations. Congregations also ask, in the midst of the realities in which they live, "Who are we? Who do we wish to become? How do we get there?"

---

[15] Ibid., 28–29.

[16] Ibid., 29. Consider, for example, the Benedictines (stability, conversion, and obedience) and Dominican friars (who profess obedience only, though the other vows are included within that vow), 29.

[17] On the virtues, I'm grateful for the work of Alasdair MacIntyre in *After Virtue: A Study in Moral Theory*, 3rd ed. (Notre Dame, IN: University of Notre Dame Press, 2007); and James F. Keenan in numerous writings, including *Jesus and Virtue Ethics: Building Bridges between New Testament Studies and Moral Theology* (New York: Sheed & Ward, 2002).

The vows are lived as a whole. We do not decide to live one vow at a time, just as we do not decide that today only my lungs will be used and tomorrow only my hands. We live and practice the vows and vowed life together. They are neither separate nor separable.

Evolution of Vows within the Lens of God's Mission

What's new with the vows? Actually, a great deal. Although the essentials of the vows remain, they are shaped by realities and charism.[18] Vows, therefore, are Spirit-driven.

Our lives are about God and following God's mission. This is our ultimate call and the source of our calls to mission. As religious we are first and foremost to be about God's mission, making God's vision of love, justice, and peace present in our world. We listen for how we are to do this. We listen to the calls of God and the cries of the people and of God's earth. We respond to these cries through the lens of our charism in religious life. While many of us hear the cries of the migrants, whether they be on the United States–Mexico border, the shores of Europe, or the edges of Syria or Bangladesh, our response will come from our charisms, the gifts of the Spirit we are given at this time and for this time. As noted earlier, charism also continues to evolve in the context in which it is lived. So how do I respond as a Religious of the Sacred Heart, in light of our call to discover and reveal God's love today? The question is also asked as a "we": How do we as Religious of the Sacred Heart of Jesus respond? What does it mean to be a Franciscan or Servite or Presentation Sister or member of any institute today in light of these needs? The essentials of our call remain, but how we live them out evolves.

At times we answered some of these questions through the lens of our ministries alone. This is changing. Reflection on the question we are being invited to today goes beyond our ministries, but certainly includes our ministries. We are being asked to go deeper and wider. In the midst of the migrant crisis, for example, what is the Spirit asking of us through our charism? What is being asked? The challenge is not to run too quickly to our usual responses. The call is to look at the reality, see the reality through the lens of God's love, hearing the cries, asking how we are called to respond, realizing that the religious imagination is far beyond our usual ways and yet works in response to what comes into our lives. There is a creativity being invited—the Spirit is creative! I sometimes wonder if we fear such creativity because we are not sure we will be able to do what is invited, to stretch beyond our current resources of persons and finances. And yet this is exactly where the Spirit is intervening and inviting us to see who else is with us and how community can contribute in this time. This can be charism widening to include our charism family—associates and collaborators in mission. It may also be an invitation to work beyond our charisms and work with those living the wider charism

---

18   See also Maria Cimperman, "A Fresh Perspective on the Vows," *Occasional Papers* 47, no. 1 (Winter 2018): 16–19 (Leadership Conference of Women Religious).

of religious life. The invitation is also to work with all in our common humanity. While we will see with our charism what is calling, how we live this out is the fruit of the Spirit. The grace is never given without consequences that can move the grace, though not necessarily in the way we would first imagine.

Connecting Call, Cries, Charism, and Vows

Our call from God and the cries around us move us to act in response through the lens of charism. We respond then through our vows, which are each lived out in prayer, community, and ministry. I offer the chart below as a way to visualize this.[19]

Connecting Mission, Context, Charism, and Vowed Life

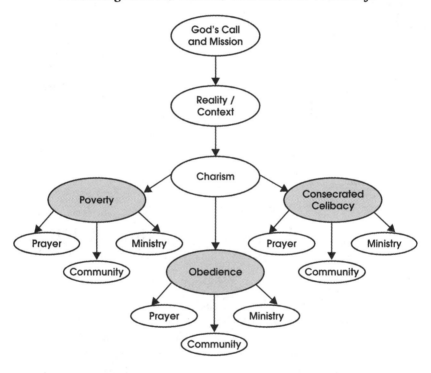

At the top of the chart we hear and respond to God's love and desire to live God's mission. In this stance of desire we hear the cries of the people and the cries of the world, for God also hears these cries. We are concerned with all that concerns God. How we respond is affected by charism and the particular gifts we are given for this time.

Some might prefer to say the reality/context (cries of the earth and cries of the people) comes after the charism lens. Either is possible. The point is that we see and

---

19   This visual is, of course, not exhaustive.

respond to the cries around us through our charism, which then affects every part of our religious life. Note now that how we respond to the realities around us affects us in every vow. Each vow in turn is lived out in prayer, community, and ministry. My vow of obedience asks for a particular style of listening that is present in my prayer, my community life, and in my ministry. The vow of celibate chastity invites a love and fidelity lived through ministry, in my prayer, and in my community; and all these will be framed by my particular charism. Likewise, the cries around us will be heard and engaged through the vow of poverty in my prayer, community, and ministry. All areas are involved in some way. All is interconnected. Sandra Schneiders's description of religious life resonates:

> Religious Life is a Life.
> A total self-gift.
> All that I am, with nothing held back.
> From the moment of my profession
> To my last breath.[20]

The vowed life is an all-encompassing, engaging, and grace-filled way of life. We are constantly evolving, and God is constantly creating something new in us and in religious life. The challenge is to keep following the lead of this Spirit, even as we sometimes get tired or discouraged. This is where community of all kinds is an essential help to us. We can only do this together, though each of us lives this in her own context.

Keys for Seeing the Vows

In this final section I offer twelve points to help ground us for looking at the vows individually and together. Here there is a brief explanation of each. Each is developed in the chapters that follow.

1. *Vows are dynamic.* Though grounded in scripture and tradition and the Constitutions of each congregation, they are constantly evolving according to our times, contexts, and needs. Thus, the call of obedience in the Democratic Republic of Congo asks something of religious living in the DRC that is distinct from the call of obedience in South Korea or Canada at this moment.
2. *Vows are linked to one another and to all areas of religious life.* We do not live poverty only in our personal life without poverty affecting those for whom we pray and where we put some of our time and relational energy. The vows are all linked to how we pray, live community, and serve in ministry.

---

[20]   Sandra Schneiders, IHM, presentation, "The Charism of Religious Life," Giving Voice Conference, June 2002. Author's notes.

3. *Vows are meant to be edgy.* They are to stretch us in all ways, taking us out of our comfort zones. We will always be walking a fine line between finding a way to live the vowed life and hearing the inviting calls to growth. When we find ourselves in a rut, we are losing track of our call.

4. *Vows link us to the margins and peripheries.* Because our gift of charism is the way through which we respond to the signs of our times through our relationship with God, we bring this gift and the gift brings us to the edges where God awaits us, alluring us forward.

5. *Vows are lived personally, communally, and congregationally.* It is equally important to ask how a community is living celibate chastity as how an individual is living this vow. The congregation will also have its way of visibly witnessing where the heart moves it in obedient response to God's calls. At the same time, if the individual is not living the vows, something is lost to the group. This is especially important when we look at communal discernment a bit later.

6. *Vows are to witness to the mystical-prophetic dimensions of life.* The relationship to God in daily life and the response to the areas that cry for response are linked in consecrated life.

7. *Vows demand accountability.* Although it is true that we cannot, on the one hand, judge how each is living celibate chastity or obedience, or poverty, we are called to grow in each of these areas. They are areas that ask for personal as well as sisterly or fraternal reflection. It would be interesting to ask others how they see the vows lived in us. Not only to ask one another but to ask those outside of our vowed life: "How do you see the Good News of poverty visible in my life?" It is helpful on at least an annual basis to name a goal or striving for each of the vows and to periodically reflect on where one is in relation to the goals. This again takes us to the dynamic nature of the vows.

8. *The vows and vowed life are eminently relational.* Indeed, the vows are all about relationships. The vowed life encourages our closeness to people, especially those at the margins, to all creation, and to God.

9. *Vows speak to the extravagance of God, who gives freely and offers fully.*

10. *The vowed life is paschal.* We model our lives on Jesus of Nazareth who put his life in relationship with those on the margins, who offered a way of loving that was beyond the capacity of some to imagine, and who loved even amid misunderstanding, judgment, unjust and cruel suffering, and death. We also know and follow the Risen Christ who continues to be in relationship beyond death, who forgives and is reconciling. Our lives are also paschal.

11. *The vows point to the eschatological.* Our lives lived in love speak of the value of giving our love forth fully and freely, pointing to our ultimate goal of union with God in and beyond earthly life. Our vows point to our desire to love as God loves. Because of love we put ourselves at the disposal

of others, to live *disponibilidad* (radical availability) freely and in the most radical way possible.

12. *Our vows are to be a source of joy.* Our vows are to be Good News, and Good News is a source of joy. Our lives are to reflect joy and serve as Good News for ourselves, our communities, the people of God, and God's creation.

None of this is possible without God. All is possible with God. The vowed life is lived with others. We grow to the extent that we open ourselves to what God and our sisters and brothers can teach us in this school of love. In the next few chapters, I look at each of the vows in more detail.

Questions for Reflection and Discussion

1. Virtues are both dispositions and practices. When considering the vows today, which dimension of virtue (disposition and practice) do you find inviting you?

2. Which key linked to the vows resonates with your experience?

5

THE GOOD NEWS ABOUT
CONSECRATED CELIBACY

Before reading this chapter, it would be helpful to read the sections on celibacy in your congregation's Constitutions. Then reflect on the following:

- What do your Constitutions say about consecrated celibacy?[1]
- How is the vow named?
- What do your Constitutions say about celibacy in general?
- What scriptures, if any, are used? Why would this be important?
- What is the spiritual wisdom in your Constitutions about this vow?

Describing Our Lives in Love

Next, as we begin our look at the vow of consecrated celibacy, take a few minutes to reflect on the following questions. As you look at your life up to this moment:

- What have you learned about love?
- What loves have shaped and influenced your life?
- How has your love widened in these years of religious life?

These questions are an invitation to bring your life to our conversation about the vows. Nothing is done in a vacuum, and we bring our wonderful and challenging memories, experiences, and realities to the call to consecrated celibacy. When we talk about the vows, we are talking about how we have learned to love, listen, discover, and respond to what is calling now. These are also some of the key questions about our experiences of love, as we realize that love can grow throughout an entire lifetime. This does not ignore that sometimes we struggle with love, loving, and relationships, and that we also make mistakes. Yet love is our goal and longing, to be offered in freedom as it opens us up to the fullness of the Reign of God who is Love.

---

[1] This may not be the name of this vow in your Constitutions and other documents. I look at the components of various definitions in this chapter.

Sometimes people outside of religious life, and perhaps even some within religious life, look at this vow and think of it as a "Just Say No!" vow, when in actuality it means "Just Say Yes to Love." The vows are to be Good News for us, for our communities, and for the people of God and all creation. In order to see this good news more clearly, it helps to look at various dimensions of the vow of celibacy. We need to explore what helps us be healthy, humble, and generous in love.

In this chapter I look at various ways of defining and describing this vow.[2] We ground the vow in virtue and the various contexts in which we live it. Particular areas that cry out for consecrated celibates to be Good News in our world will be highlighted, always with the encouragement to see what the call is in the particular context in which you live. I look at this vow as a virtue within the framework of the preceding chapter: God's mission, call, cries, charism, and vows lived through prayer, community, and ministry.

Well-lived, consecrated celibacy is a witness to the Good News in the midst of the cries and longings around us. The sexual abuse crisis in society and within the Catholic Church[3] continue, asking all of us to look at how we are living healthy human sexuality and how our dynamics of power and authority are either building the Reign of God or are destructive of it. All forms of consecrated life must address this crisis, and we will do far better if we do so together, across life commitments. Unjust uses of power and authority must be addressed in gender relations and other areas. Although one chapter cannot provide a comprehensive response, I offer some beginnings, keeping in mind that the challenges must be addressed across all the vows.

Defining Our Terms[4]

There are many ways of naming this vow—including, but not limited to, celibacy, celibate chastity, or consecrated celibacy. You may have found some combination of these terms in your congregational Constitutions. I offer some general points about the wording of the vow to help us see what the vow means and perhaps does not mean or presume.[5] As in all areas of life, the understanding

---

[2]   I offer some historical context, but the purpose of this book is not to give a history but to invite contemporary calls to the vows. There are others who have worked already on the historical elements. See, for example, José Rovira Arumí, CMF, *Evangelical Counsels and Consecrated Life: Three Charismatic Ways to Follow Christ* (Quezon City, Philippines: Institute for Consecrated Life in Asia, 2015).

[3]   The Roman Catholic Church is not the only denomination struggling with this crisis, but it is the denomination within which Catholic religious life is situated, and so I focus on it here. Certainly my points apply more broadly.

[4]   I draw here from Arumí's *Evangelical Counsels*, especially Chapter 3.

[5]   For example, the term "vow of virginity" has also been used, but although I mention it here, it is not one I focus on in this chapter. The vow of virginity designates a person in religious life who is a spouse of Christ or soldier of Christ. There is a presumption here about

of this vow has evolved and continues to evolve.

Three words are used often, separately or in some combination, to name this vow: consecrated, chastity, and celibacy. But what do we mean by these terms? I will unpack these words, for each has something to offer us, and although each has some essential elements, no one word is complete as a description of our vow.

Consecrated

Each Christian is consecrated by baptism. To consecrate is to declare something sacred, to devote or commit someone to a way of life, usually with a religious purpose. Baptism brings us into the Christian community, with a commitment to grow in the life of discipleship. As Christians we are all consecrated first through baptism, belonging to God. This is a common denominator for all Christians.

Chastity

Chastity is a choice to live in a manner that sees God's grace in all creation and to live in a way that is faithful to one's commitments in light of God's vision and mission. Chastity speaks to fidelity to our faith lives and commitments. All are called to be faithful to their deepest values. Arumí offers this: "Who is a chaste person? Chaste is he/she who lives his/her sexuality in the right way according to the Gospel and to his/her state of life and vocation. . . . And, since every Christian has been consecrated in his/her baptism, we can say that his/her chastity whatever his/her state of life be, is consecrated too."[6]

One can be married and chaste or unchaste, and this chastity includes all the aspects of one's married life. Here again we are looking at virtues—dispositions and practices. One can be in religious life and be faithful or unfaithful to our commitments. This includes all areas of our lives as well—relational, physical, emotional, spiritual. Living chastity fully is a lifelong process; there is no one way to live it. Our call is to live this as a Christian community, people on a journey into the depths and breadth of God, in right relationship with all.

The term "consecrated" connects us to all the baptized, while "chastity" connects us to the wider community living in fidelity.

Celibacy

Celibacy is a way of living out the call to chastity and consecrated life in relationships with God, ourselves, and others. Celibacy is a way of loving, not a denial

---

the state of life of the person before religious life. Virgin would be someone who has never been genitally sexually active. Today, in many congregations the requirement is not about never having been sexually active but rather that someone has had a significant period of time before entering religious life during which the person was not sexually active.

6   Arumí, *Evangelical Counsels*, 98–99.

of loving. As in every form of life, in religious life there are choices and decisions about how we live. Some ways of intimacy are encouraged. Some ways are not. Each type of life commitment, including living celibate chastity as a religious, does better with support.

The word celibacy also refers to someone who abstains from marriage and from sexual intercourse. On its own, celibacy can look simply like negation (i.e., I do not marry or have a genital sexual relationship). For religious this cannot be the extent of it. The word celibacy, in religious life, needs to be amplified. Two possibilities are *celibate chastity* and *consecrated celibacy*. Celibacy needs a reason. Certainly, persons can be celibate and very generative, such as teachers in a classroom or relatives who care for their younger relatives. But in religious life, celibacy without a compelling spiritual reason—beyond even ministry or community living—will be insufficient for most people to maintain over one's life in a way that witnesses love and the source of Love, God. Celibacy in religious life is to witness to God's mission, God's reign.

Consecrated Celibacy or Celibate Chastity

As a way of bringing in the essential aspects of this vow, I suggest naming the vow *consecrated celibacy* or *celibate chastity*[7] in order to witness to the Reign of God. These denote a way of loving that names one's commitment and desire to live and love with fidelity one's commitment to God and service to others. Both ways of naming the vows speak of a fidelity to God lived through the Christian tradition in the world today. Rather than a form of negation, celibacy points to our deepest commitments and values. Consecrated celibacy denotes a baptismal commitment and way of life within religious life or consecrated life.

What is most important in all these descriptions is a sense of the "why" of consecrated celibacy or celibate chastity. It is for the sake of God's mission, God's vision for society and all creation. This doesn't mean that people who are married or single aren't living this commitment. It does mean that for religious their primary life commitment is to make visible God's love beyond family or ministry and in an ever-widening sense of relationship, in building community, in outreach, and in

---

7   Both "consecrated celibacy" and "celibate chastity" are used to refer to this vow, but for the purposes of consistency in this chapter I will use "consecrated celibacy." Suzanne Breckel describes four elements that are included in most definitions of celibate chastity: "1) it has to do with pursuing and developing ways of loving that are non-genital; 2) it needs to be rooted in the spiritual life; 3) it needs to be connected vitally to one's call in life and one's call to ministry; 4) it has to do with a style of life wherein one chooses to not be coupled." Found in Sean D. Sammon, FMS, *An Undivided Heart: Making Sense of Celibate Chastity*, 20th anniv. ed. (North Charleston, SC: Create Space Independent Publishing Platform, 2013), 111. Suzanne Breckel gave this compilation in a lecture: "Sexuality, the Celibate's Response" (unpublished lecture, National Assembly of Religious Brothers meeting, Providence, RI, 1977).

prayer. The gift of consecrated life is that we declare ourselves to be available to areas of need, to go beyond ourselves and even our own communities, to reach out to where there are wounds, suffering, and yearning for new or more abundant life. We come not as saviors but as ones who seek the Beloved and who by our lives point to God's priorities and strive to make them visible.

Perhaps the most important point about the vow is that *the spiritual life is key to living this vow*. Living this vow with integrity, with wholeness and holiness, requires an active and holistic spiritual life. All dimensions of ourselves are included in the conversation with God. This is how we stay healthy and grow. At the heart of celibate chastity is a desire for union with God. From this flows love of others. We witness to this love in action, but it flows from our interior depths. Whether we came to know God through the love of others or came to love others as a response to God's love, or a combination of these, a relationship with God, spiritual life, is essential for living consecrated celibacy.

To this end we regularly ask questions such as, "What is God doing in the midst of my life these days? What is the Spirit inviting, pruning, culling, and opening? How am I loving in this context?" I find that persons with a passion for God do indeed also have a passion for humanity and creation. And these passions are continually shaped in spiritual practices and a spiritual life that dedicates space for God. We make meaning of celibate chastity through our spiritual lives. This meaning making is crucial.

Living consecrated celibacy in community requires finding ways to hear one another and create with one another, even as each generation has particular gifts to offer. Each one is needed. Each must offer what she or he can. This is generativity. We need the relationships of all individuals and age groups, though due to personality and other elements of culture we may lean in different directions. The more we dialogue with one another, the more we help and learn from one another.

Celibate chastity or consecrated celibacy witnesses to God as one's primary love and to giving all to God's mission. There are internal and external dimensions. Participation in God's mission requires, as we saw in Chapter 3 on contemplation, an encounter and ongoing relationship with God. This is the interior dimension. Different scripture passages have been used over time to offer some hints of what following this way looks like for religious. Some have used scripture and the language of the Song of Songs (e.g., "My beloved is mine and I am his")[8] or the Psalms (e.g., "O God you are my God, I seek you, my soul thirsts for you")[9] to speak of this relationship. Some religious have used spousal imagery to name this vow in light of their relationship with God (i.e., Bride of Christ). The relationship with God is the primary love, from which all other loves flow and have their proper alignment. When God is the center of my life, all other loves are in right relationship.

Our lives also witness not only what God has done but also what God will do—and is even now doing among us. This is the external dimension. Participation

---

[8]   Song of Songs 2:16.

[9]   Ps 63:1a.

in God's mission brings even the mystical dimensions of one's relationship with God into the prophetic dimensions. Our lives lived in love both denounce what is contrary to God's vision for the full flourishing of all creation and also announce and point to God's desires for the fullness of all life. The many examples of Jesus's encounters with others shows us that love widens both our hearts and the foci of our concern and actions.

Finally, it is important to note that while all Christians are called to the evangelical counsels of poverty and obedience, only some are called to the vow of celibacy for the sake of the Reign of God. And while chastity is for all to live, chastity lived as celibacy is not. Some live celibacy with or without a religious or spiritual focus, but without a spiritual meaning, it would be too empty to sustain someone in religious life. For religious it cannot simply be something that goes with the territory. It must be more.

As we have seen above, the vow of consecrated celibacy must be lived through prayer, community, and ministry. This is common to all three vows. It is in the living of all these areas of our lives that we find integral consecrated life in action. These areas are not separate but mutually assist one another. We do this for one another in ever widening circles of relationship.

What Is the Good News about Consecrated Celibacy?

As I have said earlier, each vow and aspect of religious life is, in its context, framed and reframed in response to God's evolving call, with the essentials intact. The vow must reflect the Good News of the Gospel, the message of Jesus pointing to God's mission and vision. Living out the great commands to love God and to love our neighbor is a learning process. We learn by doing, reflecting, and continually practicing. It is essential that we long—and are called—to love as God loves and as Jesus points to in his love. The calls and cries of this time help us see the dimensions of the vow that seek embodiment and articulation.

Consecrated celibacy is a virtue, requiring both actions and attitudes; this is a dynamic process. The vowed life requires effort, practice, desire, ongoing reflection, and discernment (personal and communal). We know from John 3:16 that "God so loved the world" . . . and so loves us. But we are still on the journey of loving the world as God loves—fully, unconditionally, and passionately. We are in the process of living this vow, and as with any process and virtue, this takes time and practice. Our call is to live the process ever more completely and fully in response to this particular time.

We live our responses to this time publicly as well as personally and communally. This is an opportunity to proclaim the Good News about consecrated celibacy. This vow is to be Good News for the people and for creation. We do not here point to ourselves but to how God is longing to love and is loving all God's creation. We offer ourselves accountably to God and our brothers and sisters as we pronounce this vow with our lives. Consecrated celibacy is also to be Good

News for our communities and our congregations. Our lives lived in love have a life-generating effect in our communities. We provide support to one another and offer a way of together discerning how and where we are being called. Finally, the vow must be Good News for ourselves. Good News doesn't necessarily mean easy—Jesus's life was hardly easy—but Good News does mean it is worth our very lives. In fact, if there is no growing edge for us with each vow, we can bit by bit lose the flexibility required for this time. The vow of celibacy cannot be simply what goes along with the other dimensions of religious life.[10] The vow is a key to our ministerial, communal, and prayer lives, our relational lives. Any other understanding makes the life unsustainable over time.[11] Remember the vows are *dynamic*, constantly evolving and calling, a continual gift of the Spirit. The vows, like our lives, call us to interior conversion, internal transformation, and external revitalization.

Ten Markers of Consecrated Celibacy as Good News for Our Time

I offer markers of the vow of consecrated celibacy that are being called forth for our time, in light of the cries and calls of the world and church around us.[12] We may hear these writ large or in our particular locations, but they all call us to witness the Good News as communities of hope. I offer here a "thin" version of key dimensions of consecrated celibacy today. This "thin" version is filled out by each person and community in response to the cries and contexts in which they live. As you read these, consider what the markers might look like in your local context and in the larger contexts in which you engage with others.

1. Consecrated celibacy is a space of creativity. Love allows us to witness what is happening (the mysticism of open eyes) and still imagine another possible world into action. Our lives create spaces where the words of Isaiah take hold of us: "I am about to do a new thing; now it springs forth, do you not perceive it? I will make a way in the wilderness and rivers in the desert" (Is 43:19). The author of Isaiah alludes to the Exodus event and tells people that there is more. "Do not remember the former things or consider the things of old" (43:18). Our lives are witnesses to God creating the new in unexpected places, even where there are deserts and deep valleys. As such, our vow brings us to radical openness to others.

---

10 Mark Falkenhain, OSB, "Living Celibacy: A Proposed Model for Celibacy Formation Programs," *Human Development* 34, no. 2 (Summer 2013): 23–29.

11 See ibid., which encouragingly points out that how we may see the vow in our early formation is to evolve. See also John Mark Falkenhain, *How We Love: A Formation for the Celibate Life* (Collegeville, MN: Liturgical Press, 2019).

12 This doesn't mean that people outside religious life lack these gifts. I simply name these as elements of the vow(s) that are needed today and that are part of the gift of living the vow.

The vow of consecrated celibacy points to God's boundless creative possibilities, present and future. Margaret Scott, OSB, writes that "it is through consecrated chastity that we rechannel procreative, physical energy into a creative life force that enters into communion with all that is and with the Holy."[13] Nothing is beyond the scope of possibility; rooted in the world, we work to make visible the Good News of God's message. Pope Francis was calling this forth when he asked religious to "Wake Up the World."[14] The prophetic dimension of consecrated life enjoins creativity and religious imagination.

When I consider one of the great needs in my local world of south side Chicago, that of finding ways for young people to feel connected as worthy sons and daughters of God, celibate chastity asks me to imagine into creation new ways of showing love and care for young people in the midst of great poverty, drugs, and gun violence. New ways of being community can create models of conflict resolution beyond the current responses to conflict and violence, which too often include a school-to-prison pipeline. The work of the religious and collaborators in the Precious Blood Ministry of Reconciliation in Chicago's Back of the Yards and Englewood neighborhoods is an example of love in action that flows in response to a cry and is then lived out through a charism into action and attitudes that change persons and can change systems.[15] This is where the charismatic flow of our vows is most visible.

2. Consecrated celibacy points to eschatological hope, the telos (end or goal) of our lives. Consecrated celibacy points beyond ourselves to a reality that includes us but is far bigger. Our lives are to be signs of the new heaven and the new earth God is creating and inviting us into.[16] Our vow speaks to the purpose of our lives, which is to proclaim God's love through our lives. Jesus's life, death, and resurrection point to a way of life and relationship that extends even beyond our time on earth. In religious life today most of our congregations can name those women and men who preceded us and who pointed to a way of life that was a loving response to the world around them—a vision and way of hope, love, justice, mercy, and peace. Most lived quotidian lives that spoke of extraordinary faith, hope, and love. They pointed to God and continue to do so beyond their physical lives.

An eschatological awareness gives us the humility to realize that as consecrated life evolves, how it will look is beyond our imagining. Even at this moment relationships with our partners in mission are beckoning more deeply and fully. With God we know there is always more. Good News indeed! With eschatological hope we

---

[13]   Margaret Scott, OSB. "Greening the Vows: *Laudato Si'* and Religious Life," *Way* 54, no. 5 (October 2015): 86.

[14]   See Antonio Spadaro, SJ, "'Wake Up the World!' Conversation with Pope Francis about the Religious Life," *La Civiltà Cattolica* (2014) I, 3–17, trans. Donald Maldari, SJ (revised January 6, 2015), https://onlineministries.creighton.edu.

[15]   See https://www.pbmr.org.

[16]   I am grateful to Margaret Scott's work on this. See "Greening the Vows," 84.

can boldly risk and contribute to what is calling forth for God's mission. In God our lives are both beacons and beckonings.

3. Consecrated celibacy is inherently about all dimensions of our relational lives. Relationship—how we relate to one another and all creation—is essential to this vow. It truly is all about relationships. This is a stance that requires continual conversion. A phrase used by many religious groups is that we have "hearts as wide as the world,"[17] and that indeed is the call. This marker includes radical openness to the unexpected, which leads us beyond our usual circles. Our own circles continue widening here, and by our efforts others widen as well. This is the movement of integral religious life that includes Pope Francis's reminder of integral ecology. We are one in this.

Jesus of Nazareth is our premier example of the Good News of relationality. While a man of his culture, Jesus's relationship with God offers us a window into what is possible. He shows us what it is to be in relationship with a God who knows and loves us. Through Jesus's words and actions we see how we are to be in relationship with others.

The parable of the Prodigal Son is a wonderful example. During retreat one year I discovered that the word prodigal means extravagant. Before that I always thought prodigal meant someone wayward or who abandoned relationships and responsibilities. Yes, this younger son had asked his father for his inheritance and then squandered it away, only to realize later in difficult times that he needed to return home, trusting that even being treated like the servants there would be a better life than his now. The term "prodigal" opens up descriptors of the father, who is extravagant, generous, and loving beyond the imagining of both sons. The younger son begs forgiveness and receives love in abundance. The older son comes to find the limits of his own capacity for generosity, even as we sense the father does not give up on his eldest. We, the daughters and sons of God, are invited to imagine what the extravagant love that is consecrated celibacy is calling us to in our world today. Relationships lead us to building bridges.

The next three points develop the call to relationship, engaging both Gospel calls and clarion cries.

4. Consecrated celibacy's call to relationship requires entering into the suffering and woundedness of the other. The vowed life is an invitation to participate in the Paschal Mystery in prayer, community, and ministry. It is not that we bring God to the places of suffering and vulnerability; God is there before us. Our call is to witness, to embody, to incarnate Love of the other. Sometimes this means solidarity with the other, waiting for the other to name the need and direction. Sometimes this means standing at the foot of the cross with the person. Often our presence is all we can do to take the suffering person from the cross. Here gentleness is needed

---

17   For example, this phrase is used by my own congregation, the Religious of the Sacred Heart of Jesus and Sisters of Notre Dame.

especially. Crosses have nails and they must be removed carefully so as not to add to pain.

Entering into the places of suffering, margins, exclusion, and woundedness is a particular call of religious life, whatever a community's charism may be. How and what you do is dictated by charism, but that you DO respond is the key. *Religious are called to be exactly where others are not or cannot be. This is the radical nature of celibate chastity and all the vows.* We come to incarnate Good News where it is needed. This also reminds us that our lives need to be touched by "the other" in need, including all of creation, whether in full-time or in volunteer ministry. This changes our hearts, too. This is part of the conversion, transformation, and revitalization of religious life that the Spirit continually calls forth. At times only this can get us out of our self-absorption or the ruts that keep us bound.

Of course, such presence demands preparation and work from us, including self-knowledge of our own wounds and healings. My favorite definition of mercy is "a willingness to enter into the chaos of another's life in order to respond."[18] Our call is to embody mercy. This sounds good in theory, but in reality this call can be daunting and we may resist. This is normal.

Years ago, on the first day of my thirty-day Ignatian retreat, I was without a thought in my head about suffering. I was actually just enjoying the unusually warm and beautiful November weather in Italy as I walked on a lovely garden path, when I heard clearly as if spoken aloud: "Maria, if you know the love of Christ you can suffer." Yikes! The phrase made no sense to me at the moment except that I could feel its truth. I was no stranger to suffering. Walking with a family member who suffered had taught me a lot about both suffering and accompaniment. Yet I think God knew my resistance about entering into the suffering of others. I shared the phrase with my retreat director and she too was caught by the phrase—she invited me to let it be and see what the rest of the retreat would offer.

The truth of that statement is now clear: only with love can we bring love to the places of suffering, places where we encounter persons on the margins and peripheries. It is only with love that we can see poverty of all kinds (physical, psychological, structural) and respond. The phrase "Maria, if you know the love of Christ you can suffer," made more and more sense as I went through the Ignatian Exercises, falling in love with God all over again, walking with Jesus as he walked, staying at the cross as he suffered, and meeting the Risen Christ on the road and on the shores.

Accompaniment isn't always what we imagine. Religious life in much of North America and Europe continues to experience the aging and death of more of our elders, sisters, and brothers who are wisdom figures. The call is to walk alongside them as well, to be in relationship with them, and love them in all ways we can. This

---

[18]   I learned this from Jim Keenan, SJ, while in graduate school, and I find myself sharing this definition often. It resonates with many. For further information, see James F. Keenan, SJ, *The Works of Mercy: The Heart of Catholicism*, 3rd ed. (Lanham, MD: Rowman & Littlefield, 2017).

love does not keep us at home, however, but must also move us to see and respond to the needs and losses of others around us. These realities also call us to act in our time *for this time*. Just as those before us, we are called to discern the road ahead and walk together with those given to accompany us on the journey. Here we can imagine the conversation on the road to Emmaus where we hear the Risen Christ speaking through our realities to help us see and go forth afresh. Jesus is our invitation into the dying and rising of life together.

It is also in the space of accompaniment of persons on the margins, entering into their reality as we can, finding the courage to denounce injustice and announce God's vision for all. Pope Francis explains that Jesus "hopes that we will stop looking for those personal or communal niches which shelter us from the maelstrom of human misfortune, and instead to enter into the reality of other people's lives and to know the power of tenderness. Whenever we do so, our lives become wonderfully complicated."[19] In the midst of all this, we shall see wonders.

5. Our vow of consecrated celibacy requires us to live integral ecology, that is, to live in right relationship with the entire earth community. There is a clarion call to a greater respect and care for our common home at this time. In *Laudato Si'* Pope Francis has made it very clear that the cries of the people and cries of the earth are interconnected: "We are not faced with two separate crises, one environmental and the other social, but rather one complex crisis which is both social and environmental. Strategies for a solution demand an integrated approach to combating poverty, restoring dignity to the underprivileged, and at the same time protecting nature."[20] A proper relationship with all brings us to that same understanding as God's response to creation: "And God saw everything that he had made, and indeed, it was very good."[21] Seeing creation this way brings us to care for that which we love. Margaret Scott describes this well:

> Religious consecration is penetrated and shaped by an awareness of and commitment to the integrity of creation. An ecological spirituality brings to the vows new significance and meaning. It places itself at the heart of vocation so that every dimension of our being—our loving, having and wanting—can become ecological actions, as we are gradually transformed so as to love, to serve and to reverence creation.[22]

Note the reference to gradual transformation.

Jesus of Nazareth is our guide here, one who was familiar enough with the earth and animals to include them in his teachings (e.g., references to sheep, farmers

---

[19] Pope Francis, *Evangelii Gaudium* (*The Joy of the Gospel*), 270, http://w2.vatican.va.

[20] Pope Francis, *Laudato Si'* (*On Care for Our Common Home*) (2015), 139, http://w2.vatican.va.

[21] Gen 1:31.

[22] Scott, "Greening the Vows," 85.

planting and sowing, walking along rivers and shores).[23] We find in Jesus an attentiveness to all creation. As we practice seeing as Jesus sees, caring as Jesus cares, we come to see ourselves, as Jesus did, as part of and caring for all. Indeed, consecrated celibacy "binds us irresistibly to this Christ, empowering us to love what he loves. . . . It reminds us that we are part of everything and that we are most like Christ when we reverence the earth and all its peoples lovingly, when our hearts are broken by what touches and moves the compassion of God, who hears 'the cry of the earth and the cry of the poor' (*Laudato Si'*, 49)."[24]

Much of the work on evolutionary consciousness and scientific lenses to help us understand creation and our place in the evolving universe holds great possibility for enlarging and deepening our understanding and experience of the God who is Ultimate Mystery.[25]

6. *Consecrated celibacy calls us to interculturality.* In offering us such a diversity of gifts in our world, consecrated celibacy opens us to learning how God loves. Going beyond an appreciation of our own cultures to appreciate the cultures of others, religious life has an organic richness in its diversity of membership. Yet there is still a call to conversion to interculturality, the newness toward which the Spirit is inviting and persistently calling us. This is certainly true in the United States, where increasingly members not of the majority cultures are joining congregations. This is a gift of God to our time, not a difference to be tolerated but an offering toward the new communities God desires to create among us. The movement is from appreciation for the dignity of difference and diversity of people to an open-heartedness to the other who offers the gifts of cultural and other diversities.[26] As we open our hearts to one another and grow in knowing, appreciating, and engaging one another with all the gifts each offers, new community is formed.

The implications are endless. Engaging interculturally will influence our ministries, whether parishes, schools, social ministries, health care, or anywhere else. How we love one another and commit to creating community with one another shapes not only the future but affects our current ways of doing ministry. Our ways of praying will be enriched and perhaps transformed as we invite one another to sharing intimately here as well.

The impact is far-reaching. As Adriana Milmanda, SSpS, writes: "The very experience of being and accepting 'difference' questions and develops new and creative forms of inclusion of those whom the political, economic and religious systems force towards the margins and the frontiers of our societies, communities

---

[23]   I am grateful to Scott and others for these images and reminders.

[24]   Scott, "Greening the Vows," 85–86.

[25]   See the writings of Ilia Delio, OSF, and John Haught, which are wonderful examples of this work.

[26]   I am grateful to my colleagues Roger Schroeder, SVD, and vanThanh Nguyen, SVD, for their work and efforts in interculturality. I develop the topic of interculturality further in Chapter 6 on community.

and churches."[27] Anthony Gittins, CSSp, in his essential text, *Living Mission Interculturally*, writes that nothing less than the future of international congregations is at stake here:

> Given the global demographic changes that have occurred in the lifetime of today's senior members, the future of international religious communities must increasingly and intentionally become intercultural. Indeed, without the tectonic shift from "international" to "intercultural," there will be no viable future for international religious orders. Unless we can live together interculturally, we shall fall apart, retreat into our respective cultural groups, or continue half-heartedly, perhaps professing unconvincingly what we do not really live.[28]

As we do strive to heed the call to intercultural living in a world with such great gifts of diversity, we hear God's invitations to religious life, and this is good news. "The aim of consecrated life will not be to maintain itself in a permanent state in the different cultures it meets but to maintain the permanence of evangelical conversion in the heart of the progressive creation of an intercultural human reality."[29] The call and the invitation are clear.

7. Healthily living the vow of consecrated celibacy requires regular times of silence and solitude. This does not remove someone from outward care and affection but helps to hone one's loves properly. Henri Nouwen wrote that when, in solitude, you discover your belovedness by God, you see the belovedness of other people and call that forth.[30] It is in the deep listening of our lives that we grow the capacity to enter another's life with compassion. Knowing who and how we are in God affects all else. For many of us, there will be a continual challenge and tension between outreach and the interior life. Attending to the interior life gives us the capacity to have healthy boundaries and respond out of one's belovedness.

Again, we must be rooted in the spiritual life to live this as Good News. This is where we can hear, "This life must be worth everything or it's not worth it," and answer the question, "Is it still worth it?" It is worth everything. In prayer and solitude we can hear what the "everything" is that is being asked of us. In our solitude and silence God speaks if we listen.

---

[27] Adriana Carla Milmanda, SSpS, "Inserted Life: The Radical Nature of an Incarnated Spirituality," in *Intercultural Living*, vol. 1, ed. Lazar T. Stanislaus, SVD, and Martin Ueffing, SVD (Sankt Augustin: Steyler Missionswissenschaftliches Institut, 2015), 48.

[28] Anthony J. Gittins, CSSp, *Living Mission Interculturally: Faith, Culture, and the Renewal of Praxis* (Collegeville, MN: Liturgical Press, 2015), 2.

[29] Congregation for Institutes of Consecrated Life and Societies of Apostolic Life, *New Wine in New Wineskins: The Consecrated Life and its Ongoing Challenges since Vatican II* (Nairobi, Kenya: Paulines Publications Africa, 2017), 40.

[30] See Henri Nouwen, "From Solitude to Community to Ministry," *Leadership Journal* (Spring 1995).

It is important to acknowledge that there is a challenge to living this vow. We need both times of healthy intimacy with others and intimacy with God. Sandra Schneiders correctly observes:

> Celibacy is somewhat like high diving in that it springs from a particular charism (or spiritual "talent" that is not due to nor achieved by the person so gifted) and requires an enormous expenditure of personal resources in ascetical and spiritual practice to actually reach the ideal to which one is called. But like the talented diver who must practice and train at high intensity to achieve what most mortals regard as truly beyond human capacities, the person who lives consecrated celibacy over a lifetime is not a freak or oddity or abnormality. But no one would maintain that celibacy (or high diving) is a universal gift or is easily attained by anyone who is willing to put forth a little energy.[31]

All this is true. Yet it will be love that will give us the way. Loving others and allowing ourselves to be loved—by God, others, and creation—balances our desires. As we said in Chapter 2, a primary relationship with God helps us grow our capacity to love in right relationship according to our commitments.

Many live this call in community life, and in the midst of this we must cultivate a healthy and holistic way of living prayer, ministry, and community. Solitude and silence assist with integrating one's passion and energy as much as community and ministry do. Times of silence and solitude attune us to God's concerns, align us with God's loves. We also find in Jesus's life the pull toward time with God and time with people. Often in the Gospels we read of Jesus going off to pray. Sometimes it was with the apostles, but often enough he was alone. So, too, is our call to silence and solitude in the midst of our frenetically paced and noisy world. This witness is Good News, to us, our communities, our church, and our world.

8. Consecrated celibacy is meant to enflesh the person as an embodied relational agent. It is crucial to treat each person and all creation as sacred. I offer here a description of the person as agent, and then I offer a few points on relationality and embodiment.[32] Essential to any vision of the person is that one is an agent. The person as *agent* is a dynamic subject with participatory and self-determining capacities for living out one's loves and desires. The agent as *subject* is in opposition to person as object. The term *object* removes the person from the heart of decision-making, while *subject* defines the self to be a central starting point for discernment and decisions. The agent is a subject who acknowledges the inherent and integral good of each person and the dignity with which each person is to be regarded and treated.

---

[31]   Sandra M. Schneiders, IHM, *Selling All: Commitment, Consecrated Celibacy, and Community in Catholic Religious Life* (Mahwah, NJ: Paulist Press, 2001), 130.

[32]   Much of this is found in Maria Cimperman, *When God's People Have HIV/AIDS: An Approach to Ethics* (Maryknoll, NY: Orbis Books, 2005), especially Chapter 3.

In addition to being the starting point for decisions, the agent must also have self-determining capabilities for discernment and decision-making. This is because a capacity for self-determination gives meaning to choices and commitments. Self-determination necessarily flows from freedom. Commitments can be freely chosen with respect for one's self as well as for others. This freedom for self-determination is not disembodied, without social context, personal ties, or history.[33] It is instead a freedom *for* relationship and *in* relationship. Self-determination affirms responsibility in relationships and considers the complexities of decisions. The moral agent is to "act according to his or her conscience, in freedom, and with knowledge," and the "other" is also to be respected as an agent "capable of acting with the freedom of an informed conscience."[34] Self-determination requires that one is an active, engaged, and free *participant* in discussions and decisions.[35] Self-determination requires freedom, including a free and informed conscience.

What is the purpose of this freedom? It is for love. Agency is for the sake of *love*; it is about the love of self, God, and the other, in a continually spiraling movement. Only the agent as self-determining subject can answer the question: "Who will I love and how?" Loving oneself, knowing oneself as loved by God and other(s), as well as loving one another and God and caring for one's self, are all part of agency. There is an activity as well as a receptivity in this description. The agent in freedom chooses love out of her desires. The agent in freedom is situated.

The agent is also a *dynamic* subject, capable of growth and a deepening of one's loves and commitments and actions. Just as cultures, societies, and institutions are capable of change and therefore growth, so too is the person. The dynamic nature of the person allows for an incredible possibility for good in relationships and situations that the agent as subject can incarnate. While realizing that every person is capable of failing to love, I propose that the dynamism here essentially focuses on the person's capacity and activity of love. I certainly recognize the reality of evil, bad intentions, and wrong acts. They are found in the inequalities and structural injustices that assail so much of our world and promote inequalities of all kinds. However, the constructive element of dynamism is to acknowledge sin and failure to love[36] while working for good. This is the positive anthropology we are called to support and create.

---

[33] Margaret Farley distinguishes a feminist notion of freedom and autonomy from the problematic Kantian autonomy that is more disembodied and non-relational, in "A Feminist Version of Respect for Persons," in *Feminist Ethics and the Catholic Moral Tradition: Readings in Moral Theology*, no. 9, ed. Charles E. Curran, Margaret A. Farley, and Richard McCormick, SJ (New York: Paulist Press, 1996), 169.

[34] Richard Gula, *Reason Informed by Faith: Foundations of Catholic Morality* (New York: Paulist Press, 1989), 68. Citing Aquinas, Gula writes: "The Catholic tradition has been clear that we cannot speak of morality in any true sense apart from human persons who are able to act knowingly and willingly (cf. *ST.* I–II, prologue)," 68.

[35] Participation also has as an aim the removal of coercive elements from decision-making.

[36] I am grateful to James F. Keenan, SJ, who has developed the understanding of sin as a failure to bother to love. James F. Keenan, SJ, *Moral Wisdom: Lessons and Texts from the Catholic Tradition*, 3rd ed. (Lanham, MD: Rowman & Littlefield, 2016), 29.

Seeing the person as dynamic acknowledges the present reality of the person and appeals to the best that one is and can be. This dynamic character of the agent offers time and room for growth. The dynamic nature of the agent is essential for constructing a positive ethics rooted in the person's reality. Agency thus speaks deeply to all layers of relationship.

The very nature of God is relational; God is relationship. Roberto Goizueta reminds us that in the Trinity we learn about the "intrinsically and constitutively communal character of God."[37] Mercy Oduyoye sees the unity in diversity of the Trinity as a helpful model for relationships among individuals and the community. She writes that "we find the Persons in constant and perfect mutual relationship and we are reminded of the need for properly adjusted relationships in our human families, institutions, and nations."[38] Each person of the Trinity is distinct and yet equal.

Using Trinitarian imagery, theologian Catherine Mowry LaCugna offers us an image of community and how we are to live: "We were created for the purpose of glorifying God by living in right relationship as Jesus Christ did, by becoming holy through the power of the Spirit of God, by existing as persons in communion with God and every other creature."[39] The way we are to relate brings us into community with all. Nontando Hadebe, linking *ubuntu*[40] and Trinitarian understandings of community, furthers the implications of such community and communion. She writes that "to be made in the image of the Trinity means that relatedness, difference, equality, interdependence, and community define what it means to be human."[41] These descriptions offer us ways to see ourselves in God and to imagine how we are to be with all creation.

The relational agent who is embodied knows that one's whole person demands respect. All elements of the embodied person are sacred. All spiritual, emotional, physical, psychological, social, sexual, and cultural aspects of relating to one another as embodied, sexual persons must be treated with respect and dignity. All this

---

[37]   Roberto S. Goizueta, *Caminemos con Jesús: Toward a Hispanic/Latino Theology of Accompaniment* (Maryknoll, NY: Orbis Books, 1995), 66.

[38]   Mercy Amba Oduyoye, *Hearing and Knowing: Theological Reflections on Christianity in Africa* (Maryknoll, NY: Orbis Books, 1986), 140.

[39]   Catherine Mowry LaCugna, *God for Us: Trinity and the Christian Life* (New York: HarperCollins, 1991), 319. This quote was on the remembrance cards given at Catherine LaCugna's funeral.

[40]   *Ubuntu* is a Bantu term meaning "humanity." The *Oxford Learner's Dictionaries* defines *ubuntu* as "the idea that people are not only individuals but live in a community and must share things and care for each other," and notes that "The concept of *ubuntu* involves deep concern for others and having sound morals." https://www.oxfordlearners-dictionaries.com.

[41]   Nontando Hadebe, "Toward an *Ubuntu* Trinitarian Prophetic Theology: A Social Critique of Blindness to the Other," in *Living With(Out) Borders: Catholic Theological Ethics on the Migrations of Peoples*, ed. Agnes M. Brazal and María Teresa Dávila (Maryknoll, NY: Orbis Books, 2016), 214.

requires our freedom (another process); capacity to love and be loved; self-knowledge; capacity and commitment to growth; capacity to reflect, assess, and change; spiritual life and practices; and discipline of mind, heart, and body.

The world needs persons living a healthy sexuality that acknowledges the holistic blessing of our bodiliness: physical, psychosexual, sensual, and holy. This is a growing edge in religious life as well as in much of our world today. The witness of persons who can be in healthy relationships in which all are subjects and not objects, is crucial. Understanding ourselves as sexual persons who understand our physical, emotional, psychological, and social needs and desires and who are able to live intimate, chaste, and celibate relationships is a freeing invitation of relationship to others. It is impossible to sufficiently underscore the value of this witness in the innumerable places where people are used as objects and relationships are superficial or exploitive. This is a call to all who desire to live chaste lives.

That this is a challenge in the Catholic Church is clear. Too many headlines over the years reflect the sexual abuse scandals in the church. We are in process and not the experts. If our lives are to be public witnesses, then it is also time to publicly invite and engage the conversations and encounters with the wider church and all people of good will on how we are to live our human sexuality in a manner the affirms the full human dignity of each person and all people. We must learn from one another.

We continue to learn about areas of human sexuality through all the disciplines. All areas of psychosexual living are part of a growing literature that we must not fear but must engage thoughtfully and with our deepest values. Celibate chastity is asked of all religious, regardless of one's gender identity or sexual orientation identity, but if such aspects of one's life cannot be discussed somewhere, we are diminished. Not speaking about an area as close to us as ourselves doesn't change the realities and questions. We need to integrate this into our lives in religious life. Not speaking forces any discussion to go underground, which is rarely healthy for a person, congregation, institution, or church. Yes, such discussions are complicated and not necessarily easy. The church can and must hold the questions. The people of God must hold these questions. Jesus held all questions, and so must we.

The call to consecrated celibacy will at times be physically, psychically, and spiritually very challenging. A yearning for physical intimacy is natural and normal. Vowed consecrated life asks us to find ways to respond to these longings in ways that support deeply spiritual and profoundly human living. At times this requires creativity, and at all times it requires the practice of self-discipline. We are all people who are longing all of our lives, but the longings differ according to age, experience, and contexts. Sharing with trusted friends and spiritual accompaniment are important. Respectful, dignity-supporting relationships do happen without physical genital relationships. Friendships are graces. Religious life must offer a way of being in relationship and intimacy that is chaste and celibate. It is to intimacy that I now turn.

9. Intimacy is essential for living consecrated celibacy. So much of living in constant activity or even constant contact can make living more functional than desirable. The call of our lives, however, is to intimacy. All people are invited to intimate relationships. For religious all intimate relationships are welcomed and even encouraged except genital intimacy or intimacy that does not support living consecrated, chaste, and celibate lives.[42]

Psychologist Lynn Levo, CSJ, who conducts workshops around the world, offers the following types of intimacy with the reminder that only genital intimacy is not acceptable for religious.[43] The others are encouraged. As you read these, note which ones are a regular part of your life and which ones invite you.

- Emotional Intimacy (being tuned to each other's wavelength)[44]
- Intellectual Intimacy (closeness in the world of ideas)
- Aesthetic Intimacy (sharing experiences of beauty)
- Creative Intimacy (sharing in acts of creating together)
- Recreational Intimacy (relating experiences of fun and play)
- Work Intimacy (the closeness of sharing common tasks)
- Crisis Intimacy (closeness in coping with problems and pain)
- Conflict Intimacy (facing and struggling with difference)
- Commitment Intimacy (mutually derived from common investment)
- Spiritual Intimacy (the we-ness in sharing ultimate concerns)
- Communication Intimacy (the source of all types of true intimacy)
- Genital Intimacy (erotic or orgasmic closeness)—this is the only form of intimacy not acceptable for men and women religious.

To the above I would add:

- Earth Intimacy (closeness or feeling integral oneness with all of creation).

Can you suggest other forms of intimacy?

Where we are in the many aspects of our lives, including developmentally, experientially, and psychosexually, will affect these inclinations. Healthy consecrated celibacy is always a process, and these areas of intimacy offer some possibilities for both growth and depth.

10. Our consecration and call to chastity invites shared support and invitation— mutuality—with our wider charism family members in other ways of life and with the

---

[42] There will also be culturally determined ways of relating intimately. For example, in my family kissing on the cheek as well as hugging was a standard practice growing up. This may not be an acceptable practice in another part of the world or even in another family. Attentiveness to practices in cultures and congregations is important.

[43] This list is part of a handout from workshops Levo has given over the years to persons in formation.

[44] According to Levo, this type of intimacy is what most people really want.

people of God also striving to live out their baptismal calls faithfully in their life realities. There is much possibility in this way of sharing and supporting one another in our life commitments and calls. Helping one another see blind spots and growing edges in our efforts to live vowed life is a gift. Supporting one another amid the common realities of life, such as healthy ways of living intimacy, is another.

Mutual dialogue, within consecrated life, within our charism families, and with all people, also helps us grow into our call. We must encounter one another humbly, respectfully, and invite conversation. We dialogue with one another about what the people of God and God's creation need from us. We dialogue about how we can serve more deeply and fully through our charisms and way of life. We dialogue about how we might live this call of consecration and chastity together. In addition, our brothers and sisters in other forms of life (widowed, married, divorced, and single) have much to offer and teach us in a mutual dialogue. These markers are the gifts and the growing edges of consecrated celibacy.

Call, Cries, and Charism

Although we all desire to live God's call to mission and to hear and respond to the calls around us, which calls we respond to and how these calls and cries are lived comes through the gifts we have received, our charism. When I discuss the vow of obedience I will look at the discernment of calls more specifically. Here I can say that charism will lead us to how we are to live the vow of consecrated celibacy so as to respond to the world's cries and offer Good News.

We live our responses to God's cries and the calls of creation through our charism, which is lived through our vows, which are manifested through our prayer, community, and ministry lives. See the chart in Chapter 4.

The responses will flow from our charism (or spirituality), through our vows, entering every area of our lives. So, for example, if my charism as a Religious of the Sacred Heart of Jesus calls me to hear and witness to the love of the heart of Christ to the wounded heart of humanity and creation, then I must find a way to be present where there is pain and suffering. My heart will shrivel up rather than widen if I do not. As I said earlier, in Chicago I hear a loud cry for belonging; people need to belong and know that their life and presence matter. This cry calls me outward to build communities of belonging, to include all in prayer, and to find some way in ministry of responding in welcome. These are personal, communal, systemic, and structural calls and movements.

My call is also in community. It is true that the wounds outside our communities can also be found inside them. If we are trusted with each other's loves we will also be trusted with each other's pains. Consecrated celibacy lived through my charism asks me to attune myself to my sisters and the wide Sacred Heart family—and beyond—in our communities and gatherings. Sometimes this is where the greater challenge resides, for we may live with people whose wounds are clear yet not open. All we can do is provide the space for love to be present. Being present is a way of "doing" love. In community some years ago I lived with a sister who was grieving the suicide of a family member. Words fail at such times, but presence, gentleness, and quiet kindnesses were part of all of us living with her. We tried, without naming it, to hold her in a blanket of love. People signed up for extra cooking slots, cleaned areas that were not on their responsibility list, and just attuned themselves to what might be helpful. I don't know if the sister ever noticed it, but that wasn't the point. Loving is the point of consecrated celibacy.

Whatever my ministry, the charism must also be lived through my vows. Consecrated celibacy calls me to welcome not only people in need but to find ways to care for the earth in need. Intention matters. When I can drive or take a bus and I choose the bus for the sake of the resources we cannot continue to use so irresponsibly, I respond with my heart. How and what I teach and write about also speaks to my vow of celibate chastity.

Free people are also joyful people. What does celibate love poured out to the world look like? There are some commonalities. We would see women and men of prayer who respond to the unmet needs of our day. The love would go where hope is seemingly absent. *Disponibilidad* (radical availability) will characterize these religious women and men. Their energy moves us beyond institutional maintenance to responding to signs of the times. The good news is that such efforts will require vision, imagination, and creativity, with both systems and persons engaged. The clarity of vision and efforts to live this personally and communally will be lived transparently, freely, in solidarity, and with joy.

And so we go—to consider the Good News about community.

Questions for Reflection and Discussion

1. How would you define the vow of consecrated celibacy now?
2. What do you see as your growing edge in living this vow?
3. What do you need to put in place in order to live consecrated celibacy intimately, holistically, and dynamically? Consider this in relationship to God, self, community, church, and world.

6

LIVING COMMUNITY

Doors and Destinations

Before reading, reflect on the following:
- What has community life taught you?
- What does your constitution say about community?

The subtitle of this book is "Creating Global Communities of Hope." Creating community is both local and global, for what we seek on the local is also what is needed on the global. And what we create on a global level affects our ways of looking at what is needed and possible on a local level. Additionally, our call as Christians is to build communities of hope, so our task has particularly, although not exclusively, Christian overtones. Building community is part of our participation in the mission of God. Building Christian community has always been important, and in this time it is particularly so. Some persons and nations are closing doors and building walls even as the cries for a just and loving world and building the Reign of God remind us that communion is our ultimate destination.

In this chapter I consider community through the metaphors of doors and destinations, and I consider some biblical elements of community. In addition I look at the edges calling us more deeply into community, to see the edges calling as invitations.

Community as a Door

Many countries and cities now have posters of the various types of doors in their neighborhoods. Doors of Dublin. Doors of Boston. Doors of Barcelona. Doors of Guadalajara. We enter through doors. Some doors are colorful and ornate while others are simple and plain. Doors may have bells or knockers. Some doors are locked and others are ajar or wide open. Many doors in the United States are a standard size, built so most can enter them, although sometimes special needs require a larger doorway. Doors are of different sizes in different countries. Older houses may have certain types of door and more modern ones other types. Doors are significant.

91

Community as a door is an apt metaphor for several reasons:

1. Community is a door we must choose. We have to choose to enter community, to go through the door and enter it fully. Sometimes we only know what it will involve and ask as we live into community. We must walk through the door. Every time someone joins a community or leaves a community, we enter a new community and open a door of opportunity.

2. Community is a door to growth. Entering community is to go into the door of knowing ourselves, with our strengths and vulnerabilities. The more self-knowledge we have, the more we know what we may offer and also what we would ask of community. Life in community teaches us much about ourselves and about others. The opened door calls forth our malleability.

3. Community is the door to creating a *common home*. The door we open goes first to the whole community, not to our individual rooms. We come into a common home, not my home.

4. Community is a doorway to forgiveness, healing, and reconciliation. We learn the art of relationship in community. In relating to one another we come to know that community lived well heals, calls forth, and teaches. Community gives us a place to be ourselves and to live into our best selves. This will invariably mean that we will need to be forgiven as often as we will need to forgive.

5. Community is a door to mutuality. We all enter the same door, and we all have the same key to get into the door. While some in the community may serve as conveners and organizers, gone is the day of one person seen as "superior" to anyone else. The desire is for mutuality. Communication between people shows us what mutuality looks like. For example, I used to live with someone who always wanted to give a reason for not doing something or going to something. I personally found no need for this. I trusted she would choose well. I realized later that she needed me to know and to care why she would or would not do something. It was about keeping her present in my life. I am now grateful for the kindness of her explanations. That speaks to communication and mutuality for her and is a way of being in relationship.

6. Community is a door we allow others to enter. Community is more than a house; it is a home. A home is not just a structure but a tapestry of relationships. When a place is a home, when this is my home, there is another set of doors we enter.

   I remember a time when I was feeling especially vulnerable while dealing with some challenges. I was far more sensitive to who was coming into my community, and I knew there were people I could not easily invite. Whether others came or not, I had to trust that my community would also hold me. This can be a reconciling space if it is first a safe space, a home. Home is where we work through life.

7.   Community is a doorway to hospitality. When someone enters a community, we practice hospitality until the other feels at home. We are sensitive to the needs of the new person, attentive to ways she can engage in conversation, enter into prayer with the group, or offer initiatives. It means she can also help set the agenda, whether of conversation or the menu. Hospitality calls upon all to listen and hear. To allow all to be at home.

Community as Destination

As wonderful as doors are, they are not the ultimate destination but a means to access it. Communities exist to announce and build the Reign of God; they are to lead us toward it. Our own destination is participation in building the Reign of God.

1.   Community as destination is community in pursuit of the outward call, leading us together toward our goal, which is God. Community with God as its goal helps us become more like God, though always mindful that we are flawed.

2.   Community leads us to love of God *and* love of neighbor. When we know our primary relationship is in God, we can love our neighbors in healthy ways. Being in relationship with our neighbors brings us into relationship with all creation. Community links us with the entire earth community, and this too changes us. We see all as gift of God and as interconnected.

3.   Community is dynamic. Each time we build community, the call is to go outward and build more. The question is always: Where are we to build community next? And how? We answer these questions as we respond to the places where hope, mercy, love, peace, and reconciliation are needed. This is where and how community is built.

4.   Community as destination means we are required to go where the other has much to teach us about community. We do not go presuming we are the creators. Often where we go is beyond our current capacity to imagine, and so community creates new possibilities in us. We witness to and participate in what the Spirit longs to create among us all.

5.   Community is the space where forgiveness and reconciliation happen.

It is good to remember that the Risen Christ went through doors to reach the disciples and rebuild community among them. He also took them beyond their limits and called them to proclaim in deed and word the Good News to the ends of the earth.

Shifting Landscapes

This is a wonderful time to look at community life because so much is calling as old ways are crumbling. So much is in movement. Therefore, it is a great time to look again at what the essentials are and what is now being invited in light of the calls of our time. What is being asked of us? Certainly, we are being asked to awaken our religious imagination. Our charisms and the cries around us give us direction for the answers to our questions of "What are we to do? And how?" In all areas of consecrated life, community is lived out through our vows, in prayer, and in ministry.

Community is to create the environment that leads people to their deepest longings and God's deepest longings. This builds community. Here again we have the converging of call, contemplation, and cries.

We live this in the midst of shifting landscapes. Some of these landscapes include the following.

1. The massive shifting of numbers of religious in the United States, which affects community living options. There are fewer religious in many places, which means that community living itself also asks for our creativity. This may mean looking at community life across congregations and even across forms of life. While community living with members of other congregations is not new, there is a new call to intentionality about what kind of community is being asked for in this time. We cannot simply repeat what has been but must ask where life is needed in our communities (doors) and how we create community wherever we are (destinations). The call to community may very well invite new ways of living gospel values for the sake of God's mission.

2. Increasing diversity in a number of communities. We shall see in the next section that this presents calls for openness and conversion to each and all. Here is where the Spirit is creating the new among us that we cannot yet fully see.

3. The importance of location—geography matters, and we must again ask if and where we are is marked by the margins or edges of society. Intentionality is necessary.

Seeing the Spirit's invitation in this time can change everything. What if we could imagine the new being created as an invitation from God? Is this time calling for restructuring or re-creating in community? Binding or loosening? Can we see what is dying, a particular way we have been living community, as a pathway to the new life calling? This may include more mobility and more openness to considering with whom we live, perhaps persons outside our regions, congregations, or consecrated life. These are growing edges and opportunities today.

More dynamic structures need to be constructed, allowing for greater adaptability for living according to the needs and cries around us. This is an opportunity to ask what our charisms are inviting us to and moving toward creating it. Structures may be less concrete and more mobile; again, intentionality is essential. The attitude of *ad experimentum* is needed for members and leader-members.

Communities that take seriously the call to be missionary disciples will be able to transform persons and structures. In *The Joy of the Gospel,* Pope Francis gives us such beautiful ideas, not only for our institutional church but for local churches and communities: "I dream of a 'missionary option,' that is, a missionary impulse capable of transforming everything so that the Church's customs, ways of doing things, times and schedules, languages and structures can be suitably channeled for the evangelization of today's world rather than for her self-preservation."[1] I find here a clear invitation to community life, inviting transformation in all.

Biblical and Theological Foundations of Community

Scripture offers us further insights into community. We read in the beginning of Genesis that God created humanity in God's image, creating them as male and female.[2] From the beginning we were created to be in relationship. God/Love created out of love and created us for relationship with God and with one another. Acknowledging the human dignity of each individual created by God is the basis for all relationships.

In Genesis we are reminded that God chose to bring a people rather than an individual into a special covenantal relationship, as when he declares to Abram: "I will establish my covenant between me and you, and your offspring after you throughout their generations, for an everlasting covenant, to be God to you and to your offspring after you."[3] The call is for us to build community as God is building community. Sandra Schneiders reminds us: "It was with the Hebrews as a people, as a community, that God made an everlasting covenant at Sinai (Ex 24)."[4] Note that community is built out of vulnerability, where God enters. God is intimately connected with both the individual persons and the community. God's involvement continues into the life and death of Jesus, through the Gospels, and forward to our time and beyond.

The "visitation," the meeting of the pregnant Mary and pregnant Elizabeth serves as a particularly instructive image of community.[5] Here are two women who need each other. Each has been told that she has new life within her, and because of

---

[1]   Pope Francis, *Evangelii Gaudium* (*The Joy of the Gospel*), 27, http://w2.vatican.va.

[2]   Gen 1:1–30.

[3]   Gen 17:7.

[4]   Sandra M. Schneiders, IHM, *Selling All: Commitment, Consecrated Celibacy, and Community in Catholic Religious Life* (New York: Paulist Press, 2001), 279.

[5]   See Lk 1:26–57; Mt 1:19–25.

the unexpected circumstances, each needs the other with whom she can share this news. That both women, one young and one older, are pregnant reminds us that all of the members in our communities can bear new life. The Spirit was active in each one's life, and they knew it. At the same time, each needed the other for support. Each affirmed the life in the other. The embrace of the two women was new life touching new life. How beautiful that we read of Elizabeth telling Mary that the infant in her own womb leapt upon hearing Mary's voice! Both women said "yes" to Holy Mystery, and God responded with life. So it is with us. In the visitation story we see that God was with each personally just as the call and invitation of each of us was personal, offering and awaiting a response.

In addition, although the depiction of this scene is that of just two women meeting, it is historically and culturally not probable that Mary would have traveled alone.[6] She would have had at least another person with her. Elizabeth would also have had others in her home. In their encounter, the women were praising God together. We, too, praise God individually, but we also do so communally, and liturgy reminds us of our call to community. Paul Wadell expresses this beautifully: "With worship *we enter the world of God* so we can come to know ways of God and become active participants in the Reign of God."[7] In community we witness to the Good News of God's constant creativity.

Through the life of Jesus, we learn about building communities with the values of the Reign of God. Jesus invited, engaged, touched, healed, enjoyed, celebrated, taught, prayed, loved, and served. The Gospels are replete with such stories. He taught with word and example, and then commissioned men and women to preach the Good News and live by this Good News of God's love and desire for us.

Jesus's primary love was his God; from this love flowed all other loves. So it is with us. The context of religious life is community; within the community we search for God and live out love of God and love of neighbor in our responses. Schneiders reminds us that religious life is communitarian, not because it is religious, but because it is Christian.[8] And while community is foundational to religious life, gospel values are its fundamental rule of life. Schneiders notes that the "model for community relationships is the relationship that Jesus established with his immediate followers, namely evangelical (i.e., gospel) friendship."[9] What this looks like varies according to the charism of each particular group. The particular lens of gospel values that each charism offers also moves the direction of the community.

---

6   See Elizabeth A. Johnson, *Dangerous Memories: A Mosaic of Mary in Scripture* (New York: Continuum, 2004).

7   Paul J. Wadell, *Becoming Friends: Worship, Justice, and the Practice of Christian Friendship* (Grand Rapids, MI: Brazos Press, 2002), 20.

8   See, for example, Sandra M. Schneiders, IHM, *Finding the Treasure: Locating Catholic Religious Life in a New Ecclesial and Cultural Context* (Mahwah, NJ: Paulist Press, 2000).

9   Schneiders, *Selling All*, 278.

Intercultural Encounters and Building Community

It is good to remember that the human Jesus also grew in his understanding of community and of the other. A powerful illustration of Jesus's conversion in this regard is the story of the Canaanite woman.[10] Jesus, a male Palestinian Jew, encounters the Canaanite woman, an outsider to his cultural groups. Jesus first tells her he was "sent only to the lost sheep of the house of Israel." He directed the twelve apostles as they were to go forth in mission to "stay away from the Gentiles and don't go to any Samaritan town."[11] Yet we also know that Jesus healed both Jews and Gentiles. As Adriana Carla Milmanda, SSpS, adds: "He did meet foreigners and outcasts. Today we know that he also invited women to be his disciples. He even came to engage some of them in theological conversations, he admired the faith of a Canaanite woman (Mt 15:28) and of a Roman Centurion (Mt 8:10) —under whose rule the Jewish people were at the time of Jesus' birth." Milmanda continues, "Furthermore, he even used the Jews' historic enemies as an exemplary model in one of his best-known parables (The parable of the Good Samaritan)."[12]

The question then is: How did the human Jesus, with his own cultural biases and views of the insider and outsider, move from excluding the other to including all people as part of God's reign?[13] What happened? Let's look at this encounter more closely.

Jesus was walking and a woman called out, shouted at him, to heal her daughter. Jesus ignored her; the woman persisted. When he told her that he was not sent to her people, she still persisted, not daunted by his rejection but compelled by love for her daughter. When Jesus insults her by speaking of her as less than human, she still calls on him to do what is most important to her, heal her daughter. She saw in Jesus someone who could save her daughter, and she was willing to take on the structures and cultures that were preventing him from saving her daughter's life.

The mother was insistent. Jesus listened and finally heard what she was asking. It is significant that Jesus said that the woman had great faith. He went beyond responding to persistence and healing her daughter simply to have the woman stop asking and go away. Jesus finally heard her, realized the woman had faith, and that

---

[10]   Mt 15:21–28; See also Mk 7:24–30, the story of Jesus's encounter with the Syrophoenician woman.

[11]   Mt 10:5.

[12]   Adriana Carla Milmanda, SSpS, "The Intercultural Journey of Jesus," Keynote presentation at "Engaging Our Diversity: Interculturality and Consecrated Life," Conference of the Center for the Study of Consecrated Life (CSCL), November 2–5, 2017, at Catholic Theological Union, 3. A wonderful version of this presentation is also found at http://www.ctuconsecratedlife.org.

[13]   I appreciate that Milmanda would say it in this way: "How did a culturally biased Jesus move from an ethnocentric mindset to an intercultural mindset. . . . From ethnocentrism to ethno-relativism . . . from exclusion of the 'other' to the radical and egalitarian inclusiveness of God's Kindom?" Ibid.

he had missed it. Jesus was willing to be wrong about a cultural other, a woman, a Canaanite, someone he would not ordinarily engage.

Everything changes at this moment. Jesus recognizes that the Canaanite woman is a part of God's vision of the oneness of all creation. She was teaching Jesus about the Good News, for she already knew it! This encounter with her changed Jesus.

To the extent that we are willing to encounter, not just meet but encounter, come to know at a greater depth than simply basic or superficial elements, we will come to know one another better and create the community that is longing to be created by God. Something new can emerge.

When we encounter one another at the level of culture and come to know each other with both our differences and similarities, we will be able to build community through diversity. Anthony J. Gittins, CSSp, notes that culture is "'the [hu]man-made part of the environment': what social groups do to the worlds they inhabit."[14] As part of his description, Gittins writes, "Culture is 'an enduring social reality.' Cultures rise and decline, flourish and die, and none is static or immortal; implications for intercultural living should be obvious. Culture is transmitted gradually over time, through the generations: an ongoing process rather than a simple social fact."[15] Our faith is expressed culturally. This level of knowing our own culture, communicating what we know, and learning about the culture of others is critical to consecrated life. Let us now look a bit more at how diversity affects community.

As mentioned in Chapter 5, Anthony Gittins writes that religious communities need to become intentionally intercultural.[16] Gittins looks at intercultural community through a theological lens, writing, "Theologically speaking, intercultural communities consist of members drawn from diverse cultural backgrounds but sharing a single charism and an intentional commitment to fellowship, motivated not simply by pragmatic considerations but by a shared religious conviction and commitment to a common mission."[17] This common charism and commitment help the group members offer the wisdom of their own cultures. Over time this creates a new culture that has benefited from diversity and creates a new community. This new community flows out of the diversity toward what is needed in community, religious life, the church, and the world today.

Interculturality requires conversion, awareness, and an openness to being transformed. These then move us toward transformative action and living. All are needed as participants in this effort. Gittins reminds us that "intercultural living,

---

[14]   Anthony J. Gittins, CSSp, "Beyond International and Multicultural: Mission and Intercultural Community Living Today." Keynote presentation at "Engaging Our Diversity: Interculturality and Consecrated Life," Conference of the Center for the Study of Consecrated Life (CSCL), November 2–5, 2017, at Catholic Theological Union.

[15]   Ibid.

[16]   Anthony J. Gittins, *Living Mission Interculturally: Faith, Culture, and the Renewal of Praxis* (Collegeville, MN: Liturgical Press, 2015), 2.

[17]   Gittins, "Beyond International and Multicultural."

then, is a faith-based and lifelong process of conversion, emerging as a require-ment of members of intentional, international religious communities.[18] But healthy intercultural living depends on the level of commitment and support generated by the wider membership."[19] The growth process requires an awareness of one's own cultures and preferences as well as the capacity to see others' cultures and to appre-ciate the gift each offers. This is a process that continues throughout life, and the process must be intentional. This takes time—it is a matter of coming to know one another more deeply and integrally. Gittins notes that "the ability to live *with*, and not simply *despite* cultural differences is a hallmark of an intercultural community. Diversity is good, since God made it intrinsic to creation."[20] Committed commu-nity members can create good space for growth into intercultural community. Over time a new shared culture emerges, one that has meaning for all members and for the new group created.

A friend once offered a jazz ensemble as an image of how interculturality is formed.[21] When jazz musicians gather to create music, they often begin with a piece of music that they all recognize; from there, different individual musicians with a diversity of instruments offer distinct contributions at different times. They may all be playing at the same time, with one person taking the lead for a bit, building on what has come before. A new piece of music is thus created by the intermingling and contribution of each to the whole.

Although the road to true interculturality may not be necessarily smooth or linear, this image can help us see how a new way of living is created. When all the persons involved are heard and each culture is appreciated as valuable, there is a movement that brings forth the motivation, effort, and value in a way that creates a new culture. This is done with the deep desire to follow God's call within the reality in which we live, and to respond to the cries around us. Through our charism God is creating a new community, with implications for our living, praying, and minis-tering. And the creation of this new community affects how we live the vows.

For example, if the cry around me in Chicago is from persons on the margins wanting to feel that they belong, my charism naturally opens me to ask how we may build communities of belonging so that all feel God's love and the love of others. When diverse persons come together, forming community means that we come to know the other and their diversity as gift and offering to the whole. In the offerings, community is transformed. Not only is there a sense of belonging, but something new can be created as well. Where people belong and share their stories, healing

---

[18]   Intercultural living constitutes a challenge and opportunity for many other people working and ministering among people of several or many languages and cultures. Though by no means will all of these people learn the skills and virtues mentioned here, dedicated ministers will resonate with many aspects of intercultural living, and may find much insight into how to respond to the challenges they face.

[19]   Gittins, "Beyond International and Multicultural."

[20]   Ibid.

[21]   I'm grateful to Lucianne Siers, OP, for this image.

happens and relationships are built. From this we can learn something about what intercultural encounters can offer us. Everyone is changed in the encounter as new relationships and understandings emerge. From these new relationships and understandings, actions can then emerge.

A key point for both interculturality and community is that everyone is needed. The "inters," as I like to call them, are present in all areas of community—religious life today is not only intercultural, but also intergenerational and intercongregational. And it is in the intercultural connections that we can also learn about the gifts of generations. Christa Parra, IBVM, speaking from her cultural perspective, shared that her Mexican American extended family included her grandparents.[22] The grandparents were respected and part of everything, and the children were also valued. Parra's family situation affects her way of looking at relationships within her congregation and in her ministry. One of the realities of this time is that the generational cultures will need to look at the calls in the world and how to live them together, though not equally or in the same manner. It does not work to have the majority age group dictate what all are called to. Neither is it helpful to have only a small group discern for the whole. Each person must offer what is possible, even as the direction and discerning will carry different weight depending on how it must be lived out. Every voice must be respected and engaged.

New members remind us of the need to "mind the gap" between (1) who we say we are and do, and (2) who we really are and what we actually do. Our congregational Constitutions call us to our best, and while we don't necessarily meet this measure all of the time, there cannot be too great a gap between what we say and what we do. Years ago Franciscan Peter Cantwell wrote a wonderful article titled "Why Newly Professed Religious Leave."[23] He drove the point home that our actions must match our words quite effectively. We must "walk the talk." There is an emerging way we will live community with the people both in and beyond our own communities.

Community life is asking for transformation from the mind-set of "we've always done it this way" to asking how we will be community in light of our world, our God, and our own longings regarding community. As we explore how we will be community in the future, we continue to widen the circle. To walk this journey requires that we do mind the gap, living more closely what we believe, even as the ideal always calls us forward. We must include our newest members in whatever ways possible. It may mean inviting them to an existing group to which you belong or joining an initiative they offer.

Intergenerational dialogue is key for facilitating the transformative (ad intra and ad extra) call of community. The urgency is named in the Congregation for Institutes of Consecrated Life and Societies of Apostolic Life (CICLSAL) 2017

---

[22]   Christa Parra, IBVM, speaking in her own words at Catholic Theological Union, September 13, 2018.

[23]   Peter Cantwell, "Why Newly Professed Religious Leave," *Review for Religious* 62 (2003): 379–401.

publication, *New Wine in New Wineskins: The Consecrated Life and Its Ongoing Challenges since Vatican II*. The goal of the guidelines is to assist congregations in responding to this time in history. Early on, the document states:

> With healthy realism, we must note first of all the persistent high number of those leaving the consecrated life. It is important to shed light on the main reasons for these departures which are happening not only among those after the initial stages of formation (profession, ordination), but also among those who are advanced in age. This phenomenon is now observable in every cultural and geographic context.
>
> It must be clearly stated that this is not only and always a crisis of an affective nature. These crises are often the results of some outlying disappointment at living an inauthentic common life. The deviation between what is proposed in terms of values and what is actually lived can even lead to a crisis of faith. There is the risk that an excessive number of perceived pressing and overvalued activities neither allow for a solid spiritual life nor nurture and sustain the desire to remain faithful.
>
> In some communities where the numerically dominant older members struggle to adopt a style of spirituality, prayer, and pastoral activity required by the new evangelization, there is the risk of undermining the hope of the already isolated younger members for a truly promising life. This frustration might at times suggest that leaving is the only way for them to prevent succumbing to hopelessness.[24]

Clearly community is not the only issue; there are ministry and prayer implications as well. Nor is this only about one generation; these shifting times are affecting every generation. Attitudes range on a spectrum from a fear of change to concerns about not being able to stay if there is no change. These tension points are gifts, for they remind us something *must* be addressed for consecrated life to continue to participate in the Reign of God.

In *New Wine in New Wineskins* CICLSAL asserts that sociological research shows that young people do have gospel values and the capacity to make serious commitments: "They are open to transcendence and capable of being passionate about causes of solidarity, justice, and freedom." The document also notes: "With standardized ways which are all too often culturally out of context and excessively absorbed in the management of works, the consecrated life runs the risk of not anticipating the deepest desires of the young. This creates a void that makes generational interchange ever more difficult and the necessary intergenerational dialogue too hard."[25] This is a critical point, and each congregation and context must examine

---

[24]   Congregation for Institutes of Consecrated Life and Societies of Apostolic Life, *New Wine in New Wineskins: The Consecrated Life and Its Ongoing Challenges since Vatican II* (Nairobi, Kenya: Paulines Publications Africa, 2017), no. 12.

[25]   Ibid.

how this applies to them. Among many institutes around the globe, religious life culture has a workaholism that needs to be tempered with intentional community presence and spaces with which to widen community. For this to happen, we must be present to listen, hear, and respond to one another.

Years ago, a friend shared a poignant story. She was a college professor, well respected and liked in her discipline and among students. In speaking with a student one day, she asked the student if she had ever considered religious life; she had so many of the qualities for this vocation. The student paused, thanked her for the compliment, and then said, "All I see is you working. I don't think that can be the only part of my life." This was a conversion moment for my friend, and while it took some time, many of us found her gradually allowing more time for other areas of life, including time to be more present among her students. In her later years she said it actually made her a better teacher and a better friend.

Dialogue is critical for community building among all generations. Often when we listen and hear from one another in a caring, respectful way, new possibilities can emerge. Renewed efforts (including learning new ways for dialogue) are essential, for here the Spirit is leading. Pope Francis's efforts to engender dialogue increasingly include a focus on synodality, a mutual listening, and dialogue to hear and respond to the urgent calls of our time. Two examples are the 2018 Synod on *Young People, the Faith and Vocational Discernment* and the 2019 Synod on the Amazon. In some gatherings, a greater emphasis is placed on contemplative dialogue. The more these practices of dialogue become virtues—both dispositions and practices—the more we will also see effects in a community's daily life.

Living the gospel call to community is what is at stake. What we hear from Pope Francis about the witness of community in *The Joy of the Gospel* is essential:

> I especially ask Christians in communities throughout the world to offer a radiant and attractive witness of fraternal communion. Let everyone admire how you care for one another, and how you encourage and accompany one another: "By this everyone will know that you are my disciples, if you have love for one another" (Jn 13:35). This was Jesus' heartfelt prayer to the Father: "That they may all be one . . . in us . . . so that the world may believe" (Jn 17:21).[26]

This is what community looks like. Diversity and oneness, unity in diversity. In consecrated life, community is our intentional way of building the Reign of God.

Community, Change, and Transformation

The love of God, to which we open ourselves, enables us to live such communion. When we do so, everything is affected. What shows up when we open

---

[26]   *Joy of the Gospel*, 99.

ourselves to God's love? Joy, newness, and a capacity for change and transformation. We hear quite explicitly from Pope Francis:

> What does the Gospel bring us? Joy and newness. To what is new, newness; to new wine, new wineskins. To not have fear of making changes according to the law of the Gospel. This is why the Church asks us, all of us, for a few changes. She asks us to leave aside structures bound to collapse. They are useless! And get new wineskins, those of the Gospel. The Gospel is newness! The Gospel is a feast! The fullness of the Gospel can only be lived in a joyful heart, in a renewed heart.[27]

Note all that is at stake in this way of living personally and communally: joy; newness; leaving aside what no longer serves and which is to collapse; a renewed heart; freedom.

What does all this ask of us? To hold all lightly and attend carefully to the call of God and the Spirit as we discern how the charism seeks to be lived today. We come again to interior conversion, internal transformation, and external revitalization. Even structural change requires openness. Interior conversion and internal transformation affect the externals of community and ministry, and vice versa. Freedom, love, and joy help us imagine beyond where we are today to what the Spirit is calling forth most deeply and widely. The Spirit moving us through the gospel and our charisms will transform our community, prayer, and ministry—each of us, all of us, and all that affects us and that we affect. Such is the transformative power of the Spirit. While acknowledging "the temptation to adjust oneself tactically in order to avoid the continuous challenges of the conversion of the heart had already been present in the history of the Church,"[28] we are called to so much more. When we follow the Gospel message, consecrated life will constantly engage the new.[29]

Three Critical Areas for Conversion, Transformation, and Revitalization

Gender Relations, Clericalism, and Sexism

I cannot leave this chapter on culture and community without also looking specifically at one more necessary cultural engagement needed, the area of gender relations in all its multiplicity. As of this writing the global church is yet again

---

[27]   Pope Francis, Morning Meditation in the Gospel of the *Domus Santae Marthae*, Rome (September 5, 2014). I am grateful for this reference, quoted in *New Wine*, no. 10.

[28]   *New Wine*, no. 2.

[29]   *New Wine*, no. 3, says it beautifully: "The Gospel's message cannot be reduced to something purely sociological. We are dealing instead with a spiritual orientation which remains always new."

embroiled in sexual abuse scandals. This time there is more focus on church leaders who remained silent or hid abusive practices at the cost of lives. Retired Cardinal Theodore E. McCarrick was formally removed from the clerical state in 2019 after a canonical process found him guilty of sexual abuse of minors.[30] The Vatican announced that he was found guilty of "solicitation in the Sacrament of Confession, and sins against the Sixth Commandment with minors and with adults, with the aggravating factor of the abuse of power."[31] For decades this very public and well-known cardinal had coerced seminarians to sleep with him.

In other news Australia completed a multiyear Royal Commission into Institutional Responses to Child Sexual Abuse investigation, and reports from across Europe continue to erupt with accusations. Pope Francis had to reverse course on his original defensive position regarding priests and bishops accused of abuse cover-up in Chile. A bishop in India is under investigation for the rape of a sister.

Pope Francis gathered the heads of the bishops' conferences to Rome in February 2019 for a Summit on Clerical Sexual Abuse. All gathered listened to survivors of abuse and experts. In May 2019 Pope Francis promulgated a new church law mandating the Roman Catholic Church worldwide to report cases of clergy sexual abuse.

There is again a clear call to the new wine and new wineskins approach for the people of God in the church. This is the same call we hear from the #MeToo movement of women naming oppression in the workplace, social gatherings, and homes. There is no place where conversion, transformation, and revitalization are not needed. The need is on an individual level as well as communally and systemically.

To create local and global communities of hope, women and men in consecrated life must also respond to the scandal of women and men not being treated with equal dignity and human rights. Women and men religious can offer another way through our own efforts. We begin by listening to one another in safe, honest, open-minded and open-hearted ways. It is important for those in formation, particularly formation toward ordination, to participate in listening circles among the laity, who make up the majority of the church.

The need for change in gender relations is clear, and it is called out by Pope Francis's comments and by CICLSAL. The need is for an ongoing process with specific, measurable goals and objectives. Centuries of unequal gender relations will take time to transform, and we will need to continue the call for conversion beyond the necessary externals. Our congregations can contribute to another way of relating, but we must first acknowledge the present reality. *New Wine in New Wineskins* correctly states that "we have inherited style of life, organizational and government structures, vocabularies, a collective imagination, and a mentality that emphasized profound differences between man and woman instead of their equality

---

[30]   Chico Harlan, "Ex-Cardinal McCarrick Defrocked by Vatican for Sexual Abuse," *Washington Post*, February 16, 2019, https://www.washingtonpost.com.

[31]   See John L. Allen Jr., "Despite Defrocking, the Fat Lady Hasn't Yet Sung on the McCarrick Saga," https://cruxnow.com.

in dignity."[32] As a result, there need to be multiple fronts from which to deconstruct these inequalities. Interestingly, at the 2018 Synod on Young People, both young women and young men were speaking up and asking about the role of women. They wanted women to not only be participants in the synod, but also to have a voice and a vote. Young people from around the world were asking for this. Religious life must take on these inequalities in whatever sectors we are involved. There is a distance between words and actions, and we have a way to go to close that gap. To refuse to change runs the risk of gravely impoverishing the church itself. As Pope Francis has said: "We should not reduce the involvement of women in the Church, but instead promote their active role in the ecclesial community. If the Church, in her complete and authentic dimension, loses women, she risks becoming sterile."[33]

Brothers

Religious brothers can experience inequalities in their congregational community life when their congregation includes both brothers and priests. Even Vatican rules can perpetuate inequalities. For example, if a congregation has both religious brothers and priests, the named leader of the entire religious order must be ordained. There are continuing efforts to encourage Vatican officials to change this practice, but as of 2019 it is still the rule.

Even within the wider church community there can be a sense among the people that although a priest has completed his formation, something is missing in the brother's. "Why are you not ordained, brother?" is not an infrequent question, implying that ordination is the better choice and appearing to wonder whether the brother could not complete ordination formation. Clearly, education is needed on the vocation of brothers in all places. One gift of brothers is that they remind the ordained in the congregation of the primary call in consecrated life, the call to God through the congregation. Ordination is a manner of service within the call to religious life. The primary call is not ordination but religious vocation.

Systemic Wrongs and Social Sin

There are systems at work in all areas of inequality. Unless we unearth it, name it, and work to change it, we unknowingly participate or even accede to it. A story from a recent conference experience may illuminate this. In July of 2018 I participated in the Catholic Theological Ethics in the World Church conference. It was a powerful gathering of 425 Catholic ethicists from all over the world in Sarajevo, the capital of Bosnia and Herzegovina. Many topics were engaged, from refugees and migrants to violence, environment, civil discourse, and more.

---

[32]   *New Wine*, no. 17.

[33]   Pope Francis, speech at a meeting with the Brazilian Episcopate, Rio de Janeiro, July 27, 2013.

On Saturday evening a Eucharistic liturgy was held at the cathedral, which actually was not big enough to hold all the conference participants and parishioners gathering for a Saturday evening liturgy. There were a number of ordained priests at the conference, so they were invited to vest and sit in the sanctuary, in part to use all available space. The rest of the church was packed. At one moment the organizer of the cathedral space went to the second row of pews, which happened to contain only women. He asked them to move so that the priests who still needed a place to sit could sit there. This created a crisis, and the women, who now had nowhere to sit in an overfull church, left the church, visibly upset. Once they left, priests who were waiting in the sacristy came out and sat in those rows. They most likely had no idea who was unseated so that they could sit. Moments later the liturgy began.

People nearby saw what happened, but many did not. However, by Sunday morning, most people knew that a row of women had been asked to vacate their pew so that priests could have a seat. To his great credit, one of the conference organizers, Jim Keenan, SJ, spoke about this to the entire group. He said he was particularly speaking as a priest to his brother priests. Quite clearly, he named what happened as clericalism and said it had no place here or anywhere. He made the comparison to the United States at a time when African Americans were not permitted to sit in the front of the bus or sit at a soda fountain counter to be served. He poignantly reminded people that only the priests were able to sit in the sanctuary; women were not welcome there. *And now women were not even allowed to sit in the pew in the church.* This is not about culture, he said, because men and women from Asia, Latin America, Europe, Africa, and North America were all upset. It was an example of clericalism, Keenan said, even though Pope Francis reminds us that the role of the priest is to serve and not to be served. His words were first met with thoughtful silence, followed by deafening applause from many. The message was given and received.

Less than twenty-four hours later, I was at the Sarajevo airport with three other participants as we waited for our flight to Paris. The events at Saturday's liturgy came up in our conversation. We were two women (one married, one a religious) and two men (one ordained, one single). One of the men said, "But who is responsible here? The priests in the sacristy didn't see this happening. They are not responsible." After a pause, one of the women responded, "But isn't that the case with systemic injustice? That there is no one place but it is so part of everything that it is hard to pull out just one area. It's all of it." Yes, it is all of it, and all of us are called to respond to pull out the pieces and to dismantle the structure not only of clericalism,[34] but also of sexism[35] and racism that are in the

---

[34]   In brief, clericalism is an attitude of privilege over an attitude of service, because of clerical ordination. Nonclergy can also have the clerical attitude of power over another. Calling for an end to clericalism, Pope Francis wrote that it "extinguishes the prophetic flame to which the entire Church is called to bear witness in the heart of her peoples." Francis's letter to Cardinal Marc Ouellet, president of the Pontifical Commission for Latin America, March 19, 2016.

[35]   Sexism privileges men over women. For example, the UN Sustainable Develop-

very air we breathe. The call continues. In all these areas another way of being together and our best is possible.

Creating Communities of Hope on a Global Scale

Sulpician moral theologian Richard M. Gula, SS, describes community in the context of Christian spirituality. He writes that Christian spirituality is "a way of discipleship involving a personal relationship with Jesus under the power of the Holy Spirit working in and through the community of believers to bring about a world marked by justice and peace."[36] This describes the community of hope, locally and globally. We come as a community of believers, rooted in a personal relationship that leads us through the Spirit to build the Reign of God. In religious life we must build our congregation communities. This quickly and naturally leads us outward, for community is a circle that continually widens—until all are part of the circle.

We must widen community from the local to the global. The world is asking us to build and extend community. Refugees are teaching us to open our hearts, our doors, and our homes. Murder rates are asking us to put our bodies in places where life can find some measure of security, safety, or at least solidarity. Sometimes it is when we respond to those outside our local communities that we realize that the wounds outside are also present inside. God is a God of healing and love, and our openness to one another in building community creates spaces for God's healing and loving Spirit to encounter us in community. Our call to build community must take us to the edges and peripheries to witness to hope, to the life that is possible.

It is in doing so that we create a community of justice and peace that glorifies God. Catherine Mowry LaCugna's work on the Trinity reminds us of this most communal nature of our lives as well.[37] Our lives glorify God, give praise to God, and witness to who God is for us in our efforts to be in life-giving and life-affirming relationship with others, as Jesus showed us in his life. Our lives speak to our deepest longings as we seek to become one in God through the Spirit. Our lives point to what drives our love as we are in communion with God and with all creation.

---

ment Goal (SDG) no. 5, which calls for gender equality and empowerment for all women and girls, reports that "in 18 countries, husbands can legally prevent their wives from working; in 39 countries, daughters and sons do not have equal inheritance rights; and 49 countries lack laws protecting women from domestic violence" (https://www.un.org). In the United States, although the pay gap is narrowing, women working full- and part-time make 85 percent of what their male counterparts earn, according to the Pew Research Center (https://www.pewresearch.org). In other words, women would need to work an extra 40 days a year to make as much as men. It's an even grimmer picture overseas: Women worldwide make 77 percent of the amount paid to men, according to a report from the United Nations International Labor Organization (https://www.theguardian.com).

[36] Richard M. Gula, SS, *The Call to Holiness: Embracing a Fully Christian Life* (New York: Paulist Press, 2003), 21.

[37] Catherine Mowry LaCugna, *God for Us: Trinity and the Christian Life* (New York: Harper Collins, 1991).

We navigate change and challenges better as a community. Pat Farrell, OSF, reminds us that "religious have navigated many shifts over the years because we've done it together."[38] Community builds identity and resiliency.

Community and Conflict

"Relationships that have been built over time constitute the only fabric strong enough and resilient enough to keep its strands together under severe stress. One thread will simply not do it."[39] This profound point by theologian and reconciliation expert Robert Schreiter, CPPS, reminds us that it is relationship that helps us remain united at our depths when conflicts arise. Communities are built gradually, with experiences that build understanding, trust, and enough connection to keep persons and groups together when conflicts and misunderstandings arise.

Sometimes we see conflict as a failure, either in our personal relationships or in community life. What if we instead see conflict as part of the deepening of our lives? Pope Francis tells us: "Religious brotherhood [and sisterhood] with all its possible diversity, is an experience of love that goes beyond conflicts. Community conflicts are inevitable: in a certain sense they need to happen, if the community is truly living sincere and honest relationships. That's life. . . . Something is missing from communities where there is no conflict."[40]

There is a delightful practicality to these words from a man who has lived in communities of many kinds as a Jesuit. In *Joy of the Gospel* Pope Francis also writes about conflicts in families, reminding us that what we learn about conflict translates to many settings, and that others have much to teach us about conflict resolution. He offers the hope of conflict resolution as a new creation: "It is the willingness to face conflict head on, to resolve it and to make it a link in the chain of a new process."[41]

Conflict is often exactly where God desires to enter into our lives more deeply and fully. Over the years I have come to recognize that while I do not like conflict, as I dare to face it, conflict widens the doors of my heart, opening me to previously unknown possibilities and realities. I become aware of my blind spots and freedom moves in me. Willingness to grow, a desire to see the other as God sees them, and an openness to a vision beyond one's own are the virtues and attitudes we need to practice. How this happens varies with circumstances and the community. Often there are surprises.

---

[38]   Pat Farrell, OSF, "Navigating the Shifts," LCWR Presidential Address, August 10, 2012, 4, https://lcwr.org.

[39]   Robert Schreiter, CPPS, "Consecrated Life as a Reconciling Presence in the World," Chicago Archdiocesan Celebration of Consecrated Life Day, February 19, 2011, 7, http://legacy.archchicago.org.

[40]   Pope Francis, interview with Antonio Spadaro, SJ, "Wake Up the World: Conversation with Pope Francis about the Religious Life," *La Civiltà Cattolica* (2014): I:3–17, trans. Donald Maldari, SJ, 10.

[41]   Pope Francis, *Evangelii Gaudium* (*Joy of the Gospel*), 227 (see 226–30 also).

Sometimes we need to address a situation directly, while at other times the tension and conflict can be transformed by silence. Years ago a brother shared the following story:

> Another brother and I were like oil and water—we clashed at home and at school. We literally could not talk and resolve our many petty differences and we were poles apart politically, theologically, and personally. One day this brother surprised me with the suggestion that we just spend fifteen minutes together each day in silence, either in the school or community chapel. We did that very faithfully (much to the mystification of other community members!) for a semester. I can't say we became fast friends at the end of the semester, but the tension and conflict ceased and to this day I think of him with gratitude and affection.[42]

Friendship and Community

Schneiders writes that the kind of community being called forth now is that of evangelical friendship. Friendship in community is an area of relationship that religious men and women need for flourishing today. This may include those with whom we live in our own congregations, and also those beyond our home communities and congregations.

Friendship, like intimacy, is a necessary element of life. Friendship is also a gift, something no one can demand or command. Friendship is better and deeper to the extent the friends are free. Each person must have the capacity to accept or refuse the offer of friendship, along with sufficient maturity to grow in its evolution. Freedom is external as well, meaning that the friendship is not contingent on status, power, or connection. Boundaries here are meant to be freeing, so that each person can grow into unity in God and outreach toward all creation. In this kind of freeing space, friendship's possibilities are many.

I would like to offer four points about friendship and community.

1. Friendships both within one's religious community and outside one's religious community are gifts. Friendship in community is a gift because of a charism and way of life in common; this is naturally part of the relationship. Friends help each other live their congregational calls and find pleasure in time spent together and with others. Friendships are also necessary outside one's community and congregation. Friendships are built on common interests and values, and often we meet people in ministry or other gatherings of common interest and energy. These relationships also bring energy to our communities.

2. Friendship leads us toward God, toward others, and toward all creation. Ultimately, friendship leads us to Love. My closest friends have helped me understand dimensions of God's love and have enfleshed dimensions of God's love, mercy, forgiveness. Paul J.

---

[42] Though the story is offered accurately, to protect privacy, some of the details about the persons in the story have been modified.

Wadell has written extensively about Christian friendship in its many dimensions. Wadell explains that "Christian friendship envisions the reign of God. . . . Through friends sharing the life of grace, each helps make the other fit for the community of perfect friendship that is the kingdom of God."[43] Wadell utilizes the work of St. Augustine to show how friendships lead us to love God more and to love more like God:

> For Augustine, friendships should help us grow in the love of God, in the sense that through them we love God more deeply and our love becomes more godly. If our friendships with others are patterned on the friendship of God that comes to us in Christ, then through those friendships we are formed or, better, *transformed*, in the love of God so that eventually the way we love our friends resembles the way God loves us. This is what should happen through the life of friendship. We should (1) teach each other about the love of God, (2) form each other in the love of God, and (3) help each other practice the love of God.[44]

Friendships teach us about God and about Love. The sacred nature of friendship cannot be overstated.

3. *Friendship makes us more human, teaching us about Jesus's humanity and calling forth the best of our humanity.* I write in more depth about this in Chapter 8 on obedience, but I use the example of the Emmaus journey here, which begins with two disciples leaving Jerusalem. Their friend Jesus had been crucified, and they could not understand what happened. Their disappointment and grief were obvious. Jesus met them where they were and as they were. He listened to them and responded to them. He gave them a wider perspective than they had on their own. His words and presence clearly engendered some hope, for the two asked him to stay with them that evening. The Risen Christ helped them see with new eyes that yes, Jesus suffered and died, but also that yes, he has risen and was with them. Their eyes were finally opened in the breaking of the bread that evening, as they realized why their hearts were burning within them. The result? They left and returned to Jerusalem, freer to live out their humanity as followers of Jesus.

4. *Friendship makes us better community members, for friendship expands our sense of inclusivity, mercy, and compassion.* In the Gospel of John Jesus calls his disciples friends and tells them he has shared with them all he had learned from God: "No longer do I call you servants, for a servant does not understand what his master is doing. But I have called you friends, because everything I have learned from my Father I have made known to you."[45] The call is for us to do the same.

The Risen Christ teaches us much about mercy, compassion, and forgiveness. We see this in the post-resurrection scene at the seaside when the Risen Christ

---

[43]   Paul J. Wadell, *Becoming Friends: Worship, Justice, and the Practice of Christian Friendship* (Grand Rapids, MI: Brazos Press: 2002), 84.

[44]   Ibid.

[45]   Jn 15:15.

speaks to Peter, referencing his denials and healing Peter, calling him forth to servant leadership. Three times Peter denied Jesus and three times Jesus asks Peter if he loves him. Each time Peter says that yes, he loves Jesus, and each time the Risen Christ then tells Peter to feed the sheep, tend the lambs. The Risen Christ, who knew pain beyond all measure, entrusts Peter with serving and tending to the people. Peter was being offered a new story, another opportunity, by the one who loves him. Friendship in community offers the same.

Much has always been needed for living and creating community; our time now asks even more of us. In the midst of brokenness and crumbling, we are asked to create bonds with one another. When we can see what binds us together there is strong motivation for living community. Living community then is both a door and destination. In building community, we are creating communities of hope wherever we are, local and globally.

What Can I Give?

I conclude with this quote from scripture scholar and my Religious of the Sacred Heart sister Lyn Osiek, who preached the following on the occasion of her Silver Jubilee:

> About community: I have learned that it takes many forms, and that it can always be lifegiving if we have the good sense not to expect from it what it cannot give, and if we begin with the question, "What can I give?" rather than "What can I get?" Religious life takes discipline, and much of that discipline goes into community life: to be there, to be open, to be generous, even—especially—when you don't feel like it. An important discipline that I have learned is: always assume good motivation on the part of others unless proven otherwise.[46]

Questions for Reflection and Discussion

1. What would vibrant, life-giving and life-receiving community look like?
2. How would you create it and then offer it to another?
3. In light of community we ask:
    a. What is the world longing for?
    b. What does our church need?
    c. For what does the locale in which I live hope?
4. What does your charism offer here? Is it mercy? Is it courage, open-heartedness to the neighbor? Is it accompaniment in some form?

---

[46]   Carolyn Osiek, RSCJ, Homily for Silver Jubilee, November 26, 1995.

7

Poverty in a World of Plenty

A genuine personal and emotional conversion to the world of the poor—who constitute the majority of humankind—becomes absolutely necessary if we are to grasp the meaning of Christianity today and to respond to this time in which we are called to live.[1]

Before reading, reflect on the following:
- How do you define the vow of poverty?
- What do your Constitutions say about evangelical poverty?
  - How is the vow named?
  - What scripture passages, if any, are used? What is the significance of this scripture?
  - What is the spiritual wisdom in your Constitutions about this vow?

Although women and men religious publicly profess the vow of evangelical poverty, the call to live evangelical or gospel poverty belongs to all the baptized. As with all prophetic calls, the first step is an encounter. Pope Francis reminds us that our encounter with Jesus also brings us to an encounter with the people and earth made poor.

God's heart has a special place for the poor, so much so that he himself "became poor" (2 Cor 8:9). The entire history of our redemption is marked by the presence of the poor. Salvation came to us from the "yes" uttered by a lowly maiden from a small town on the fringes of a great empire. The Saviour was born in a manger, in the midst of animals, like children of poor families. . . . When he began to preach the Kingdom, crowds of the dispossessed followed him, illustrating his words: "The Spirit of the Lord is upon me, because he has anointed me to preach good news to the poor" (Lk 4:18).[2]

---

[1] Rafael Luciani, *Pope Francis and the Theology of the People* (Maryknoll, NY: Orbis Books, 2017), 11.

[2] Pope Francis, *Evangelii Gaudium* (*The Joy of the Gospel*), 197, http://w2.vatican.va. Hereinafter *EG*.

Missionary discipleship links us to God and to God's priorities, helping us see that relationship with Jesus naturally calls forth a closer relationship with not only all creation but in particular those struggling and on the margins. To witness to the Good News we must be close to people in need and to the earth. From a liberation perspective, Gustavo Gutiérrez, father of liberation theology, writes about poverty:

> An essential clue to the understanding of poverty in liberation theology is the distinction, made in the Medellín document "Poverty of the Church," between three meanings of the term "poverty": real poverty as an evil— that is something that God does not want; spiritual poverty, in the sense of a readiness to do God's will; and solidarity with the poor, along with protest against the conditions under which they suffer.[3]

Our call is to denounce the first and announce the second—this is the Good News of poverty.

Evangelical poverty is also a virtue; therefore, living it requires both dispositions and practices. This requires a continuous conversion that will move us to action. Encounter requires proximity, which then calls forth dispositions and actions of mercy, compassion, solidarity, and justice. All are interconnected in both integral ecology and integral religious life. Closeness, conversion, and action call us personally and communally into becoming communities of hope. The call is clear, even as resistance may occur. Pope Francis reminds us:

> No one must say that they cannot be close to the poor because their own lifestyle demands more attention to other areas. This is an excuse commonly heard in academic, business or professional, and even ecclesial circles. . . . I fear that these words too may give rise to commentary or discussion with no real practical effect. That being said, I trust in the openness and readiness of all Christians, and I ask you to seek, as a community, creative ways of accepting this renewed call.[4]

That we must respond is clear. *How* we must respond is open to the cries around us, our charism, and our personal and communal creativity.

The vow of poverty is probably one of the most challenging—yet freeing— calls today. The vow demands we live the tension of contradictions as we respond to a profound call to conversion and freedom. The vow is also another way to love generously, witnessing by our lives the plentiful nature of God's love.

The word "poverty" has appropriately negative connotations. For example, the famine crisis in Yemen was made stark on November 1, 2018, when the *New York Times* reported that seven-year-old Amal Hussain had died. The article begins:

---

[3]   Gustavo Gutiérrez, *A Theology of Liberation: History, Politics, and Salvation*, rev. ed. (Maryknoll, NY: Orbis Books, 1988), xxv.

[4]   *EG* 201.

A haunted look in the eyes of Amal Hussain, an emaciated 7-year-old lying silently on a hospital bed in northern Yemen, seemed to sum up the dire circumstances of her war-torn country. . . .

On Thursday, Amal's family said she had died at a ragged refugee camp four miles from the hospital. . . .

Riveting images of malnourished Yemenis like Amal—one of 1.8 million severely malnourished children in Yemen—have put a human face to fears that a catastrophic man-made famine could engulf the country in the coming months.

The United Nations warns that the number of Yemenis relying on emergency rations, eight million, could soon rise to 14 million. That's about half Yemen's population.[5]

Such poverty cries out for mercy, a willingness to enter into the chaos of another's life to respond to the other's need,[6] and for intervention on a systemic and personal level. The poverty that killed Amal is evil. The political choices that create such poverty are evil. Ironically, Amal's name is Arabic for hope. Perhaps the hope Amal now offers is to galvanize people toward awareness and action. Action needs to be personal, national, and international, engaging human and financial resources and international systemic violence. Amal's death cries out from systemic failures. Humans create systems; now we must work to transform such systems.

The outcry at Amal's plight was loud, but will it last? What would it take to make a difference? Consecrated life is called to witness to the realities happening and the "dangerous memory of Jesus"—even when others do not. The vow of poverty calls us to respond with a vision of what is possible. What a contradiction: the vow of poverty speaking to the people of plenty in our world and denouncing situations that prevent flourishing. Yes, the vows are to be Good News, not only to women and men religious but to all people. Because poverty is an evangelical counsel for all Christians, our vow brings consecrated life into common cause with many looking at this world and witnessing by our lives a different image of what is possible. This is our challenge as women and men religious, particularly in areas of the world where there are sufficient resources for all and which can be shared.

Contradictions That Call

Our very lives are to announce what we believe, yet many of us know that religious life can be yet another kind of contradiction. Our lives can look and be quite

---

    5   Declan Walsh, "Yemen Girl Who Turned World's Eyes to Famine Is Dead," *New York Times*, November 1, 2018, https://www.nytimes.com.

    6   I am grateful to James F. Keenan, SJ, for this definition. It resonates with many. For further information, see James F. Keenan, SJ, *The Works of Mercy: The Heart of Catholicism*, 3rd ed. (Lanham, MD: Rowman & Littlefield, 2017).

comfortable. Many of us are assured of food, shelter, and health care.[7] There is both humor and truthful poignancy when persons look at those in religious life taking the vow of poverty and remark, "You take the vow of poverty and the rest of us live it."

Sometimes we romanticize poverty in religious life, such as with an image of St. Francis of Assisi begging for his daily needs. There is truth in this image. I must also admit there was beauty in the practice of some of my Dominican students in San Antonio, who yearly were asked to participate in the practice of begging on behalf of the friars, a tradition in their mendicant order. I knew the students would still have food to eat even if I could not give more than a few dollars, but there is something about straightforward asking that is important. There is also the reality that religious do need to earn salaries, stipends, and fundraise in order to respond to needs in our church and world. Money is also needed to educate religious, subsidize ministries where there are economic needs, and offer eldercare for religious.

What is the good news in this? There is an appropriate tension here, and it takes great discernment to walk the way that includes having the necessary resources for living the mission and the trust and freedom that holds nothing back in calls for generosity in mission. Living poverty authentically requires attention and intention.

Some advocate for changing the name of the vow to "simple living," which seems to be a more manageable yet still challenging way of life. I suggest that calling our vow poverty is akin to Jorge Bergoglio taking the name Francis as pope. Naming yourself after a saint who lived poverty as Francis did is a daily call to live what you believe. The name calls him forth every day to build peace, to interreligious dialogue, to repair God's church, to poverty, and more. When Bergoglio's dear friend, Brazilian Cardinal Cláudio Hummes, hugged him upon his election as pope, he also said to him, "Do not forget the poor." This was an extraordinary gift and led to Bergoglio's choice of the name Francis, after St. Francis of Assisi.[8] So it is with men and women religious vowing poverty. It's an external and explicit challenge and call to us. The vow of poverty also challenges us daily—living this vow and virtue is a process of conversion.

In the Synoptic Gospels we read that after Jesus went into the desert and fasted and prayed for forty days and forty nights, the devil came to him to tempt him in three ways.[9] The temptations were to material possessions, power, and prestige. Jesus chose none of them; his practice of prayer and fasting offers us a clue to how he was able to refuse temptation.

---

[7]   This is notwithstanding the challenges in some congregations for sufficient financial resources including, for example, retirement, in the United States. There is at least a health care system (Medicaid and Obamacare) and some financial awareness of these challenges (for example, the Religious Retirement Office of the US Catholic Conference of Bishops and some philanthropic foundations assisting efforts for women religious).

[8]   See "Pope Francis Reveals Why He Chose His Name," *Catholic Herald*, March 16, 2013, https://catholicherald.co.uk.

[9]   Mt 4:1–11; Mk 1:12–13; Lk 4:1–12.

Seductions are part of our lives, too. The materialism of many of our cultures often seeks to encroach on our lives. Education, leadership positions, and even membership in religious life can be either sources of prestige that feed egos or reminders that point to the plight of the suffering. The balance is delicate and needs a regular *examen* and exposure to light in a trusting and honest community. The vows keep us honest, transparent, available, and dependent on God.

The vow of poverty is Good News for each of us, for consecrated life and for the people of God and all creation as we live it. As with each vow, the vow of poverty continually evolves as we seek to follow God's call and mission in our time and amid the current realities around us and in our world. Amid the cries around us we hear God's preferences and loves. It is through our particular charisms (personal and congregational) that we respond in prayer, community, and ministry.

It is also important to name what some might see as poverty *within* religious life in North America, Europe, and various other areas. I earlier named some of what can be seen as the dying of this time—discontinuing some ministries, closing some community houses, leaving some geographic regions, and living with fewer women and men in active ministry. How we see and live religious life is changing. Yes, there is loss and there will be further loss. As women and men of the gospel, how might we look at this? We look at Mary of Magdala's encounter with the Risen Christ for some insights. Mary experienced the violent loss of Jesus—the one she believed in was taunted, rejected by religious leaders and civic leaders, tortured, and crucified. When Mary went to the cave where his body was laid, she went to grieve and honor the body as was the cultural custom. But the body was not there:

> [Mary] turned around and saw Jesus standing there, but she did not know that it was Jesus. Jesus said to her, "Woman, why are you weeping? Whom are you looking for?" Supposing him to be the gardener, she said to him, "Sir, if you have carried him away, tell me where you have laid him, and I will take him away." Jesus said to her, "Mary!" She turned and said to him in Hebrew, "Rabbouni!" (which means Teacher). Jesus said to her, "Do not hold on to me, because I have not yet ascended to the Father. But go to my brothers and say to them, 'I am ascending to my Father and your Father, to my God and your God.'" Mary Magdalene went and announced to the disciples, "I have seen the Lord"; and she told them that he had said these things to her.[10]

Mary's grief was laid bare before the one she thought was the gardener. He calls her by name and then she recognizes him, calling him Rabbouni (Teacher). What joy! Then the Risen Christ tells her not to hold on to him, to stop clinging to him. I used to think that was terrible. Of course, Mary would want to hold on to Jesus, the one thought dead is now alive! Yet I missed something very important.

---

10   Jn 20:14–18.

The Risen Christ called Mary by name, an intimate gesture. Mary recognized his voice, another indicator of intimacy. This didn't dismiss the pain she experienced in Jesus's suffering and death, but a new vision came forth. Something she couldn't have imagined was happening. The Risen Christ called her beyond whatever she may have wanted to do, including continuing on in the way her life had been before he died. This was a new time, and he told Mary of Magdala to go to the others to tell them that she had seen the Lord and that he was going to God. The mission was continuing, though clearly in a different way than the disciples had understood. The Risen Christ asked Mary to go out to the others, to bring them together in this message.

What is the consolation and encouragement in this? The encounter, the relationship we have with our God, will lead us and be with us in the realities we face. Just as Mary had to let go of one vision and be willing to see another way, we must do the same. There is something new calling us, and we must trust that in the poverty of not seeing all before us, we can trust in the plenty that is God. So it is with us.

We will now consider some snapshots of the biblical and historical roots of poverty. And we will consider what poverty is inviting us to as we pray, live community, and engage ministry, all in light of call, cries, and charism today.

Biblical Poverty

Poverty is an evangelical counsel for all Christians, so I offer some points about what the call is for all, and then turn specifically to religious life. I am grateful for the work of Sandra M. Schneiders, IHM, Michael Naickanparampil, CSsR, Brian O'Leary, SJ, and José Rovira Arumí, CMF, for insights on this topic.[11] In the Wisdom literature, material poverty was not a good; the opposite was true. Wealth was seen as a sign of God's approval. At the same time, wealth was secondary to what O'Leary describes as "less tangible blessings such as peace of soul, a blameless reputation, health, virtue and wisdom."[12]

Justice was compromised in the period of the monarchy as power and wealth became concentrated in a few elites. The prophets came forth to address this, questioning the idea that God was bestowing blessing on those with wealth and power while judging those without. The prophets denounced the injustices and announced God's vision of opportunity for all. The prophets advocated for the

---

[11]   Sandra M. Schneiders, IHM, *Buying the Field: Catholic Religious Life in Mission to the World* (Mahwah, NJ: Paulist Press, 2013); José Rovira Arumí, CMF, *Evangelical Counsels and Consecrated Life: Three Charismatic Ways to Follow Christ* (Quezon City, Philippines: Institute of Consecrated Life in Asia, 2015); Michael Naickanparampil, CSsR, *The Biblical Basis of Consecrated Life* (Kerala, India: Oriental Institute of Religious Studies, 2015); Brian O'Leary, SJ, *Radical and Free: Musings on the Religious Life* (Dublin, Ireland: Messenger Publications, 2016).

[12]   O'Leary, *Radical and Free*, 23.

anawim, the poor ones of God, asserting that they were close to God and that God denounced those who oppressed them.

In the Gospels the concern for the *anawim* continues. For example, some have called Mary's Magnificat an *anawim* psalm.[13] We see in Jesus's life one who was utterly dependent on God and who, in his humanity, accepted all that went with powerlessness before religious and political figures. In this time, the word "poverty" also evolved. O'Leary writes that

> the word "poverty" gradually came to mean more than simply depriva-
> tion, penury and oppression. It could also imply a religious disposition:
> one that was meek, humble, gentle, peaceful and utterly dependent on
> God. The poor, the *anawim*, were the little ones, the powerless who had
> no influential protectors to fight or plead on their behalf. But they waited
> patiently for God, who alone would vindicate them.[14]

At the same time, Jesus demonstrated the freedom of following God by his words and actions. Jesus was baptized alongside the multitudes, lived among people, and in his ministry, led people to his Father through word and witness. His encounters with people—healing, feeding, listening, offering love, mercy, and even forgiving, to his last breath—incarnated his complete reliance on God's love.

Jesus's life and ministry was connected to the poor and oppressed. We see this, for example, in:

- Jesus's Liberating Mission: "To bring good news to the poor, to proclaim release to captives . . . recovery of sight to the blind. . . . To let the oppressed go free."[15]
- Jesus's closeness to those on the margins of civic and religious society: "Why does he eat with tax collectors and sinners?"[16]
- Jesus's cure of those on the peripheries: "That evening they brought to him many who were possessed with demons, and he cast out the spirits with a word, and cured all who were sick. This was to fulfill what had been spoken through the prophet Isaiah: 'He took our infirmities and bore our diseases.'"[17]
- Jesus's encouraging and healing a woman with hemorrhages who touched his cloak: "'Take heart, daughter. Your faith has made you well.' And instantly the woman was made well.[18]

---

13   Ibid., 25.
14   Ibid.
15   Lk 4:18.
16   Mk 2:16.
17   Mt 8:16–17. See also O'Leary, *Radical and Free*, 26–27.
18   Mt 9:20–22.

- Jesus's mercy and forgiveness to those who seek it. No one is beyond salvation, including those who committed criminal acts.[19]

We are reminded about where our focus is to be. Yes, the beatitudes bless those who are hungry, poor, and suffering. Yet Naickanparampil reminds us that "what is blessed in the beatitudes is not material poverty, hunger or suffering but the radical openness to God's action in the near future."[20]

Jesus's life and words serve as a message to all disciples, about what faith must be like. We can see in the story of the rich young man that some were also called to a voluntary material poverty.[21] Jesus goes even further—O'Leary reminds us that Jesus

> adopted a more radical approach to material poverty by raising the possibility of this becoming a voluntary choice, not simply a burden to be accepted. . . . (Lk 18: 28–30).
>
> Elsewhere Jesus insisted on making material poverty a condition of the apostolate. He sent out his seventy disciples with the words: "Go on your way. See, I am sending you out like lambs into the midst of wolves. Carry no purse, no bag, no sandals; and greet no one on the road." (Lk 10: 3–4). It is as if the effectiveness of the Good News is dependent on the poor lifestyle of those who proclaim it. Poverty lends credibility to the message.[22]

While not speaking to poverty per se, the early church also tried to look at both its lifestyle and its response to those in need. We see a prime example in Acts:

> Now the whole group of those who believed were of one heart and soul, and no one claimed private ownership of any possessions, but everything they owned was held in common. . . . There was not a needy person among them, for as many as owned lands or houses sold them and brought the proceeds of what was sold. They laid it at the apostles' feet, and it was distributed to each as any had need.[23]

This was a community that was aware of those who were in need and ready to reach out. Arumí reminds us, "It is not poverty that is praised, but sharing; in fact, 'there was no needy person,' that is they tried to avoid poverty. Therefore, since the beginning, it will be clear that we Christians are not in favor of poverty (on the contrary, we try to overcome it), but of the poor!"[24]

---

[19]   Lk 23:42–43.
[20]   Naickanparampil, *Biblical Basis of Consecrated Life*, 77.
[21]   Lk 18:20–25.
[22]   O'Leary, *Radical and Free*, 28–29.
[23]   Acts 4:32–35.
[24]   Arumí, *Evangelical Counsels*, 205.

Finally, we find in Paul a deep reliance on God, similar to that of Jesus. Paul writes of counting all as nothing in light of his desire to follow Jesus and his indifference to all because he knows Jesus is with him:

> Not that I am referring to being in need, for I have learned to be content with whatever I have. I know what it is to have little and I know what it is to have plenty. In any and all circumstances I have learned the secret of being well-fed and of going hungry, of having plenty and of being in need. I can do all things through him who strengthens me.[25]

These are helpful reminders as we consider religious life as well.

Poverty is knowing that one has all one needs in Christ Jesus. This is the attitude of poverty for Christians and persons in consecrated life. Poverty is a deep reliance on God. This attitude leads to actions on behalf of others. This vow frees and emboldens followers of Jesus to advocate for those suffering crushing poverty and those marginalized and left on the peripheries of society. God's abundance means that a life of chosen poverty is a life given to prophetically proclaiming such generosity. Walter Brueggemann reminds us: "Gospel love is grounded in the conviction that all we have is a gift from God who has been generous with us and we are invited to practice generosity alongside the God of the gospel."[26]

Poverty in History: A Few Snapshots

The understanding of the vow of poverty has evolved over the years and continues to evolve. I offer here a brief historical summary to illustrate how the wording and understanding of the vow has changed.

In early Christianity, Christians were living on the margins of society, and there were periods when they were persecuted. When Constantine issued the Edict of Milan in 313 CE, Christianity was finally acknowledged as a legal religion. In 380 CE, Nicene Christianity became the official religion of the state, thus Christianity now had political status. Christians had considerable influence at this time, some achieving great power and prestige. For some, this was a plus. Others, such as St. Antony (252–356), who was called the "father of Christian monasticism," were led to live their conversion in the desert, leaving all possessions behind and seeking God alone.

Poverty became a means of protest in early monasticism.[27] Renunciation of goods, manual labor, and asceticism were part of monastic life. In this context the individual had no personal possessions but the monastery did have property.[28] Over

---

25   Phil 4:11–13.
26   Walter Brueggemann, *A Gospel of Hope* (Louisville, KY: Westminster John Knox Press, 2018), 7.
27   Arumí, *Evangelical Counsels*, 207.
28   Ibid., 209.

time this too became a challenge. The line of "I don't have anything but my monastery/congregation does," continues to be a bit of a challenge, depending on how resources are used.[29]

In St. Benedict's time, hospitality and care for the sick were important practices. Sharing with the needy had a mystical quality as "monks were taught to see in the guest Christ the poor one (Rule of Benedict 36, 53)."[30] Over time, monasteries collected wealth and a prosperity crisis led to a return to the desert for some and the founding of new orders.[31] Arumí observes, however, that "because the monasteries went on possessing, even with the reformed, the same cycle repeated itself: starting in poverty, prosperity began, manual labor was despised, decadence entered." He concludes with this warning: "Unless collective divestment is taken seriously, the temptation of wealth will always be there."[32]

One of the responses to this kind of decadence in the early eleventh century was to live the example of the itinerant poverty of Jesus and his disciples.[33] Franciscan poverty was about an interior conversion and imitation of Christ, poor and naked on the cross.[34] In Jesus, they rightly saw one who came not to be served but to serve.[35] From Vatican II this understanding is also found in *Gaudium et Spes,* the *Constitution on the Church in the Modern World.*[36]

After Francis of Assisi died and over time, the cycle repeated itself in arguments among Franciscans regarding possessions and whether collective ownership was possible. The difference between the simple Porziuncola in which St. Francis is buried and the Basilica in Assisi is an example of this tension. Arumí tells us:

> Immediately after St Francis' death, discussions started about how to live the collective poverty. The solution was that Friars passed from not having anything as a matter of fact, to not having in the legal sense (the owner would be the Pope). That solution allowed Friar Elijah to build the big Basilica of Assisi, which would be in contrast with the humble "Porziuncola."[37]

---

[29]   It is important to be aware that Eastern monasticism did not evolve in the same way as Western monasticism. My comments are predominantly about Western monasticism. Eastern monasticism remained in the model of sharing all things and offering a life of protest to the dominant culture (see Arumí, *Evangelical Counsels*, 209–10).

[30]   Arumí, *Evangelical Counsels*, 210–11. See also the Rule of St. Benedict. Translation found online at http://www.solesmes.com.

[31]   Some of the newly founded communities and founders include St. Robert of Molesmes, the Cistercians; St. Bernard of Clairvaux, the Carthusians; and St. Norbert, the Canon Regulars Premonstratensians.

[32]   Arumí, *Evangelical Counsels*, 211.

[33]   Ibid., 212.

[34]   Ibid.

[35]   Mt 20:35–38. See also Lk 17:33.

[36]   *Gaudium et Spes (The Constitution of the Church in the Modern World)* (1965), 3, http://www.vatican.va.

[37]   Arumí, *Evangelical Counsels*, 214.

Evolving Language and Understanding of Poverty

The term "poverty" also evolved linguistically. I offer examples from Odo and Thomas Aquinas, historical contemporaries of Francis of Assisi.

In 1148 Odo, the abbot of St. Genevieve in Paris, which followed the Rule of St. Augustine, wrote a personal letter, explaining that "in our profession we promise three things, as you well know, chastity, sharing, obedience."[38] He described poverty as sharing, and the Latin word for sharing is *communio*. The beginning of the Rule of St. Augustine states: "You should live in the house in unity of spirit and you should have one soul and one heart centered on God. And then, you should not call anything your own, but you should have everything in common" (I.e, 3).[39] To be united in God is the essence, and with this is common ownership of goods. The word "poverty" is not used, but we see characteristics emerging toward what poverty would come to mean: sharing all and letting go of personal possessions for the sake of the one sought—God.

Thomas Aquinas actually uses the word "poverty." As O'Leary notes, in the *Summa Theologiae*, Aquinas taught that "the foundation of charity is 'voluntary poverty (voluntaria paupertas) so that one may live without anything of one's own (absque proprio)' (2a 2ae q.186, a.3)."[40]

Over time the concept and language about poverty continued to evolve. For example, from the sixteenth century on, apostolic orders such as the Jesuits, Congregation of Jesus, and Sisters of Loretto, the Claretians, the Redemptorists, Oblates of Mary Immaculate, the Salesians, and numerous others, would live a poverty of radical availability to the needs of ministry.[41] In Europe, the eighteenth and nineteenth centuries again saw a rise of religious orders responding to social needs not provided by the governments (such as catechesis, education, health care, and social and pastoral services). Even as recently as the twentieth century, we can see this impetus in the founding of Mother Teresa of Calcutta's Missionaries of Charity in 1950.

This pattern of living poverty in various ways and struggling with living the call continues in our time. Our Constitutions often give us a solid starting point, even as the gospel holds the most compelling criteria.

Vatican II and Beyond

The following are some documents from Vatican II through the present in which we can see the continuing movement of desire to live the vow of poverty amid current realities.

---

[38]   O'Leary, *Radical and Free*, 20–21.

[39]   See ibid., 21, citing Augustine of Hippo, *The Monastic Rules*, trans. Sr. Agatha Mary and G. Bonner (New York: New City Press (2004), 110.

[40]   O'Leary, *Radical and Free*, 22.

[41]   See Arumí, *Evangelical Counsels*, 281n30.

- *Perfectae Caritatis, the Decree on the Adaptation and Renewal of Religious Life.* This 1965 Vatican II document states beautifully the call and creativity asked by the vow of poverty in consecrated life:

   Religious should diligently practice and if need be express also in new forms that voluntary poverty which is recognized and highly esteemed especially today as an expression of the following of Christ. By it they share in the poverty of Christ who for our sakes became poor, even though He was rich, so that by His poverty we might become rich (cf. 2 Cor. 8:9; Matt. 8:20).[42]

- Pope John Paul II, noting in his Apostolic Exhortation *Vita Consecrata* that "'the poor,' in varied states of affliction, are the oppressed, those on the margin of society, the elderly, the sick, the young, any and all who are considered and treated as 'the least,'" reminds us of the preference for the poor and the promotion of justice:

   The option for the poor is inherent in the very structure of love lived in Christ. All of Christ's disciples are therefore held to this option; but those who wish to follow the Lord more closely, imitating his attitudes, cannot but feel involved in a very special way. The sincerity of their response to Christ's love will lead them to live a life of poverty and to embrace the cause of the poor.[43]

- *Starting Afresh from Christ: A Renewed Commitment to Consecrated Life in the Third Millennium* (Congregation for Institutes of Consecrated Life and Societies of Apostolic Life) (2002) mentions some challenges to living poverty, such as the "insidiousness of mediocrity in the spiritual life, of the progressive taking on of middle-class values and of a consumer mentality."[44]

- *Passion for Christ, Passion for Humanity* (2005), the result of an International Congress on Consecrated Life, calls forth the external demands encompassing the freedom of the vow of poverty: "to go beyond our frontiers to proclaim Jesus Christ through inculturation, inter-religious and inter-confessional dialogue; to express our option for the lowly and excluded ones in society; to explore new means of communication: a mission and an option for the poor (poverty)."[45]

- Pope Francis, in *Evangelii Gaudium* (*The Joy of the Gospel*), further links our call as disciples to the transformation of the world so that all the

---

[42]   Vatican Council II, *Perfectae Caritatis* (*The Decree on the Adaptation and Renewal of Religious Life*) (1965), 13a, http://www.vatican.va.

[43]   Pope John Paul II, *Vita Consecrata* (1996), 82, http://w2.vatican.va.

[44]   *Starting Afresh from Christ: A Renewed Commitment to Consecrated Life in the Third Millennium* (Congregation for Institutes of Consecrated Life and Societies of Apostolic Life), 12, http://www.vatican.va,

[45]   *Passion for Christ, Passion for Humanity*, International Congress on Consecrated Life (Boston: Pauline Books & Media, 2005).

vulnerable are protected, including the earth. He writes, "An authentic faith . . . always involves a deep desire to change the world, to transmit values, to leave this earth somehow better than we found it. . . . The earth is our home and all of us are brothers and sisters."[46]

These are but a few examples of how poverty is described. O'Leary tells us that "through all this evolution there has been a constant need to reinterpret the ideal of poverty in creative yet authentic ways in light of emerging charisms and shifting apostolic goals. Changing social, political and economic systems also require a rethinking of how best to realize this ideal."[47] Today, too, poverty continues to be lived out in response to the cries of our time. Our closeness to these cries often determines the depths to which we live poverty in disposition and action. These are important notes to remember as we now move to considering living poverty today and *for* this time.

Poverty Today

The call of poverty in a world of plenty continues today and is shaped by the call of God, the cries of the people and earth, and lived through our charisms and contexts. Through the lens of virtue we see that prayer, community, and ministry enflesh the vow of poverty in dispositions and practices called for today.

Crucible Exercise: A crucible is a metal or ceramic container in which metals or other materials can be melted or subjected to very high heat.[48] For this exercise, write on a sheet of paper all the elements that you consider part of consecrated life today. If you wish to focus on your congregation, write down all the elements that you consider to be part of your congregation or institute. Then place all of the elements into the unheated crucible.

Imagine the crucible heated up. It has melted all but the most essential elements of religious life today. Sit with this for a few minutes. Allow the crucible to cool. What is left? When all but the most essential elements of religious life are gone, what is left? Write down what remains in your crucible.

---

[46] *EG* 183.

[47] O'Leary, *Radical and Free*, 33. He adds: "This continuous development has been possible because poverty is not a clear-cut, unambiguous, clearly definable value that can only ever be lived out in one specific way. . . . Especially in apostolic institutes where the central identifying element is mission, there is need for a flexibility and adaptability of structure and behavior. This involves the relativizing, but emphatically not the elimination, of the commitment to material poverty" (ibid., 34).

[48] The *Oxford English Dictionary* defines crucible as (1) a ceramic or metal container in which metals or other substances may be melted or subjected to very high temperatures; (2) a situation of severe trial, or in which different elements interact, leading to the creation of something new. See https://en.oxforddictionaries.com.

The elements most often mentioned after this exercise are:

- God, Jesus, and/or Spirit
- Charism
- Gospels—Scripture
- Love
- Community
- Generosity
- Service
- Constitutions

Sometimes people mention priorities, but specifics in terms of a building, ministry, community place, or motherhouse are not usually included. The exercise helps us clarify what is essential to religious life and what is not. Next I look at three areas where poverty is to be prophetically lived.

Poverty and Prayer

Once we hold lightly to all but God, we can live the vow of poverty and all the vows more deeply. I consider some biblical images to help us see how the virtue of poverty can be lived through prayer. Poverty is first and foremost about relationship. We learn from Jesus's life about what our priorities are to be and how we live relationship.

The Presentation in the Temple

In this episode in Luke[49] we learn about belovedness and belonging. This passage tells the story of Mary and Joseph presenting the infant Jesus at the temple. They followed the law of their tradition, which required that the firstborn son be consecrated to the Lord.[50] At the temple they meet Simeon, who was promised by God that he would live to see the Messiah. Holding the infant in his arms, Simeon praised God for this gift. "Simeon blessed them and said to his mother Mary, 'This child is destined for the falling and the rising of many in Israel, and to be a sign that will be opposed so that the inner thoughts of many will be revealed—and a sword will pierce your own soul too.'"[51]

The image of Mary and Joseph presenting their son to God is profound, for it signifies that Mary knew that Jesus wasn't all hers, that he belonged to God. She was his mother, yes, but this reminds us that the other, even her own child, does not belong to us but to God.

---

[49] Lk 2:21–40.
[50] Ex 13:2, 13.
[51] Lk 2:34–35.

Prayer brings us to this space of giving all to God, recognizing that even our loves are not our own. When we love others and gifts in this way, we are free to love deeply, fully, and openly. St. Madeleine Sophie Barat, RSCJ, founder of the Religious of the Sacred Heart of Jesus, is known to have looked upon a lovely flower and then said, "You are beautiful. But you are not my God." Poverty leads us to freedom if we know to whom we belong. Then all else is loved in proper relationship. Proximity, closeness to God, frees us to love all others. Prayer helps us to maintain our closeness to God.

The Woman and the Alabaster Jar

Matthew's story of the woman with the alabaster jar is an example of how we can go anywhere and do anything, including what we know will be difficult, if we can see with the vision of the Reign of God. On the journey we all need encouragement to be what is asked of us.

> Now while Jesus was at Bethany in the house of Simon the leper, a woman came to him with an alabaster jar of very costly ointment, and she poured it on his head as he sat at the table. But when the disciples saw it, they were angry and said, "Why this waste? For this ointment could have been sold for a large sum, and the money given to the poor." But Jesus, aware of this, said to them, "Why do you trouble the woman? She has performed a good service for me. For you always have the poor with you, but you will not always have me. By pouring this ointment on my body she has prepared me for burial. Truly I tell you, wherever this good news is proclaimed in the whole world, what she has done will be told in remembrance of her."[52]

Using our religious imagination, I would like to suggest that this passage is not about the extravagant spending of money for the expensive ointment. It is about something far more precious: one's life. In Matthew this passage is placed between an episode when chief priests and elders are plotting to kill Jesus[53] and that of Judas Iscariot agreeing to betray Jesus for thirty pieces of silver.[54] These episodes lead up to the preparation for the Passover meal and Jesus's last supper with the disciples.

It is very likely that by this point in his life, Jesus knew that there were plots against him. He was attuned to both his critics and those who believed in him. His time in Bethany was at a friend's home where he still had a little distance from Jerusalem but was nearby. Imagine what thoughts and feelings the human Jesus of Nazareth would have had about what was to come and come soon.

It was customary to anoint after death. Here a woman offers Jesus a prelude, anointing him for his own death. She gently anoints his feet, and the connection

---

[52]   Mt 26:6–13.

[53]   Mt 26:1–6.

[54]   Mt 26:14–16.

becomes so obvious to Jesus he names it even as the disciples miss the meaning of her action. Was this anonymous woman there to encourage him to follow his call? Was it to offer him a gentleness before a time that would be anything but gentle? It is our reflective, prayerful spaces that help us walk the road that assists others in difficult moments as well as open ourselves to this journey.

Prayer, silence, and a contemplative lens help us see what poverty calls us to. How can we do that with one another? How can we encourage one another when proximity with those who are marginalized or persecuted can and does result in punishment and even death? We hear news of this regularly. On November 15, 2018, a Kenyan Jesuit, Fr. Victor Luke Odhiambo, was shot and killed by armed men in South Sudan, where he was ministering as principal of Mazzolari Teachers College. He had lived in South Sudan for about ten years. On May 20, 2019, in Nola, Central African Republic, Daughter of Jesus missionary Sr. Inés Nieves Sancho, who taught young girls how to sew so they could better their lives, was found dead, almost decapitated, in the building where she taught sewing. This happened in an area where there was known human trafficking.[55]

Although no one goes to a place deliberately to suffer, we do go to places to offer love and hope even if that means we may suffer. The line that opened my long retreat some years ago, "If you know the love of Christ you can suffer," comes to mind. This is not easy. We need encouragement for such proximity to suffering and fear. We must anoint one another, with gentleness, reminding one another of our mission in God, for God's people, and for God's creation. Jesus appreciated the woman who anointed him, and he knew she was preparing him for what was to come. Poverty is offering what we can for one another, pointing one another to God and God's mission.

It is helpful to look to our charism and spirituality to see how poverty calls. In my Sacred Heart tradition, our charism calls me to attend to the wounded heart of humanity, where God already is. I can do this when I know the call of my charism: "By our charism, we are consecrated to glorifying the Heart of Jesus: we answer His call to discover and reveal His love letting ourselves be transformed by His Spirit so as to live united and conformed to Him, and through our love and service to radiate the very love of His Heart."[56] If I allow myself to be transformed and united, I will open myself to the edges and woundedness of humanity and earth. Where it will lead is not as important as my willingness to go and radiate God's love.

Kenosis: Self-Emptying

Poverty for the sake of love requires a *kenosis*, self-emptying, and Jesus modeled this for us: "Let the same mind be in you that was in Christ Jesus, who, though he was in the form of God, did not regard equality with God as something to be

---

[55] Junno Arocho Esteves, "Pope Prays for Spanish Missionary Murdered in Central African Republic," *Catholic News Service*, May 22, 2019, https://cruxnow.com.

[56] Constitutions, Society of the Sacred Heart of Jesus, 1987, 4.

exploited, but emptied himself, taking the form of a slave, being born in human like-ness. And being found in human form, he humbled himself and became obedient to the point of death—even death on a cross."[57]

There are many other passages that speak of offering all,[58] but for now I focus on how prayer and poverty are intertwined. In his self-emptying, a surrendering all to God, the human Jesus was deeply connected to all. We have a God who, in Jesus of Nazareth, showed us the fullness and best of humanity. Instead of choosing power, prestige, and self-centeredness, God chose to show that humanity is deeply connected to others and to God; Jesus never gave up on people and pointed to the image of God in all of humanity.

Pope John Paul II also beautifully connected consecrated life to the connection between loving God and loving neighbor:

> The fact that consecrated persons fix their gaze on the Lord's countenance does not diminish their commitment on behalf of humanity; on the contrary, it strengthens this commitment, enabling it to have an impact on history, in order to free history from all that disfigures it. The quest for divine beauty impels consecrated persons to care for the deformed image of God on the faces of their brothers and sisters, faces disfigured by hunger, faces disillusioned by political promises, faces humiliated by seeing their culture despised, faces frightened by constant and indiscriminate violence, the anguished faces of minors, the hurt and humiliated faces of women, the tired faces of migrants who are not given a warm welcome, the faces of the elderly who are without even the minimum conditions for a dignified life.[59]

To live like this requires a contemplative attitude of seeing with the eyes of the Reign of God even in the midst of challenges. It is when we empty ourselves that we can live not only with simplicity but go to the edges that are crying out to know the fullness of God. It is when we empty ourselves that we can be present and take action to transform unjust systems and practices. Poverty is a profound freedom and fullness to bring the Good News to exactly where witness is needed.

Poverty and Community

The vow of poverty asks me and my community very practical and often chal-lenging questions: Where do I live? With whom do I live? What is the proximity of my community life to the margins and edges, to the vulnerabilities of persons and the earth? Am I living where hope is needed? How do I know? Do I know my neighbors? Do I know about the poverty of those around me? How? How will my neighbors experience hope? What is the call of poverty at this time?

---

[57] Phil 2:5–8.

[58] See, for example, the story of the widow's mite in Mk 12:38–44.

[59] Pope John Paul II, *Vita Consecrata*, 75.

The vow also asks questions of my congregation or institute: What do we see together as calls and cries in light of our charism? How shall we participate together in discerning these cries? How shall we participate in responding to these cries? What shall we do with our gifts of membership, the wider charism family, and financial resources in order to witness the Good News of Jesus Christ among us?

The call to create communities of hope on a global scale must include the local, the place where we relate daily. There are times when persons with whom we live in community experience their own vulnerability and poverty. This could be due to personal struggles, personality, illness, ministry challenges, or other reasons. More often than we may realize there are persons in our own communities who lack a sense of deep belonging to the group. How am I to respond and how is my community to respond, knowing that all belong and are to be made welcome?

In *Evangelii Gaudium* Pope Francis calls "communities throughout the world to offer a radiant and attractive witness of fraternal communion. Let everyone admire how you care for one another, and how you encourage and accompany one another."[60] This includes how we care for every single person and every community. We must be open to change if our models of community life are insufficient or impoverished. In consecrated life, all areas of our lives are to be open to growth and new possibilities that can build. Our communities are also reminded that "no change is possible without renouncing obsolete models so that new horizons and possibilities may arise in government, in common life, in the management of goods, and in mission."[61]

What does my charism ask of me in living poverty and community? *Disponibilidad*, which in English is translated as *radical availability*, goes far beyond being available for a quick phone call or brief walk. Radical availability is about being completely available and open to what God is alluring us toward. The disposition and action of *disponibilidad* include openness to my local community, to my congregation, and extend to all areas that ask for my own plenty to be offered. Living community and poverty means that my time is often the greatest gift I can offer, the whole of my time and attention. The edges of community are rich spaces.

The Importance of Diversity in Community

Interculturality calls me to see that I am impoverished without the diversity that my sisters offer. The interculturality that can be created from diversity is part of our evolution into the new creation God is desiring. God is continually creating, and I must be attentive and present, willing to do my part. In engaging with diversity, I will come up against my limitations and weaknesses in understanding. This is where God is trying to give me new sight. Community means that I will offer

---

60   *EG* 99.

61   Congregation for Institutes of Consecrated Life and Societies of Apostolic Life, *New Wine in New Wineskins: The Consecrated Life and Its Ongoing Challenges since Vatican II* (Nairobi, Kenya: Paulines Publications Africa, 2017), 52.

myself and my culture to the community, and together we will walk toward what the Spirit is asking of us. We are encouraged in this also by the Congregation for Institutes of Consecrated Life and Societies of Apostolic Life: "The objective of the consecrated life shall not be that of maintaining itself as a permanent state in the various cultures it will encounter, but that of maintaining the permanence of evangelical conversion at the heart of the progressive construction of an intercultural human reality."[62]

The Poverty of Sinfulness

Community life offers us great gifts in our narratives, yet poverty in community means that we must honestly attend to those narratives that are painful and even scandalous. It is easy enough to receive the accolades of our past histories. It is not so easy to touch the poverty of our sinfulness, past or present. Over the past twenty years and into today, consecrated men and women have had to account for the abusive and criminal behavior by some members and by some leaders. The sexual abuse crisis has found its way into congregations. Key to a response is a willingness to name both the sin and criminal actions of our members and in our congregations, and to work through these challenges in order to create structures and ways of seeing and acting that prevent abuse of any kind.

Some male congregations have also been working to change the impoverished view of the other in sexist cultures. One province of Dominican men added to their guidelines for acceptance of candidates the question of whether the candidate is able to appreciate women and minister with women as equals. These are efforts to change systems that further a clerical and sexist culture.

For more than twenty years, a number of congregations in the United States have also acknowledged racist attitudes and actions in their members and even in congregational policies and actions. Some groups are actively working on antiracism education and dismantling racism.

A history of owning enslaved persons is one of the poverties that some communities, including my own, are naming and seeking to respond to in a manner that is honest, just, and reconciliatory. Years ago the Sisters of Loretto acknowledged their slaveholding past and expressed regret. In the past few years, Georgetown University students called on the Jesuit community and university to acknowledge that the school would not have been built without enslaved persons, and to look for the descendants of the persons who built and worked on the grounds of the school. The acknowledgment of the social sin of slavery is leading to creating dialogue and efforts to address racism today.

In my own congregation, research led us to seek out the descendants of enslaved persons who made the ministry of some of our schools in Louisiana and Missouri possible. Acknowledging such a history is not easy, yet there are

---

[62]   Ibid., 40.

unexpected graces even in this. As we contacted the descendants of enslaved persons, it was touching that people were grateful to know about their ancestors. And what did the descendants ask of us in 2018? They asked to have the graves marked with the names of their enslaved family members. Family members also wanted to have a plaque with the names of their enslaved ancestors on the wall of the building where they had lived.[63]

There is more that we as Religious of the Sacred Heart must do beyond these acts. We can learn from others who have encountered similar histories in their congregations. There is a commitment now to study this part of our history and to begin a process of understanding and working to dismantle racism today. If our work as a community, with our partners in mission and our associates, can be even a small contribution toward the work of healing in our society today, grace is at work. This, too, is a kind of poverty and thus a space for deep conversion.

Poverty and Creation

We again are reminded that all manifestations of poverty, along with all other areas in life, are about relationships. I have spoken about community within and among persons. Community also includes creation and all of nature. Realizing that we are impoverished without creation, we must build a community of kinship with creation. We must realize that we do not own our common home but are interrelated inhabitants with all God's creation.

Inclusion and Welcome

Community also leads us to build community outward, being the doors and destinations toward widening the circles of inclusion and welcome. The community of Sant'Egidio is a wonderful example of this. A Catholic lay association, with over 50,000 members in seventy countries, the members build community among persons on the edges through relationship. The quality of their relationships is illustrated by the language they use. Persons who are made poor are not called "the poor" but "friends." I first met some Sant'Egidio members while I was living in Rome. I kept hearing them talk about "our friends" and kept wondering who they were referring to. It eventually became clear when we went to a dining room where their friends ate and received social service assistance.

Perhaps the most strikingly visual way of being and building community comes on Christmas, when in Rome, the Basilica of Santa Maria de Trastevere turns into a dining room, replete with beautifully decorated tables. I attended the Christmas Eve celebration in the church and saw a beautifully decorated banquet table at the

---

[63]   See the website of the United States–Canada province of the Society of the Sacred Heart of Jesus, for a related article, photos, and video. I encourage you to watch the powerful ten-minute video of the ritual from September 23, 2018, in Grand Couteau, Louisiana. It can be found at https://rscj.org.

foot of the altar area. In his homily the presider reminded us of who and what we are celebrating and of who is often missing from our tables. The following morning the pews were moved to the side and decorated tables were ready to serve hundreds of friends who struggled with poverty, had some form of physical or cognitive disability, or had no family and friends with whom to celebrate the day. This is the plenty that community can and must offer.

Acknowledging Pope Francis's insistence that we are to welcome, protect, promote, and integrate migrants and refugees, doing so is an example of community as door and destination. We welcome and we also build community in numerous ways. Sometimes it will by the relationships we form, at times by sharing spaces and buildings. We also build community across congregations and organizations, realizing that together so much more is possible. Community is transformed and re-created as we do so.

Hospitality is a corollary virtue to poverty, which offers space and acceptance to the other, including allowing the other to choose the direction of conversation. The practice of poverty and hospitality can also move us to genuine friendship. As Gustavo Gutiérrez reminds us, "If there is no friendship with them [the poor] and no sharing of the life of the poor, then there is no authentic commitment to liberation, because love exists only among equals."[64] This brings us to the third category, poverty and ministry.

Poverty and Ministry

The vow of poverty calls us to be present and engaged on the peripheries of society. Living poverty through the lens of ministry asks us questions about (1) where we are and why we are there, (2) where the emerging needs are and how our charism offers a response, (3) what systemic responses to systemic issues are required, and (4) how the virtue of solidarity lives in us and our institutes. This is a brief overview. I look further at areas of ministry for our time in Chapter 9.

Where Are We and Why?

When people consider women and men religious on a global scale, we are often associated with the margins and peripheries, serving needs that are otherwise unmet. We must ask ourselves regularly if this is still true. Perhaps it is even better to ask persons and groups outside of consecrated life how they see us. The question is clearly context-specific, and I invite you to look at the question through your own contexts. The question is also *not* salary-, stipend-, or time-specific. Some in consecrated life minister full-time in areas addressing direct and systemic change. Some volunteer their time directly or indirectly. Tony Gittins would call all of us who work indirectly with persons or in area of need to tithe our time. Gittins, Pope Francis, Gutiérrez, and the many others close to the peripheries, continually remind

---

64   Gutiérrez, *Theology of Liberation*, xxxi.

us of our call to be present in spaces where we can encounter those on the edges. This is one reason why I do some volunteering at the Precious Blood Ministry of Reconciliation in Chicago. I cannot teach courses in Catholic social thought or religious life if I am not also connected to the ground on which God's cries are joined with the cries of the people.

The call today is to ask how and where we are connects our charism and the vow of poverty. Some of our ministries may be among those who have considerable financial means. To stay there we must ask how our presence and ministry is intentionally serving those in great need. It may be that the school curriculum, for example, brings forth the realities of need. It may be that there is an intentional effort to do social analysis and faith reflection on challenging social issues today. These are some ways to engage the urgent cries of our time. We must still ask if we have any direct contact with those on the peripheries, and with the earth. To remain where we are, we must be very intentional about efforts for transforming systems and society. It is not enough to provide good salaries or our congregational name on an institution. And if the institutions where we serve do not still truly need us, we must ask: Where are we needed now? This moves us to the next aspect of the implications for us today.

Emerging Needs

There continue to be needs for education, health care, social services, and faith accompaniment. Religious have been part of these ministries for centuries. The question now is, are we still on the edges in these ministries, or are we remaining where the needs are no longer critical? If, for example, higher education is still a key need, how are we serving those who are excluded from opportunities? In Chapter 9 I offer an example of a Catholic junior college in the United States that was founded in order to give young people without financial resources or needed academic supports the opportunity to graduate and go on to jobs or to complete a four-year degree without taking on debt with loans. This is an example of where our commitment to live poverty in a world of plenty links our ministries and our resources to the people and areas of earth in greatest need.

Some congregations and communities are already engaging these questions. A community in Peru, already in a challenged area, looked around and realized there is yet another region that has even fewer resources, so their discernment took place among the people in both areas. I invite you to look at your national and regional context and ask where you are and what is needed. If your presence is welcome but not urgently needed, would you be willing to respond to the call to serve where the needs are greatest? If there is a tug and some resistance, you may have found an important question. If there is a longing, you are hearing a call. If there is a deep sense that you are where you can work to transform society and church, you are where the call is. Let others ask these questions of you. You will know within yourself the freedom you have.

Systemic Responses to Systemic Issues

Systemic responses are needed to address the systemic issues created by human beings. The late Joseph Cardinal Bernardin wrote that "those who defend the right to life of the weakest among us must be equally visible in support of the quality of life of the powerless among us: the old and the young, the hungry and the homeless, the undocumented immigrant and the unemployed worker."[65] When we know who the persons are and where creation is on the edges and peripheries, we can together find a way forward. Proximity to persons brings us more closely into the issues we must address as systemic. Faith and policy link us. This requires *risk-taking* and advocacy as well as transparent and prophetic engagement with all involved.

The Virtue of Solidarity

When we are most connected to those without power and those suffering and struggling on the margins, our voices are different, whether on Capitol Hill or at cathedrals in the neighborhood and parish communities. Our voices are "different" because they come from a place of authenticity and integrity. *Intentionality* is key here. *Solidarity* means that we walk alongside persons on the margins, listening intently, following the lead of those most immersed in the situations even as we, too, offer our insights, presence, and offerings. This is transformative. We must be public in our learning and walking. Our presence will speak to our values and to the values of all those whom we also call our friends. One of the gifts we will continue to discover is that we go forth ever more together, across congregations, as charism families, across charism families, and with all people of good will. With such connections, the possibilities for transformation, revitalization, and renewal are boundless.

Praying at 93

These are a few of the ways we are called to live poverty in ministry, community and prayer. I close with an offering from one of my sisters, Beatrice (Bea) Brennan, RSCJ. She served in schools in the United States and ministered in Egypt. In her later years her eyesight failed, yet her heart and mind remained engaged with the needs of the world. She reminds me that there is no "retirement" from living poverty as we pray, expand our communities, and gaze outwardly. I offer these few lines from her "Praying at 93" meditation as a way to bring together prayer, community, and ministry. I continue to learn much from her, even as now she experiences the fullness of plenty in the heart of God.

---

[65]   Joseph Cardinal Bernardin, "A Consistent Ethic of Life: An American-Catholic Dialogue," Gannon Lecture, Fordham University, December 6, 1983, 5, https://www.hnp.org.

To live this long is an amazing grace. One of its unexpected joys is how alive one can feel spiritually as the slow dismantling of other human processes goes on. The Bible speaks of "laughing in the latter day." Prayer, for me, is like that at times. And always, a song of gratitude and joy. . . .

In both the lights and darks of a psyche prone to alternating (and sometimes simultaneous) highs and lows, I rock with the paradoxes of reality. It is only God who keeps my little skiff afloat.

At a deeper, quieter level of consciousness runs an undefined awareness of God's presence, similar, I think, to that union of old married couples who may rarely or never put love into words. It has become their life.

So prayer becomes a steady underlying trust bearing me along.[66]

Questions for Reflection and Discussion

1. Scripture tells us that possessions, power, and prestige are temptations. What are your three temptations with regard to poverty? What are those of your congregation?
2. What are your graces and gifts with regard to poverty? What are those of your congregation?
3. Whose cries do you hear? Who is able to expand your listening to cries beyond where you are located? Whose context do you need to hear? What do you sense your charism is calling forth and desiring to create anew, in light of the poverty today?
4. What are the local and global implications of your responses?
5. How might you live the vow of poverty through your prayer?
6. If poverty is in a world of plenty, how might you imagine and create a response to the cries calling forth a response to your living the vows?
7. Find some members of your congregation who have lived the vow of poverty for many years. Ask them what the vow of poverty meant when each entered and how their understanding evolved over the years.

---

[66]   Beatrice Brennan, RSCJ, *Seeking the One Whom We Love: How RSCJs Pray*, ed. Kathleen Hughes, RSCJ, and Therese Fink Meyerhoff (St. Louis, MO: Society of the Sacred Heart, 2016), 8–10. This was first published in *Heart Magazine*, a journal of the US Province of the Society of the Sacred Heart.

8

COMPELLING OBEDIENCE

Walking with the Risen Christ

In the Kingdom of God, authority is recognized in those whose
character resembles that of God.
—Charlotte Sumbamanu, STJC[1]

Before reading, reflect on the following:
- What do your Constitutions say about the vow of obedience?
- What scriptures are used?
- What is the spiritual wisdom about obedience in your Constitutions?

After Jesus's death, chaos must have ensued for his followers. What did Jesus's stories about the Reign of God and his miracles mean after his gruesome death on a cross? What to make of the stories that he was risen? Their world had just crashed around them.

As mentioned in Chapter 6, two disciples left Jerusalem and were on their way to Emmaus. They were deeply disappointed, grieving, and unable to make sense of what had happened to their friend Jesus. They were talking about all this as a stranger approached them and asked what they were talking about. Incredulous that this stranger would have been so unaware, they shared that Jesus of Nazareth, a prophet mighty in word and deed, had been turned over to the chief priests and leaders and crucified. They had hoped he would redeem Israel. Their grief was evident as they shared the strange news that the women who came to the tomb found it empty.

How surprising, then, to hear this stranger chastise them for not believing the prophets and then explain how the scriptures had foretold a prophet would come, suffer, die, and enter into glory. Something must have resonated with them, for when they reached the village, they asked this stranger to join them. They wanted more. And more they received, for when they sat down to eat, this stranger "took

---

[1]   Charlotte Sumbamanu, STJC, "Exercising Authority in an Adult Community,"
UISG Bulletin 152 (2013): 47.

bread, blessed and broke it, and gave it to them. Then their eyes were opened, and they recognized Jesus; and he vanished from their sight."[2] Now they understood, saying to one another, "Were not our hearts burning within us while he was talking to us on the road, while he was opening the scriptures to us?"[3] And then what happened? The two returned to Jerusalem; but it was a different Jerusalem, and the story they now knew was very different from the one they had previously believed.

The Emmaus journey offers key elements for reflection about the vow of obedience. In brief, the vow of obedience:

- Engages us in the midst of life;
- Focuses us on God's mission. Obedience leads us to the Reign of God and God's mission with the Risen Christ. As we walk with the Risen Christ we are offered a bigger picture, a deeper and wider lens. In John's Gospel we read that the Risen Christ appeared to the disciples, said to them "'Peace be with you. As the Father has sent me, so I send you.' When he had said this, he breathed on them and said to them, 'Receive the Holy Spirit.'"[4] We have the gift of the Spirit with us. It is with the Spirit that we discern where we each individually and together are called. This is a gift that
  - is relational;
  - requires mutual listening and hearing;
  - requires openness;
  - requires a response;
  - takes time, is a journey;
  - connects us to core values and experiences;
  - requires community and leads us to community.

All of these elements remind us that the vow of obedience is also a virtue, consisting of both dispositions and practices toward listening, hearing, and responding to God's call amidst the calls around us.

In this chapter I delve into various elements of obedience for our time, including the role of communal discernment. In the last part of the chapter I look at current calls in relation to the role of leadership and authority, and in response to abuse of power.

A Historical Note on the Vow of Obedience

It is helpful to get a sense of some of the perspectives on obedience that have emerged in various forms of consecrated life. José Rovira Arumí, CMF, writes about authority and obedience that is either more vertical (obedience to God) or horizontal (obedience to community or another person). There is also obedi-

---

[2] Lk 24:30–31.
[3] Lk 24:32.
[4] Jn 20:21–22.

ence that looks more internally (to one's community) or externally (to mission that extends outward, including outside the community).[5] I briefly offer a few broad descriptors of the vow to demonstrate the variety of ways obedience has been seen at different times.[6]

Obedience to another person was not prominent in early monasticism. The call was to listen directly to God. The hermitical life was also purposely distant and removed from contact with most or all people so that the individual would listen solely to God. The focus was on a personal search for God and God's will. Some people did go to another person seeking wisdom, guidance, or formation in their search for God, but this was often temporary. As monasticism with a focus on community (cenobitic monasticism) evolved, community allowed for people to listen for the voice of God together. In some communities[7] obedience was mutual obedience (among equals) and was for an orderly and peaceful way to live life together. The gospel was a clear criterion for obedience, and over time as rules for living out obedience were written, these, too, were sources from which to determine the call of a person and a congregation.

It is interesting that titles bespoke how authority or leadership was seen and what obedience meant. Some spoke of the abbot as father, while others called everyone brothers. Some spoke of ministers, those who serve, while others used the language of superior for the person who was the leader of the community. This language reveals roles at the time,[8] perhaps more than at present.[9] In some congregations the belief was that God's will was found in the decisions of the superior. By the time of Vatican II, the emphasis in most congregations was that all members are equals, bound by a common obedience to God and seeking God's will. As Pope John Paul II wrote in *Vita Consecrata*:

> The equal dignity of all members of the Church is the work of the Spirit, is rooted in Baptism and Confirmation and is strengthened by the Eucharist. . . . Everyone in the Church is consecrated in Baptism and Confirmation. . . . In addition to this basic consecration, *ordained ministers* receive the consecration of ordination in order to carry on the apostolic ministry in time. *Consecrated persons,* who embrace the evangelical counsels, receive a new and

---

5   José Rovira Arumí, CMF, *Evangelical Counsels and Consecrated Life: Three Charismatic Ways to Follow Christ* (Quezon City, Philippines: Institute for Consecrated Life in Asia, 2015), 312.

6   This is not meant to be a comprehensive historical overview. Additional history may be found in Arumí's book (*Evangelical Counsels*) as well as in histories of different congregations.

7   Arumí, *Evangelical Counsels*, 305.

8   Ibid., 319.

9   Today some institutes have changed their language to more accurately reflect roles (i.e., from superior general to congregational leader), though to someone outside the group what the role is in actuality may not be clear (e.g., moderator of a congregation).

special consecration which, without being sacramental, commits them to making their own—in chastity, poverty and obedience—the way of life practised personally by Jesus and proposed by him to his disciples.[10]

In 2008 the Congregation for the Institutes of Consecrated Life and Societies of Apostolic Life (CICLSAL) published *Faciem tuam*, stating: "Exercising authority in the midst of one's brothers or sisters means serving them, following the example of Christ."[11]

Today we can find all of these understandings present in various groups in consecrated life. Different institutes have different practices that come from their own histories and sources. Now is a good moment for institutes to look at their histories and see how practices emerged. Different national and cultural contexts also influence practices, but in all, obedience is first and foremost to God. Even so, we are always journeying as we search for God's voice amid the cries around us and the wisdom of community seeking also to listen, hear, and respond to the call of God. It is worthwhile to look at one's congregational history and the evolution of the vow of obedience.

Obedience for Today

As I consider religious life *for* the twenty-first century, I look at the fundamentals of the vow of obedience and see the vow in light of and in response to the cries of the world (which are also God's cries). I then consider some implications in light of charism lived through prayer, community, and ministry.

The word "obedience" comes from the Latin word *obo* ("in the direction of ") and *audire* ("hear"). Obedience implies a deep level of listening. It is a wholehearted listening accompanied by a response. Jesus tells us: "My mother and brothers [and sisters] are the ones who hear the word of God and act on it."[12] Obedience is a posture of listening to God, both an attitude and a practice. We must first be hearers of the gospel if we are to become doers of the gospel. These two elements also converge profoundly in living the vow of obedience. We must listen to God and to the cries within and around us.

To Whom Shall We Listen?

The encounter between Jesus and the two disciples walking to Emmaus offers much wisdom for obedience. First, note that we live obedience in the midst of daily life, in the midst of ordinary time as well as extraordinary time. The disciples knew Jesus in the days when his preaching and healings gathered crowds and when

---

[10]   Pope John Paul II, *Vita Consecrata* (1996), 31, http://w2.vatican.va.
[11]   CICLSAL, *Faciem tuam*, 2008, 17b.
[12]   Lk 8:21.

his arrest and crucifixion scattered even his closest followers. They were no doubt sharing memories of Jesus as they walked, trying to understand what it all meant. What they had heard and seen during Jesus's life was now overlaid with a reality they hadn't imagined.

Then comes the Risen Christ, a seeming stranger. He enters their conversation first by listening. They would have described who Jesus was for them, what he did, and what he meant to them. They would have shared stories and explained what had just happened, including that the women who went to the tomb were claiming he had risen. The disciples would have taken at least some risk sharing with this stranger, for they were not far from where Jesus had been killed and could be in danger themselves.

Only after listening did this stranger speak. The disciples now listened to their companion reference their tradition and scripture as a way to understand what had happened in a new way. Perhaps they heard echoes of Jesus's earlier words about the fact that he would suffer, die, and be raised. Their experiences, real as they were, were transformed. Obedience requires a willingness to listen and hear what is said. What they were hearing also connected to their faith tradition and to the vision of the Kingdom Jesus had spoken of while among them. Truth resonated among them. The listening and hearing went both ways.

A relationship and openness to one another formed when the disciples asked this stranger to stay with them as they stopped for the evening. They wanted more time with him. Note the mutuality here. The disciples asked their companion to remain with them and he responded to the invitation. That evening, when they gathered to share bread and wine, they saw, heard, and felt Jesus alive among them. In the breaking of the bread, they connected to the message of Jesus again. What was their response? They went back out, returning to the community in Jerusalem to share what they had seen and heard, and to share Jesus's message of the Reign of God.

Where Do We See and Hear God?

The Emmaus story illustrates the very steps of obedient listening and responding to the call of God. As we look at the call of consecrated life today, we see how we must listen to the voice of God that resonates from our own encounters with Jesus and through scripture. Our relationship, rooted in love and mutuality, takes time to develop. Responding to a particular call also can take time. When they recognized Jesus with them, the disciples knew what to do next: return to Jerusalem. They were re-grounded.

The Emmaus story shows us that God also comes to us in the form of strangers, the other. We must, as the disciples did, be open and listen. We open ourselves to encounter the God of Mystery by looking beyond the familiar or comfortable voices to those calling for more from us, calling to us with refrains resonant of the gospel calls to justice, peace, liberation, and mercy. These become mystical encounters. Antonio Pernia, SVD, reminds us:

Mysticism is built on the conviction that God is not like us, that God always has an "other face"—the unfamiliar, mysterious face of God, the face of God that is revealed to us when we come face to face with the one who is different from us, namely, the poor, the stranger, the foreigner, the refugee, the migrant, the displaced people, the unwed mother, the single parent, the one affected with HIV-AIDS, the faith-seeker, the unbeliever, the non-Christian.[13]

We come to see that the encounter with the other is not first our gift, but rather a gift of God to us for the sake of God's mission. The call, then, is to do what the Emmaus disciples did: to listen and hear. Peruvian liberation theologian Gustavo Gutiérrez aptly notes: "Working in this world of the poor and becoming familiar with it, I came to realize, together with others, the first thing to do is listen."[14] This also means that we intentionally get close so the other can choose to reveal God's message of flourishing for all to us.

German theologian Johann Baptist Metz writes about the mysticism of open eyes,[15] which calls us forth when we encounter the other, particularly the suffering other. Life changes in these encounters. The cry goes out to God, and at the same time the outward cry in solidarity creates spaces in us to hear God's response. We can then move from our listening to God to responding with action. Austrian theologian Martha Zechmeister, CJ, writes that we must listen particularly to those who suffer, for their suffering gives them an authority to which we must respond in some way. In her article, "The Authority of Those Who Suffer,"[16] we are reminded again, as Jesus's life reminds us, that our neighbors both near and far are included in our call to fidelity with God.[17]

Earth, our common home, is another place that God reveals Godself to us. In *Laudato Si'*, Pope Francis reminds us that "[the earth] now cries out to us

---

[13]   Antonio M. Pernia, SVD, "Interculturality and Leadership in Consecrated Life: The Theological Significance of Interculturality," CSCL Conference (2018), Chicago, Catholic Theological Union (unpublished draft).

[14]   Jennie Weiss Block and Michael Griffin, eds., *In the Company of the Poor: Conversations with Dr. Paul Farmer and Fr. Gustavo Gutiérrez* (Maryknoll, NY: Orbis Books, 2013), 166.

[15]   See Johannes Baptist Metz, "Theology as Theodicy?" in *A Passion for God: The Mystical-Political Dimension of Christianity*, trans. J. M. Ashley (Mahwah, NJ: Paulist Press, 1998), 69 (orig. German: 1990).

[16]   Martha Zechmeister, CJ, "The Authority of Those Who Suffer," *UISG Bulletin* 152 (2013): 59–71.

[17]   Metz particularly calls us to remember the neighbor from a distance, for we can easily forget and deny our duty to those in need simply because we do not see the other directly. Certainly we do that easily enough by not reading certain news or by not watching online or on television suffering that is particularly challenging. However, when we do listen, look, and allow the reality of the neighbor's suffering to permeate us, grace moves—often in unexpected ways, and even with unexpected others. Such is the grace of God!

because of the harm we have inflicted on her by our irresponsible use and abuse of the goods with which God has endowed her."[18] Francis also tells us: "The earth herself, burdened and laid waste, is among the most abandoned and maltreated of our poor."[19] Pope Francis writes in stark terms about how destruction and famine affect earth and earth's people.

Our interconnectedness with all creation is also our interconnectedness with the God who is revealed in creation. Mysticism is an openness to encounter the God of Mystery who is present all around us. As obedience leads us to where we must next walk, mysticism takes us beyond ourselves. While we go beyond what we know when we open ourselves to the mysticism of encounter, there is something in us that realizes this is familiar, this is where we belong and are called to be at this time.

We find in our encounter with the other some direction for our call to obedience. From the preceding chapter on poverty, we know our witness must be to the good news of God's freeing love for all creation. The mystical call is accompanied by a prophetic call to denounce all that is not building up God's creation and to announce the way forward. Obedience is to God's mission, and God's mission is to all creation, particularly where creation suffers.

Our call to obedience must bring us to the margins. The mystical and the prophetic converge here. In earlier chapters we have seen that God hears the cries of the poor and cries out against the injustices they suffer. Moses was called upon to free the Israelites from slavery. The prophets who came after him cried out, denouncing injustice and announcing God's vision for the fullness of human dignity and justice.

In the New Testament, we clearly see Jesus's choices. Pope Francis writes:

> God shows the poor "his first mercy." This divine preference has consequences for the faith life of all Christians, since we are called to have "this mind . . . which was in Jesus Christ" (*Phil* 2:5). Inspired by this, the Church has made an option for the poor which is understood as a "special form of primacy in the exercise of Christian charity, to which the whole tradition of the Church bears witness." . . . We are called to find Christ in [the poor], to lend our voice to their causes, but also to be their friends, to listen to them, to speak for them and to embrace the mysterious wisdom which God wishes to share with us through them.[20]

Note how Pope Francis reminds us that those who struggle have much to teach us about the suffering Christ and about injustice, and that they also offer us friendship. It is important not to interpret "to speak for them" as a substitute for inviting them to offer their own voices. There will be times when we will bring to our meetings

---

18   Pope Francis, *Laudato Si'* (*On Care for Our Common Home*) (2015), preface, http://w2.vatican.va.

19   Ibid., 2.

20   Pope Francis, *Evangelii Gaudium* (*The Joy of the Gospel*), 198, http://w2.vatican.va. Hereinafter *EG*.

and deliberations what we learn from our brothers and sisters. The call is to widen the table as well as to be attentive to who is missing from our tables.

God's preferential option asks us to hear the cries of the poor and to work to transform the systems that create situations of poverty and oppression. These realities call us to respond in how we live each of the vows, but the vow of obedience asks very particularly for us to listen and hear with God's eyes, ears, and heart to the cries around us. From his experience of living in close proximity and relationship to the struggling people of his diocese in Rustenburg, South Africa, South African Bishop Kevin Dowling, CSsR, asserts that

> the raison d'être of the vows is to proclaim and bring about the Good News of the reign of God and this especially among the vulnerable, marginalised and poor of the world, and indeed the marginalised and alienated in the Church. The vows exist in function of a living critique of the different forms of personal and social sin which diminish/destroy the person, the family, the community, the planet. And so, the goal in living the vows is to become ever more authentically a prophetic sign and presence of God's reign in the midst of Church and world.[21]

Something happens when we see and hear from the periphery. In an interview with *La Civiltà Cattolica*, Pope Francis said: "I am convinced of one thing: the great changes in history were realized when reality was seen not from the center but rather from the periphery. It is a hermeneutical question: reality is understood only if it is looked at from the periphery, and not when our viewpoint is equidistant from everything."[22]

Women and men religious, steeped in scripture and tradition, will follow obedience's particular call through their institute's charism, Constitutions, and traditions to discern the calls from geographical, spiritual, and other peripheries. Pernia reminds us what is possible when we open ourselves to such encounters with the other:

> Gazing at God's face, we acquire the heart and the eyes of God, so that we begin to gaze at the world with the eyes of God. When we do so, we see

---

[21]   Kevin Dowling, CSsR, "Revisioning Religious Life for the 21st Century in a Global Context," talk given at the Annual General Meeting of the Conference of Religious of Ireland, June 4, 2015. At the beginning of this section he says: "With the developments at Vatican II and afterwards, the theology of baptism and the promotion of the universal call to holiness and so forth, there had to be a re-visioning of the fundamental call and meaning of the religious life. . . . The vows also could no longer be understood in terms of what could basically be described as a set of norms and ascetical practices in view of achieving a state of holiness or perfection."

[22]   Antonio Spadaro, SJ, "'Wake Up the World!' Conversation with Pope Francis about the Religious Life," *La Civiltà Cattolica* (2014) I, 3–17, trans. Donald Maldari, SJ (revised, January 6, 2015), https://onlineministries.creighton.edu.

the world differently, we see the world in a new way—enemies become friends, separating walls become open doors, strangers become brothers or sisters, borders become bridges, diversity leads not to differences and conflict but to harmony and unity. So, mysticism, which arises out of mission, leads back to mission.[23]

We are all transformed when we see and hear from the periphery. Mysticism and prophecy converge as our hearts become as wide as the world our home.

What Is Required for Living Obedience?

I offer seven requirements for living obedience. This is not a "how-to" list, but it includes elements that institutes and congregations need to have in place in order to live obedience for the calls of God in this time.

Freedom is first, the sine qua non for obedience. Only persons who are free within themselves can profess and witness healthy obedience. Canon law mandates that each person professing solemn or perpetual vows or promises declare that she or he is professing in *full freedom*. We are always growing in our freedom, but the vow of obedience requires that we are promising voluntarily and without reservation.

Interior freedom is essential for mature, responsible obedience. While this is a quality that grows in us throughout our lives, obedience in spirit as well as in action requires lifelong growth as interiorly free persons. What does it mean to be interiorly free? Psychologist Ted Dunn, who has worked with a number of congregations in their efforts to listen to the Spirit, offers a helpful description.

Simply put, interior freedom is a state of mind and heart that allows your inner truth and wisdom to be known, accepted and assimilated. It is like a chamber inside yourself, where your truth and God's truth merge. Your freedom to accept the truth, the size of this interior room, is in direct proportion to your readiness to receive the truth. The greater one's room is, the greater is one's ability to seek and accept the truth. If you are frightened of what the truth might bring, ambivalent because it might be disturbing, then the chamber shrinks. If, on the other hand, you are ready to receive the truth no matter the cost, then the room is enlarged. Your interior freedom is determined by how well you have prepared your heart, readied yourself to listen and worked with the fears that can otherwise constrict the truth and render you unfree.[24]

---

[23] Pernia, "Interculturality and Leadership in Consecrated Life," 10.

[24] Ted Dunn, PhD, "Interior Freedom," *Human Development* 33, no. 2 (Summer 2012): 6. Dunn offers these practices toward greater interior freedom: "1) Ease the defenses that constrict your truth and conceal self-knowledge; 2) Return to your touchstone faith experiences—those moments and places in your life where you best meet God; 3) Play with possibilities, think outside of the box, and suspend your judgment; 4) Explore your own

What is our freedom for? Love. Freedom must move us to be *active participants* in our congregations, ministries, communities, and our life of prayer. Passivity is deadly for community and erodes the generosity that flows from freedom for love.

Second, obedience requires that our love be directed to God's mission, which brings us to depth of relationship with God and love of neighbor.[25]

Third, intelligent obedience, not blind obedience, is asked of us. Intelligent obedience brings forth all our capacities for love and service. Intelligent obedience is not consonant with the logic of the world but lives out of the logic of love.

Fourth, ongoing formation is essential. In *New Wine in New Wineskins: The Consecrated Life and Its Ongoing Challenges since Vatican II*, CICLSAL states that "formation must last a lifetime"—it is not just a sabbatical program, a pilgrimage to a foundation site, or a workshop or academic course. Rather, "Ongoing formation should be oriented according to the ecclesial identity of the consecrated life. . . . The task is one of reinforcing, or often of rediscovering, their appropriate place in the Church at the service of humanity."[26] However, the CICLSAL document also notes that

> we must admit that a culture of ongoing formation does not yet exist. This lacuna is the result of an incomplete and narrow mentality regarding ongoing formation. Hence, there is little sensitivity to its importance. Likewise, the involvement of the individual with it has been minimal. On the level of pedagogical praxis, we have not yet found concrete programmes, either at the individual or communitarian levels, which translate into a real journey of growth in creative fidelity, and have significant and lasting effects in actual life.[27]

Fifth, models of obedience and practices that are no longer useful must be renounced. The horizon is what can best serve the gospel at this time. Invoking *Perfectae Caritatis* and stating that all areas of consecrated life are to be examined, CICLSAL reminds us that "no change is possible without renouncing obsolete models so as to be open to new horizons and possibilities regarding government, the common life, the administration of assets, and mission." And further, "In no way can we remain with an attitude that knows more about maintenance than about the authentic redevelopment of styles and behaviours."[28]

---

resistance in order to gain insight and become freer from it; 5) Visualize what liberation would look like beyond the struggle, to be radically free."

[25] This topic was discussed in Chapter 3 on the contemplative dimension of consecrated life.

[26] Congregation for Institutes of Consecrated Life and Societies of Apostolic Life (CICLSAL), *New Wine in New Wineskins: The Consecrated Life and Its Ongoing Challenges since Vatican II* (Nairobi, Kenya: Paulines Publications Africa, 2017), Introduction. Cf. *Vita Consecrata*, 70.

[27] CICLSAL, *New Wine*, no. 35.

[28] Ibid., no. 22.

Examples of this kind of impasse occur when all decision-making power is centralized or when there is little change in community and institute leadership.[29] Sometimes this happens because of fear of change and sometimes because we cannot see who else might serve.[30] In all these areas, the call is to the prophetic imagination. We must do this together in order to hear the Spirit speaking.

Sixth, there is a requirement to listen and respond to the edges of need. CICLSAL quite strongly challenges and encourages ministerial responses to the urgent cries of this moment:

> The rich multiplicity of ministries that the consecrated life has exercised in the last decades has undergone radical redesigning due to social, economic, political, scientific, and technological evolutions. The same goes for state appropriation of works historically associated with the consecrated life. All this has changed the way consecrated persons relate with the context in which they live and their typical way of dealing with others. *In the meantime, new and unprecedented emergencies have caused other needs to explode. They still have not been responded to and continue to knock at the door of the creative fidelity of all forms of consecrated life.*[31]

This will require of us an attitude of *disponibilidad,* radical availability.

The seventh point is that we must do this with creativity and boldness in all areas of consecrated life. We must find new ways of evangelizing in our time. We must respond from the virtue of obedience, the dispositions and practices of open listening that move us to action. What Pope Francis calls for in *Evangelii Gaudium* is a call to us as well: "Pastoral ministry in a missionary key seeks to abandon the complacent attitude that says: 'We have always done it this way.' I invite everyone to be bold and creative in this task of rethinking the goals, structures, style and methods of evangelization in their respective communities."[32] Again, there is a hopefulness and invitation to creativity even as there will be a letting go of what has been. The call is to see where the needs are *today* and to respond.

Moving toward More Relational Models of Leadership and Membership

Recognizing that institutes have had many different models of leadership and membership, there is a strong emphasis today on relational models of obedience. Declaring that "a service of authority that fosters collaboration and a common

---

29   Ibid.

30   Some congregations whose membership is small may imagine only the same few people serving.

31   CICLSAL, *New Wine,* no. 7. Emphasis added.

32   CICLSAL, *New Wine,* no. 30, citing Pope Francis, *EG* 33.

vision of the fraternal lifestyle is to be encouraged,"[33] *New Wine in New Wineskins* also references the 2008 document, *The Service of Authority and Obedience*, which underlines that the point of leadership is service: "The authority of the religious superior must be characterized by the spirit of service, in imitation of Christ who 'came not to be served but to serve' (Mk 10:45)."[34] We must seek to embody "the behaviour inspired by Jesus the servant who washes the feet of his disciples so that they might have a part in his life and in his love."[35] Washing feet and feeding sheep are compelling images of servant leadership, done out of love, as Jesus modeled for us.

A relational model between those in elected or appointed leadership and the whole of membership is also a model of the inbreaking of the Reign of God in the world. While acknowledging the legitimate role of authority in society, church, and religious life, Sandra M. Schneiders offers that:

> Religious, by their vow of obedience, undertake to create and live a different kind of political life in which there is no hierarchy, in which all participate as equals, where coercion is not the normal *modus operandi* of leaders and nor is heteronomous submission the way of the members. This new way of organizing power for the empowerment of all affects in radical ways the relationship of Religious with God, with one another in community, and with those they serve in ministry, and as a result gives prophetic witness to a new reality that is coming into being, the Reign of God in this world.[36]

Although religious life ad intra has its own specificities, the lived vow of obedience is to also be Good News for the church and world. Mary John Mananzan, OSB, underlines this and offers a reminder that four key principles offered by Vatican II are participation, collegiality, subsidiarity, and accountability.[37] For congregations and communities, the participation of as many as possible, in a manner that regards the contributions of each as valuable, is necessary and must be encouraged. Whenever possible, local groups should take the lead and responsibility for decisions made even as accountability at all levels of religious life are

---

[33]   CICLSAL, *New Wine*, no. 43.

[34]   CICLSAL instruction, *The Service of Authority and Obedience* (*Faciem tuam, Domine, requiram*), May 11, 2008, 14b.

[35]   CICLSAL, *New Wine*, no. 21. Cf. CICLSAL, *Service of Authority and Obedience*, 12.

[36]   Sandra M. Schneiders, IHM, *Buying the Field: Catholic Religious Life in Mission to the World* (New York: Paulist Press, 2013), 105.

[37]   Mary John Mananzan, OSB, "Post–Vatican II Perspectives on Religious Leadership," *UISG Bulletin* 152 (2013): 5–6. Thank you to Samuel H. Canilang, CMF, for this reference in his book *Service of Authority in Religious Life: For the Life and Mission of a Church which "Goes Forth,"* ICLA Monographs no. 18 (Quezon, Philippines: Institute for Consecrated Life in Asia, 2018), 38.

to be offered as the norm. Nevertheless, there are some areas of discernment and decision-making that may not be appropriately made public. Here we must trust the current leadership of members to make Gospel-based decisions. This does not preclude conversations and questions, but we acknowledge that members in leadership are given this authority to act on behalf of the whole. This authority is necessary for timely decision-making.

Quantum Leadership

Samuel M. Canilang, CMF, describes the model offered by Joanne Schuster, SFP, as "a new model of leadership—quantum leadership, which is *holarchical*." He notes that, in Schuster's words, "Quantum leadership 'emphasizes free-flowing interaction and codetermination. That is, members influence the internal dynamic as much as the internal dynamic influences the members.'"[38] Quantum leadership represents a paradigm shift for some and a way of living leadership and membership for others. Schuster contends: "Today's religious congregations no longer see themselves as simply obedient agents of the hierarchical church. Rather, they see themselves as interconnected parts of the whole church: an interconnection of hierarchy, priests, vowed religious and church members, all of whom form a morphogenic field." She notes that this field is "invisible, intangible,"[39] but it is nonetheless a real connection.

It is useful to see the space between hierarchical and quantum leadership as a continuum. Consider where you, your congregation, and your leadership might be found. It is helpful to do a self-evaluation first and then to dialogue with others about how they see these areas in themselves, in leadership teams, and in how the congregation actually functions.[40] There are many models, and each institute and team must see what is best for this time.

The Call of Leadership and Authority Today

The call of obedience, as discussed above, has particular dimensions for the life and flourishing of a community or institute. I offer seven key elements regarding the service of leadership and the flourishing of community.[41] First, any form

---

[38]   Joanne Schuster, SFP, "Quantum Leadership of Religious Congregations: A Model for Interesting Times," *Human Development* 33, no. 4 (2012): 25. Quoted in Canilang, *Service of Authority in Religious Life*, 47.

[39]   Schuster, "Quantum Leadership," 23.

[40]   Sometimes what we say or write is not how we or our organizations actually function. Especially valuable here would be the voices of people who are connected to the institute but not actual members, for they might offer further insights on what is perceived and how.

[41]   I think some or many of these areas can be applied to ministries and groups that require a community.

of leadership must be grounded in listening to God and helping others listen to God. Any authority must be at the service of God and for the service of consecrated life. The service of leadership does not mean that a person in leadership will know what God is saying to others. Instead leadership will create an atmosphere in the congregation and community for each person and for the group to listen, hear, and respond to God's calls. The spiritual life of the community is first and foremost; without spiritual life, community and ministry will struggle or fall apart. It is notable that the call to listen deeply, to live in relationship with God's vision is not only the call of consecrated life but of the whole church and all those in servant leadership in the church. The actual title of the pope is *servus servorum Dei*, servant of the servants of God.[42] Pope Benedict XVI, at the beginning of his pontificate, said, "My real program of governance is not to do my own will, not to pursue my own ideas, but to listen, together with the whole Church, to the word and the will of the Lord, to be guided by him, so that he himself will lead the Church at this hour of our history."[43] So it is with us.

Second, leadership is at the service of the Spirit and so must continually be attentive to the evolution of the charism in a particular time and place. Creating communities of hope on a global scale requires this, for our fidelity and responsiveness to the Spirit's movements is transformative for us, our congregations and institutes, and the world. Knowing ourselves as interconnected means each small community affects the church and the world. There must also be attentiveness to the mission of the congregation, the whole of the consecrated life (prayer, community, and ministry) that has as its call announcing and incarnating God's vision for the world.

Third, leadership in congregations must build communion. Each congregation is, and will continue to be, a community in diversity and a call to union, oneness of heart and spirit. I remember realizing the wisdom of this when early in my years in the Society of the Sacred Heart a sister shared that when leadership calls us to *Cor unum*, one heart, it is a strong call to us to come together. Significant to the society's history are narratives in which it was the intense effort to live *Cor unum* that kept us together during times in which we experienced great division. A spirit of communion helps members work toward a larger good.[44]

Fourth, leadership promotes the flourishing of each person, promoting the dignity of each and encouraging the freedom to be our best selves for the service of God. Members need to be known and to know they belong. While responsibility for much of the personal work belongs to the individual person, leaders and

---

42   I am grateful to Arumí for this reminder! See *Evangelical Counsels*, 296.

43   Pope Benedict, homily at inauguration mass upon becoming pope, April 25, 2005, https://www.tldm.org.

44   That something is "for the good" is an important factor here, because there are times in congregations when the greater good happens when there is a movement to create a new entity. This is done for the good of God's mission rather than simply because one group does not want change.

communities are responsible for connecting with one another, for knowing one another as much as possible,[45] and for building communion with one another.

Fifth, it follows then that leadership connects the community with the wider church and the world. Because consecrated life is intricately connected to the life of the church, leaders are at times bridges with other ecclesial leaders and a link between members and the wider church. There is much co-learning that longs to be galvanized in the church today. Members who serve in leadership are called to bring forth the living wisdom of their institute to the world and to make possible collaboration and co-learning to serve God's mission.

Sixth, those in leadership are tasked with keeping key questions at the forefront of the institute. These questions are about mission, not maintenance. As we have seen earlier, the call is to respond to the Spirit's call in prayer, community, and ministry *for this time*. Because no one person or team of persons can see all that is needed or possible, it is essential to have "wisdom persons" nearby who can offer perspectives that can deepen and widen discernment. Wisdom persons may or may not be congregation members, but these individuals should know the mission of the congregation well. Leadership must also point to callings on the horizons—and at times, the members will pull leadership toward the horizons, and their service is to utilize their voice and authority to call forth the institute, whether to discernment or to action. What no longer serves must be let go in order to receive the calls emerging from the Spirit crying out and leading us into transformation.

Finally, today's leadership is called to prophetically denounce what is not of God and announce a vision of God's loving goodness in the world. Just as our vows are public, ecclesial events, so is every form of consecrated life. By our prayers, communities, and ministries we both announce the Good News of Jesus Christ's mission and denounce anything that demeans God or any aspect of God's creation. Consecrated life is about testing the spirits of good and evil in the world and responding to unmet needs. In this time consecrated life is called to build unity, courage, confidence, and hope-filled communities, and to denounce any attempt to destroy persons or creation in word or deed, efforts to stir up fear and mistrust, and all forms of violence. We instead are to engage in peacebuilding. These are calls within our congregations, church, and society; they affect all areas of creation. How all of this is lived will be through the flow of the charism given to each form of consecrated life and adapted to the needs of this time. As we have seen, the community we have, and must nourish, is an intercultural one.

Call to Interculturality

Diversity of cultures and generations must be seen as a gift for this time, asking us all to listen together anew. *New Wine in New Wineskins* offers the example of a situation in which we see "on the one hand, a few dozen elderly members tied to the classic

---

[45] This is not about invading one another's privacy, but about caring for one another enough to want to know each other deeply.

cultural and institutional traditions which have been hardly altered; on the other hand, a large number of young members from different cultures who are agitated and feel marginalized, and who no longer accept subordinate roles."[46] This is not an isolated situation. New models come forth when we realize that the gifts of persons before us are God's invitation to the continually emerging future. Note the hopeful, dynamic horizon described by CICLSAL: "It is becoming increasingly clear that what is most important is not the preservation of models but rather the willingness to re-examine, in creative continuity, the consecrated life as the evangelical member of a permanent state of conversion out of which insights and concrete choices flow."[47]

There is a great gift here in the movements that are happening in religious life today. Recognizing the gift requires skills and dispositions for seeing with new lenses. What is at stake? *Vita Consecrata* reminds us: "The consecrated life is at the very heart of the Church as a decisive element for her mission, since it manifests the inner nature of the Christian calling and the striving for the whole Church as Bridge towards union with her one Spouse."[48] And *New Wine in New Wineskins* calls on the prophetic dimensions of religious life as "the sign and fruit of its charismatic nature, making it capable of inventiveness and originality."[49]

How do inventiveness and originality emerge? When we work together, willing to change what we must for the sake of the Reign of God—it is then that we see wonders. So much is possible here! In addition to the diversity within our membership, the diversity among the people with whom we collaborate in mission and those we are privileged to serve offers all institutes possibilities for this conversion, transformation, and newness.[50]

One description of the kind of obedience asked of leadership is found in *Keep Watch*, the 2016 letter by CICLSAL on the occasion of the Year of Consecrated Life:

> We are not called to a preoccupied and administrative leadership, but a service of authority that, with evangelical clarity, guides the journey to be undertaken together and in unity of heart, within a fragile present in which the future is waiting to be born. We do not need "simple administration"; what we need is to "walk after them, helping those who lag behind and—above all—allowing the flock to strike out on new paths."[51]

---

[46] CICLSAL, *New Wine*, no. 13.

[47] Ibid.

[48] Pope John Paul II, *Vita Consecrata*, 3.

[49] CICLSAL, *New Wine*, no. 32.

[50] This is not to place the same rights and responsibilities for a congregation or institute on those with whom we minister or serve. It is, however, to remind us that all congregations have the gift of diversity around them. Some congregations may have less internal diversity than others, but diversity still exists and must be nourished. There may be more diversity than one imagines if one intentionally seeks to discover the gifts of one's fellow members.

[51] Congregation for Institutes of Consecrated Life and Societies of Apostolic Life, *Keep Watch!* Letter for the Year of Consecrated Life. A Letter to consecrated men and women journeying in the footsteps of God. (English 2015).

Whatever their role in a congregation, each individual must walk toward new paths through prophetic listening, hearing, and responding. This brings us full circle to the mystical call at the beginning of this chapter. *New Wine in New Wineskins* brings the mystical and prophetic together:

> The nature of the consecrated life as a sign which has distinguished it within the journey of the People of God throughout history, places it in a privileged position within the dimension of evangelical prophecy. This prophetic dimension is the sign and fruit of its charismatic nature, making it capable of inventiveness and originality. This requires contin- uous availability to the signs coming from the Spirit to the point of listening to the still soft breeze (cf. 1 Kgs 19:12). This is the only attitude that permits the recognition of the mysterious ways (cf. Jn 3:8) of grace to the point of being reborn to a new hope through the fruitfulness of the Word (cf. Jn 4:35).[52]

When we each listen to the Spirit, we can together discern how we are being called as a congregation to live our mystical-prophetic call. It is to communal (and personal) discernment that I now turn.

Communal and Personal Discernment

Our call to living obedience to God within our congregational charism is enfleshed in our prayer, community, and ministry. We live this personally and as members of our community. This moves us to communal discernment, which is the way in which a community or congregation hears the Spirit's voice calling and responds. This is a critical area for congregations to articulate and practice. The recent Synod on Youth and its accompanying documents also emphasized the need for young people to learn discernment.

All congregations discern, but there is a lacuna in explicitly articulated meth- odology or process. Ignatian discernment is a well-articulated process and is used not only by religious orders but people in many walks of life and even other faith traditions. However, the Spirit's creativity is boundless, and the call now is for more forms of consecrated life, within their spiritualities and traditions, to offer their methods of discernment as Good News for the people of God. This will not only assist all people, but it will also assist the institutes themselves in expressing their particular way and seeing how it flows through their charism.

Discernment both personal and communal is an essential component of obedi- ence. Decisions are made as a result of the process of communal discernment. This is the final step before action is taken. What follows are some basic points about communal and personal discernment. They are meant to be filled out or thickened through each institute's particular charism and spirituality.

---

[52]   CICLSAL, *New Wine*, no. 32.

It is also important to note that communal discernment encompasses the whole of our lives, including the internal dimensions. As consecrated life is called to an interior conversion, internal transformation, and external revitalization, all areas of religious life ultimately require ongoing discernment, including communal discernment.

Discernment, is, according to Schneiders, "a difficult process required in any situation in which we must make a judgment or decision about *what is the right thing to do in the present situation.*" She then emphasizes, "Notice, the question is not about what is, in principle, right for a theoretical subject in some generic situation . . . but rather what *I* am called to do, *here and now*, in response to the *concrete situation* in which I find myself." She also clarifies that "discernment is never an isolated process. Even when the decision being made primarily affects the individual rather than the community it is *always communal* in the sense that a valid conscience decision must take into account the persons and groups to whom one is related in the relevant situation, the influence of one's decision." Finally, she notes that discernment "is not simply a matter of 'making up one's own mind,'" and that a person exercising careful and prudent discernment "recognizes the need to '*form one's conscience,*' that is, to consult, to familiarize oneself with the biblical, moral, historical, and theological data relevant to the issue . . . to attend to good example, to examine circumstances carefully and do whatever else is possible to bring to bear in the decision-making process all the data relevant to the situation."[53]

As Schneiders notes, there is a difference between discernment and decision-making. However, the two are related in certain ways. In brief:

- Discernment can be in service of a decision but not the other way around.
- Decisions that need to be made call us to discernment.
- Discernment is what we perceive as the will of God and the possibilities in service as a result.
- Decision-making is what you do.
- Discernment is a climate of soul.
- Decision-making is task driven.

Pope Francis offers three verbs to describe discernment: to recognize; to interpret; and to choose.[54] To recognize means to notice what is moving in you, from external observations to internal feelings. This is reading the signs of the times in us and around us. Such a reading requires some interpretation, sorting through what in it is grace, what is invitation, and what is temptation. Ultimately, discernment leads us to greater love, toward how to manifest that love, and to greater participation in God's mission of love in our world today. We then must make a choice and act on it. This doesn't guarantee we will be right, for we are humans, but the process

---

53   Schneiders, *Buying the Field*, 563–64.
54   *EG* 51.

of discernment keeps us growing in our goodness. Discernment is a process to be practiced for the entirety of our lives.

Communal discernment, or discernment in common, is a process whereby a group desires to together hear what the call is from the Spirit. Many books have been written on this,[55] so I offer here simply a few notable points.[56]

- Communal discernment requires personal discernment, a sharing of what moves in the individuals.
- Communal discernment requires each person to be willing to share authentically. This movement asks for a sharing in community that makes us vulnerable. It calls for transparency.
- Communal discernment is a way of holding one's perspective lightly. Each one offers her ingredient into the process, listening deeply to what is coming forth. Discernment is not a puzzle in which each individual piece is put together to make a predetermined whole, but rather the visioning of the picture to which we are called by God. These ingredients and offerings create the space for the vision to be named and heard. Something is missing if anyone withholds the gift each one is. The diversity of the individual gifts is needed for movement toward the new whole.
- Discernment is not about being right but the offering of ourselves in prayer and in person.
- Discernment is not about consensus. When a prophetic voice speaks, we are called to recognize it and feel its pull. There can be more than one prophetic voice. Testing of the spirits in discernment is to ask whether this voice will take us toward God.

Communal discernment as a way we live obedience requires open-heartedness, and obedience is incomplete without a living response.

Abuse of Authority

We are in a moment when we realize the need to acknowledge that sometimes authority within the church and within consecrated life has failed in its call to care

---

[55] See Henri Nouwen et al., *Discernment: Reading the Signs of the Daily Life* (HarperOne, 2011); LCWR, *Occasional Papers* 43, no. 2 (Summer 2014); Brian Gallagher, MSC, *Communal Wisdom: A Way of Discernment for a Pilgrim Church* (Melbourne, AU: Coventry Press, 2018); Timothy M. Gallagher, OMV, *Discerning the Will of God: An Ignatian Guide to Christian Decision Making* (Chestnut Ridge, NY: Crossroad, 2009); Elizabeth Liebert, *The Way of Discernment* (Louisville, KY: Westminster John Knox Press, 2008); Suzanne Farnham, Joseph Gill, Taylor McLean, and Susan Ward, *Listening Hearts: Discerning Call in Community,* 20th anniv. ed. (1911; New York: Morehouse, 2011).

[56] I am very grateful to Mary Sharon Riley, RC, for her wisdom on this topic.

for and serve its people and the people of God. The institutional church continues to suffer from the actions and effects of abuse—sexual, emotional, and verbal—in and by its members. The sexual abuse of minors and vulnerable persons, anywhere, at any time, and by anyone, is egregious and criminal. In this twenty-first century we are still uncovering more instances of this sin and the crime of abuse by persons whose role was supposed to be to serve and protect. In addition to direct abuse, in some places there are discoveries of cover-ups within the hierarchy and other ecclesial, social, and political systems that perpetuate the abuse.

As this book was written, the abuse of power by a United States cardinal became public, along with stories of the cover-up of his abuses, both overt and indirect. This is a scandal and sin in our church, though certainly abuse is not limited to any one religious tradition or nation. Neither are women and men in consecrated life exempt from committing such abuse. Some are also survivors of abuse. Efforts continue to be made to locate and respond to the survivors of abuse anywhere in the church or consecrated life.[57] This is an important step, but it is not sufficient.

Schools and educational centers are increasingly teaching students about appropriate and respectful behavior. Formation programs must also include education about healthy sexuality, and about abuse and safety for persons in the ministry of formation, leadership teams, and those in the process of formation. Particularly among persons in the process of formation in an institute, persons in formation ministry, accompaniment, spiritual direction, and leadership have an unequal power relationship due to their authority and role. Persons in the process of formation must also be educated about healthy sexuality, appropriate relationships, and setting their own boundaries. This information must be shared with any who have contact with persons in formation, including bishops, priests (diocesan or religious order), teachers, and others. What for some is obvious about appropriate boundaries is not so for others.[58]

It must be clear that:

- Obedience is never to be blind obedience.
- Obedience is never to be abusive, or to acquiesce in abuse, whether in word or action.
- The abuse of power requires a response.
- Abuse takes many forms, including but not limited to physical, sexual, emotional, and verbal abuse. This can happen in physical proximity or through social media. All are equally reprehensible.

---

[57]   This is, of course, a need in all areas of society, including in families. For the purposes of this book I am focusing on the Roman Catholic Church and consecrated life.

[58]   This is an important area for review or teaching for any in these ministries. Boundaries such as not having meetings or spiritual direction/accompaniment in bedrooms need to be taught regularly, for persons in formation and leadership roles of influence by their very nature fluctuate. It is better to not assume.

- Abuse of power can be manifested in any area of congregational life, including but not limited to economics, ministry and community appointments, bullying, or sharing information inappropriately.

Women in the Church and Abuse of Power

On November 23, 2018, the International Union of Superiors General (UISG) issued their public statement, *UISG Declaration against Any Kind of Abuse*, in which they explicitly condemn abuse: "Abuse in all forms: sexual, verbal, emotional, or any inappropriate use of power within a relationship, diminishes the dignity and healthy development of the person who is victimized." The statement goes on to declare:

> We stand by those courageous women and men who have reported abuse to the authorities. We condemn those who support the culture of silence and secrecy, often under the guise of "protection" of an institution's reputation or naming it "part of one's culture." We advocate for transparent civil and criminal reporting of abuse whether within religious congregations, at the parish or diocesan levels, or in any public arena.
>
> We ask that any woman religious who has suffered abuse, report the abuse to the leader of her congregation, and to church and civic authorities as appropriate. If UISG receives a report of abuse, we will be a listening presence and help the person to have the courage to bring the complaint to the appropriate organizations.[59]

Pope Francis assembled the heads of bishops' conferences in Rome for a Vatican summit on clerical sexual abuse in February 2019. One of the speakers was Sr. Veronica Openibo, SHCJ, a Nigerian superior general of the Society of the Holy Child Jesus and member of the executive board of UISG. In compelling language, she called the church to be transparent and proactive in facing sexual abuse. She also reminded all that abuse in the church is found on every continent. Openibo lamented, "Clerical sex abuse is a crisis that has reduced the credibility of the Church when transparency should be the hallmark of mission as followers of Jesus Christ."[60] She continued: "We must acknowledge that our mediocrity, hypocrisy and complacency have brought us to this disgraceful and scandalous place we find ourselves as a church. We pause to pray, Lord have mercy on us!"[61] Openibo also called for more effective processes across the entire church

---

[59]   See the full statement at the UISG website: http://www.internationalunionsuperiorsgeneral.org.

[60]   The quotes are all from the text of the presentation by Sr. Veronica Openibo, SHCJ, on February 23, 2019, at the Vatican Summit on Clergy Sexual Abuse. See https://www.catholicnews.com.

[61]   Ibid.

based on research in human development as well as civil and canon law, for the safeguarding of minors. Then clear and comprehensive safeguarding policies and guidelines in every diocese should be placed visibly in various parish offices and published on the internet. There must be better handling of the cases through face-to-face, transparent and courageous conversations with both victims and offenders, as well as investigating groups.[62]

She saw some hope for change, she said, as she watched Pope Francis's handling of the Chilean bishops' scandals and saw how he learned and changed his thinking and actions. With some tenderness, she described Pope Francis's method of discernment in that case: "I admire you, Brother Francis, for taking time as a true Jesuit, to discern and be humble enough to change your mind, to apologize and take action—an example for all of us."[63]

The call is clear that change must happen and that the entire church must be part of creating the change. This, too, is the call of prophetic obedience: listening to the cries of God and the cries of the people of God and responding by denouncing abuses everywhere and forging a new path forward, together.

Living Deeply One's Call to Love

Obedience is about living deeply one's call to love. When we love, all else can follow. At the heart of our vocation we long to give ourselves away; we long for a way of life that is worth *everything*. Sometimes it is—and we do.

I close with a quote from Maryknoll Sister Ita Ford, who was martyred in El Salvador on December 2, 1980. In a letter she wrote to her niece just a few months earlier, Ita offers a call that is to all of us: "I hope you come to find that which gives life a deep meaning for you. Something worth living for—maybe even worth dying for—something that energizes you, enthuses you, enables you to keep moving ahead. I can't tell you what it might be. That's for you to find, to choose, to love."[64]

Questions for Reflection and Discussion

1.   How does your congregation's charism affect your understanding and living of the vow of obedience?
2.   How does your congregation discern? What are elements of your communal discernment that are essential for today?
3.   How does obedience affect your prayer? Community life? Ministry?

---

[62]   Ibid.
[63]   Ibid.
[64]   From the letter of Ita Ford, MM, to her niece and godchild, Jennifer Ford, August 18, 1980, http://www.lovingjustwise.com.

4. What is your congregation or province's plan for ongoing formation? How have you participated? For what would you long in ongoing formation?
5. What are your congregation's narratives and stories of obedience? Ask others.
6. What key insights do you have about obedience? Share with someone.
7. What questions do you have about obedience? Talk with someone.
8. What do you sense the Spirit is inviting us to in light of the vow of obedience?

9

COMPELLING CALLS

Cries of the People and Cries of the Earth

The call of religious life has always been within a particular context, amid a particular need, an offering that asks all of us. Consecrated life is born of a call from God in the midst of the world with its cries and joys, hopes and fears. Founders and followers have within them the gifts of the Spirit with which to respond to the church and world, locally and globally. We respond by following the way of Jesus through prayer, community, and ministry. While ministry is often how religious life is most easily or publicly seen, prayer and community are equally important parts of the persons and congregations. Religious life and ministry cannot be sustained without them.

In this chapter I consider what these times ask of us in ministry. When we look around the world, the needs seem endless. Our call is to discern, through the lens of our charism, which of the cries around us are particularly ours. From there, the who, what, where, when, and how emerge. We are not called to do this alone—as Religious of the Sacred Heart of Jesus, Passionists, Viatorians, or Salesians, the call in our time is to respond to the calls *together*. Our responding communities will widen even beyond consecrated life, but we must begin with steeping ourselves in the cries of God and the cries of all creation. Reading the signs of the times is essential; we do this together as well as personally, sensing where the call is and asking to follow the lead of the befriending Spirit. As we do so in freedom, our creative religious imagination sheds further light for the next steps.

Over the years I have learned that if the graces I am offered in the midst of discerning steps for ministry are joy, peace, confidence, and freedom, then I must trust that the consequences will also be joy, peace, confidence, and freedom. This does not mean that all will be easy. Touching that space of grace helps in both the long and short term.

As we look at the world, it's helpful to note the good news about the world as well as the challenges we face. These also help us determine where and how to direct our energies.

161

Hans Roslin, in his 2018 book *Factfulness*,[1] reminds us of the advances made in recent times. Consider some of these facts:

- In the last twenty years, the proportion of the world population living in extreme poverty has been cut almost in half.
- Eighty percent of the world's one-year-old children have been vaccinated against some disease.
- Eighty percent of the people in the world have some access to electricity.
- Worldwide, on average thirty-year-old men have spent ten years in school. Women of the same age have spent nine years in school.
- The number of deaths per year from natural disasters over the last hundred years decreased by 50 percent.
- The majority of the world's population lives in middle-income countries, defined by the World Bank as lower-middle-income economies with a gross national income (GNI) per capita between $1,006 and $3,955, and upper-middle-income economies with a GNI per capita between $3,956 and $12,235.[2]

This is great news. It is a significant improvement over the past and thus is to be celebrated.

Yet the gaps are exactly what consecrated life[3] notices, and where consecrated life is called to focus. Despite the 50 percent decrease in the number of persons living in extreme poverty (people living on less than a $1.90 a day), over 800 million persons still live in extreme poverty. And "some" access to electricity means just that, "some." It may be neither consistent nor sufficient for the needs. And are nine or ten years of education sufficient for people everywhere? Also, these facts say nothing about the current and impending effects of climate change, which are most severe among the most vulnerable. As the phrase "mind the gap" indicates, we must note the gaps. This is the logic of religious life, the logic of followers of Jesus, who himself had a particular eye for those in need.

The gospel imperative to share the Good News engages the depths of humanity's cries for spiritual depth and meaning. We also know that love of God and love of neighbor are linked. Jesus saw everyone as part of his call to the good news of the love of God. So too, must we. Where possible, consecrated life also works in

---

[1]   Hans Rosling, with Ola Rosling and Anna Rosling Rönnlund, *Factfulness: Ten Reasons We're Wrong about the World—and Why Things Are Better Than You Think* (New York: Flatiron Books, 2018).

[2]   I have paraphrased a number of the questions and answers from *Factfulness*, 4–9. See also the World Bank's country classification data for fiscal year 2020, https://datahelp-desk.worldbank.org.

[3]   This is certainly a call to all Christians and all people of good will. My focus is on consecrated life and hence my emphasis.

conjunction with others in responding to cries. For example, there is much within the United Nations' Sustainable Development Goals (SDGs)[4] that resonates with efforts of consecrated life to serve and promote all life.[5] The United Nations defines sustainable development as "development that meets the needs of the present without compromising the ability of future generations to meet their own needs."[6] According to the UN:

> Eradicating poverty in all its forms and dimensions is an indispensable requirement for sustainable development. To this end, there must be promotion of sustainable, inclusive and equitable economic growth, creating greater opportunities for all, reducing inequalities, raising basic standards of living, fostering equitable social development and inclusion, and promoting integrated and sustainable management of natural resources and ecosystems.[7]

The SDGs include economic, social, and ecological dimensions of sustainable development to be accomplished by 2030. Over 150 world leaders and the Vatican committed to the seventeen SDGs.[8] These goals to transform our world are:

Goal 1: No Poverty
Goal 2: Zero Hunger
Goal 3: Good Health and Well-Being
Goal 4: Quality Education
Goal 5: Gender Equality
Goal 6: Clean Water and Sanitation
Goal 7: Affordable and Clean Energy
Goal 8: Decent Work and Economic Growth
Goal 9: Industry, Innovation, and Infrastructure
Goal 10: Reduced Inequality

---

[4]   The seventeen new SDGs, also known as the Global Goals, aim to end poverty, hunger, and inequality; take action on climate change and the environment; improve access to health and education; build strong institutions and partnerships; and more.

[5]   Although the limits of this project do not allow space to go into details about all the areas in which the Vatican has questions about particular elements of the SDGs, the "Note of the Holy See on the First Anniversary of the Adoption of the Sustainable Development Goals," by H. E. Archbishop Bernardito Auza, Apostolic Nuncio and Permanent Observer of the Holy See to the United Nations, offers helpful clarifications. It must also be said that on the whole, Pope Francis has spoken in great support of the SDG efforts. https://holyseemission.org.

[6]   United Nations SDG Report, 2019, https://www.un.org. See also (Our Common Future, the Brundtland Report, 1987), https://sustainabledevelopment.un.org.

[7]   Ibid.

[8]   See https://www.un.org.

Goal 11: Sustainable Cities and Communities
Goal 12: Responsible Consumption and Production
Goal 13: Climate Action
Goal 14: Life below Water
Goal 15: Life on Land
Goal 16: Peace, Justice, and Strong Institutions
Goal 17: Partnerships to Achieve the Goal

The goals reflect the challenging fact that 836 million people live in extreme poverty, one third of the world's food is wasted, and water scarcity affects more than 40 percent of the world's population.[9]

The Catholic Church is committed to achieving these goals. In his 2015 address to the United Nations General Assembly, shortly before the Agenda 2030 and SDGs were adopted, Pope Francis said:

> We must address the causes of the distortion of development, which is what in recent Catholic social teaching goes by the name of "structural sins." Denouncing such sins is already a good contribution that religions make to the discussion on the world's development. Nonetheless, alongside this denunciation, we must also put forward feasible ways of conversion to people and communities.[10]

The Vatican's commitment to the SDGs comes with the proviso that the goals and targets it supports are in line with Roman Catholic Church teaching.[11] Catholic Social Teaching, as well as scripture and tradition, provide priorities for witness and action. Nine key themes for the church are:

1. Dignity of every person and human rights
2. Solidarity, the common good, and participation
3. Family life
4. Subsidiarity[12] and the proper role of government
5. Property ownership in modern society: rights and responsibilities
6. Dignity of work, rights of workers, and support for labor unions

---

[9] Ibid.

[10] Pope Francis, 2015 address to the United Nations General Assembly.

[11] For example, see Auza, "Note of the Holy See on the First Anniversary of the Adoption of the Sustainable Development Goals," which states that the Vatican opposes any SDG interpretation that could support abortion and other acts in opposition to church teaching. In consecrated life, we also offer support with a critical eye to how the details of the SDG serve those who are seen as the least.

[12] This tenet of Catholic Social Teaching holds that nothing should be done by a larger and more complex organization that can be done as well by a smaller and simpler organization.

7. Economic development
8. Peace and disarmament
9. The preferential option for the poor, marginalized, and vulnerable.[13]

These all inform our thinking by offering a scope of rights and responsibilities that call to us as human beings. These foundational principles of justice and fidelity bring us to the response of religious life.

Call of Consecrated Life

Congregations and individual members of consecrated life ask ourselves: What is ours to do? Where is our witness to the Reign of God needed? To these questions I now turn.

What are we to do? According to Pope Francis, we are to "Wake Up the World." The call to "Wake Up the World" was sounded on November 29, 2013, at a meeting with the Union of Superiors General in Rome. In that conversation, Francis said:

> The Church, therefore, must be attractive. Wake up the world! Be witnesses of a different way of doing things, of acting, of living! It is possible to live differently in this world. We are speaking of an eschatological outlook, of the values of the Kingdom incarnated here, on this earth. It is a question of leaving everything to follow the Lord. No, I do not want to say "radical." Evangelical radicalness is not only for religious: it is demanded of all. But religious follow the Lord in a special way, in a prophetic way. It is this witness that I expect of you. Religious should be men and women who are able to wake the world up....
>
> You should be real witnesses of a world of doing and acting differently.[14]

Discerning where we are to go and be is not new. It is gospel-based and flows from our Catholic social tradition. CICLSAL, in *New Wine in New Wineskins*, reminds us:

> The originality of the Gospel (Mk 10:43), which the consecrated life wants to prophetically incarnate, passes on concrete attitudes and choices: the primacy of service (Mk 10:43–45) and the constant movement toward the poor and solidarity with the least (Lk 9:48); the promotion of the

---

13   I am grateful to Thomas Massaro, SJ, for this basic articulation, found in his book *Living Justice: Catholic Social Teaching in Action*, 3rd classroom ed. (Lanham, MD: Rowman & Littlefield, 2015).

14   Antonio Spadaro, SJ, "'Wake Up the World!' Conversation with Pope Francis about the Religious Life," *La Civiltà Cattolica* (2014) I, 3–17, trans. Donald Maldari, SJ (revised, January 6, 2015), https://onlineministries.creighton.edu.

dignity of persons in whatever situation they live and suffer (Mt 25:40); subsidiarity as an exercise of reciprocal trust and the generous collaboration of everyone and with everyone.[15]

Service, solidarity, dignity, subsidiarity, and collaboration are all essential prophetic dimensions of religious life. How we actually respond will require us to hold these prophetic dimensions together with the mystical dimensions. What is being asked of us at this time is risky and uncomfortably meaningful, as it leads our charisms into the calls of this time. Religious life is being called to conversion, transformation, and revitalization, including in ministry. We are being encouraged by church leaders to be close to the cries of the world. Pope Francis consistently asks us to be close to the people and earth, to smell like the sheep and to have mud on our shoes because we are walking with and among those most in need. We must walk at the peripheries. He reminds us that such a reality check is crucial: "This is very important to me: the need to become acquainted with reality by experience, to spend time walking on the periphery in order [to] really become acquainted with the reality and life-experiences of people. If this does not happen we then run the risk of being abstract ideologists or fundamentalists, which is not healthy."[16]

When we experience these realities, we will find calls tugging at us. There is also fear at times, in terms of how we can respond to these calls: we don't have the same number of people we once had; we are older; we can't do this alone; we don't have the financial resources; we can't risk a venture that we cannot be sure will succeed; and so on. These are legitimate questions and concerns, and some will likely have a familiar ring. This moment is asking much of us.

From our church leaders we are also very particularly called forth in consecrated life. Consider how, in *New Wine in New Wineskins*, we hear quite directly:

- "New and unprecedented emergencies have caused other needs to explode. They still have not been responded to and continue to knock at the door of the creative fidelity of all forms of the consecrated life" (7).

- "New poverties question the conscience of many consecrated persons and press traditional charisms to respond in new and generous ways to these new situations and the new rejects of history. Out of this reality new forms of presence and ministries in many existential peripheries have blossomed" (7).

- "The Gospel's message cannot be reduced to something purely sociological. We are dealing instead with a spiritual orientation which remains always new. It requires open-mindedness in order to imagine prophetic

---

[15]   Congregation for Institutes of Consecrated Life and Societies of Apostolic Life (CICLSAL), *New Wine in New Wineskins: The Consecrated Life and its Ongoing Challenges since Vatican II* (Nairobi, Kenya: Paulines Publications Africa, 2017), no. 31.

[16]   Spadaro, "Wake Up the World."

and charismatic forms of discipleship [*sequela*] that are realized through suitable, and perhaps, unprecedented schemes. . . . A renewal which is incapable of affecting and changing structures—as well as the heart—does not bring about real and lasting change" (3).

- Acknowledging that it is difficult to continue to hear the Gospel anew and act upon it, we are reminded: "The temptation to adjust oneself tactically in order to avoid the continuous challenges of the conversion of the heart had already been present in the history of the Church.

  "The Lord Jesus' word helps us assume the challenge of newness which demands not only acceptance but also discernment. It is necessary to create structures that are truly capable of safeguarding the innovative richness of the Gospel so that it can be lived and put at the service of all while preserving its quality and goodness" (2).

- Pope Francis confirms us on this journey: "For new wine, new wineskins. The newness of the Gospel. What does the Gospel bring us? Joy and newness. To what is new, newness; for new wine, new wineskins. Not to be afraid of changing things according to the law of the gospel. This is why the Church asks us, all of us, for a few changes. She asks us to leave aside structures bound to collapse. They are useless! And get new wineskins, those of the Gospel."[17]

We have here a clear, direct, and hopeful call. We are being encouraged to look at our ministries and ask if we are truly where we most need to be. We must continue to evolve in response to the calls we receive.

In the remainder of this chapter, I look at four particular cries that continue to call forth our gifts, and I name some ways religious life is positioned to offer creative responses. I also offer some initiatives and examples of charisms at work.

Poverty

Pope Francis inaugurated the first *World Day of the Poor* in 2017, calling us to love: "Little children, let us not love in word or speech, but in deed and in truth."[18] In 2017 and 2018 he reminded us that loving in deed and truth includes encounter as well as action in solidarity. Relationship is critical, and Pope Francis is trying to remind us to listen anew with our hearts in "loving attentiveness":

The poor do not need intermediaries, but the personal involvement of all those who hear their cry. The concern of believers in their regard cannot be limited to a kind of assistance—as useful and as providential as this

---

[17]   Pope Francis, Morning Meditation in the Chapel of the *Domus Sanctae Marthae*, Rome, September 5, 2014; see also *New Wine in New Wineskins*, no. 10.

[18]   Pope Francis, *Message on First World Day of the Poor*, November 19, 2017, http:// w2.vatican.va.

may be in the beginning—but requires a "loving attentiveness" (*Evangelii Gaudium*, 199) that honours the person as such and seeks out his or her best interests.[19]

Pope Francis invites us to the peripheries, trusting that when we go there, something good is possible. He leads by example, demonstrating his own loving attentiveness by sitting with the homeless, sharing time with those imprisoned, and washing the feet of young offenders at the Casal Del Marmo juvenile detention facility on his first Holy Thursday Mass as pope. He invites us to our own encounters. In *Joy of the Gospel*, Francis reminds us that our encounters call us to seek the full liberation of all, and in this we, too, are liberated. Reminding us that liberation links God and the entire people of God working together, he writes: "God's salvation is a hand held out to the poor, a hand that welcomes, protects and enables them to experience the friendship they need. From this concrete and tangible proximity, a genuine path of liberation emerges."[20]

The invitation is to enter into the realities around us and with "loving attentiveness" see how to respond in love. Sometimes it happens from our own direct encounter, sometimes because of someone else's direct encounter, which calls us forth. I offer two examples: Arrupe College of Loyola University Chicago and the De La Salle Brothers.

Arrupe College of Loyola University Chicago

The college is described as "a two-year college for motivated students with limited financial resources and an interest in transferring to a four-year institution after graduation." Its stated goal is to help students to "begin their college careers in a setting designed to maximize their opportunities for academic success and leave them with little to no debt."[21]

The Jesuits have a long history in education, from primary to secondary, including schools for those with limited income. It was in the spring of 2014 when Steve Katsouros, SJ, received a phone call from Michael J. Garanzini, SJ, then president of Loyola University Chicago, telling Katsouros that he had a new call: to serve as the first dean of Arrupe College. Garanzini explained that nationally 17 percent of students graduate from two-year colleges, and often do not have the skills to complete their studies at a four-year college or university. Katsouros had experience in education, having served as president of the Loyola School in New York City and as an administrator at the University of San Francisco. Garanzini's outreach to Katsouros was a new call to create a response to a

---

[19] Pope Francis, *Message on Second World Day of the Poor*, November 18, 2018, 3, http://w2.vatican.va.

[20] Ibid., 4.

[21] See https://www.luc.edu/arrupe.

clear need in education. In Katsouros's book, *Come to Believe*,[22] he describes the Arrupe College program.

Arrupe offers a virtually free community college education, within a rigorous educational program. Free breakfast and lunch are available for those who request them, and free public transportation and tutoring are provided. It is a school where everyone truly knows you by name. The school began in 2015 and the first graduating class was in 2017, with a 95 percent retention rate of students after their first year. The school was focused on preparing students for further education AND on finding financial support for them. To this end, Katsouros contacted various universities and convinced some of them that Arrupe College students were well prepared to succeed in their institutions—he even convinced some universities to offer full tuition, room, and board scholarships to Arrupe graduates.

In addition, because its staff believes that relationships matter, Arrupe College stays connected to students who graduate and enroll in universities or begin jobs. The links are steadfast, helping each by holding all together. This type of higher education meets a significant unmet need. The hope is that their model can be replicated or at least adapted for other places of need.

The De La Salle Brothers

The De La Salle Brothers in Philadelphia began Bilingual Undergraduate Studies for Collegiate Advancement (BUSCA) at La Salle University. Begun in 1994, the program is a five-semester Associate of Arts degree program at La Salle University that "offers an inclusive, supportive learning community that focuses on the distinctive academic challenges of Spanish-dominant students." According to the program's mission statement:

> As the BUSCA students strive to develop a stronger foundational base of knowledge, improved academic and English language skills, deeper intellectual curiosity, and increased self-confidence, they are challenged by a rigorous liberal arts-based curriculum and a demanding and nurturing faculty and staff. Upon graduating with a valuable degree and sixty fully transferable credits into the bachelor's degree program at La Salle University, BUSCA graduates are equipped to pursue further education and to become lifelong learners and bilingual leaders in our communities, society, and world.[23]

As much as possible, the university works with federal and state aid to help students with need to study free of charge in the BUSCA program. The university, through

---

[22]   Stephen Katsouros, *Come to Believe: How the Jesuits Are Reinventing Education (Again)* (Maryknoll, NY: Orbis Books, 2017).

[23]   La Salle University BUSCA Mission Statement, https://www.lasalle.edu/busca.

grants and scholarships from private institutions, works to fill the gap between government aid and the total cost of studies.[24] The success of the program illustrates the De La Salle Christian Brothers' commitment. Theologian and educator Ernest Miller, FSC, shared that "three years ago [2015] La Salle undertook a Program of Strategic Prioritization in which every program in the University was ranked on a scale from 1–5. BUSCA received a no.1 rating."[25] Begun in 1994, this program is celebrating its twenty-fifth anniversary in 2019. It is important to share such news in order to galvanize further efforts.

These are innovative responses to unmet needs, and they build on a congregation's expertise. In addition, such projects are coordinated with a lot of people, and across life commitments. Connecting is key for all. The two congregations here saw potential for students and responded by creating a way to "mind the gap" between skills, finances, and opportunities.[26]

Migration

Scripture reminds us of God's care for those who are considered "other," including those who migrate because of danger and violence where they are, or because of lack of access to basic necessities. Scripture tells us:

- "The Lord your God is the God of all gods and Lord of all lords, the great, mighty, and awesome God who doesn't play favorites and doesn't take bribes. He enacts justice for orphans and widows, and he loves immigrants, giving them food and clothing. That means you must also love immigrants because you were immigrants in Egypt."[27]
- "You must not oppress foreigners. You know what it's like to be a foreigner, for you yourselves were once foreigners in the land of Egypt."[28]
- "When a stranger sojourns with you in your land, you shall not do him wrong. You shall treat the stranger who sojourns with you as the native among you, and you shall love him as yourself, for you were strangers in the land of Egypt: I am the Lord your God."[29]
- "Thus says the Lord: Do justice and righteousness, and deliver from the hand of the oppressor him who has been robbed. And do no wrong or

---

[24]   Students who are not eligible for the total package of government aid must take on a student loan or establish a payment plan with the university.

[25]   Miller is Vice President for Mission at La Salle University. The information related is from an information request email conversation on November 27, 2018.

[26]   Due to space limitations I am not addressing the area of socially responsible investing, though certainly this is a critical area for responsible witness that takes place in many congregations.

[27]   Deut 10:17–19.

[28]   Ex 23:9.

[29]   Lev 19:33–4.

violence to the resident alien, the fatherless, and the widow, nor shed innocent blood in this place."[30]

- "Do not forget to show hospitality to strangers, for by so doing some people have shown hospitality to angels without knowing it."[31]

We know the Israelites fled Egypt and slavery in order to live in freedom. We know Mary and Joseph also had to flee for their lives.[32] We also remember Jesus's teaching about judgment: "Just as you did not do for the least of these, you did not do it for me. . . . And these will go away into eternal punishment, but the righteous into eternal life."[33]

These are the dangerous memories of scripture for engagement with our time. Our time knows the experience of the other as stranger, refugee, asylum seeker, and migrant.

Global migration today is increasing,[34] as migrants and refugees travel at great peril to find safety and opportunity in a new land. This is not new. But today we find ever more countries restricting access to migrants, refugees, and asylum seekers. In the United States recently a caravan of migrants from Central America, some of whom were asylum seekers, were stopped at the border between Mexico and the United States. In response, people of multiple faith traditions traveled to the border to welcome and assist the migrants. The work continues, and consecrated life is in the midst of it, both in local and systemic efforts.

In Asia, according to the United Nations High Commissioner for Refugees (UNHCR), many Rohingya people (a mostly Muslim minority group described by the UN as "the most persecuted minority in the world") were forced to flee their homes in Myanmar in August 2017, after "violence broke out in Myanmar's Rakhine State, including the burning of entire Rohingya villages." The UNHCR continues, "Eighty percent of Rohingya refugees reaching Bangladesh are women and children, including newborns."[35]

As of November 2018, the Kutpalong refugee settlement in Bangladesh was the largest in the world, and home to some 600,000 Rohingya refugees.[36] In South America, Venezuelans are leaving their country because of political and economic instability, hoping that their neighbors to the south will welcome them. The cries are great and numerous.

---

[30] Jer 22:3.

[31] Heb 13:2. See Mt 25:35–40.

[32] Mt 2:1–15.

[33] Mt 25:34–46.

[34] The UN International Migration Report 2017 states: "The number of international migrants worldwide has continued to grow rapidly in recent years, reaching 258 million in 2017, up from 220 million in 2010 and 173 million in 2000." https://www.un.org.

[35] UNHCR, *Rohingya Refugee Crisis*, https://www.unrefugees.org/emergencies/rohingya/.

[36] Ibid.

We now have a pope whose first trip outside of Rome was to the Mediterranean island of Lampedusa, off the coast of Sicily about sixty-eight miles from the Tunisian coast. Thousands of African and Middle Eastern migrants died in these waters near Lampedusa while attempting to reach Europe to escape violence. In his homily at Lampedusa, Pope Francis lamented what he called the "globalization of indifference" and the "anesthesia of the heart," saying: "We are a society which has forgotten how to weep, how to experience compassion—'suffering with' others; the globalization of indifference has taken from us the ability to weep!"[37]

What is to be done? Timothy Scott, CSB, of the Canadian Religious Conference, writes that "in Canada, we have seen many religious who have concretely demonstrated the opposite of indifference in their ministries. We have witnessed an outreach to single mothers, immigrants, persons suffering from drug addictions and psychological disabilities, sex workers, and aboriginal women and men in the inner city."[38] But Scott also reminds us that so much more is possible:

> Francis' call for us to embrace the periphery is explicitly Christocentric. In a meeting at the Jesuit Refugee Centre in Rome, he chastised communities who were creating tourist "bed and breakfasts" from strategically-located former religious houses: "Empty convents don't belong to you; they are for the flesh of Christ, the refugees. The Lord calls us to welcome them courageously and generously into empty communities, religious houses and convents."[39]

Pope Francis says of migrants: "They flee intolerance, persecution, and lack of a future. May no one avert their eyes from their plight."[40] In Europe, the Focolare Movement, which includes vowed members, families, and youth, early on sought to find ways to welcome the strangers in their land. As Pope Francis says, we are to welcome, protect, promote, and integrate every refugee. The charism of unity in the Focolare movement is creating the welcome, protection, promotion, and integration called for by Pope Francis.[41]

Another example comes from the following story of the Focolare movement in Germany, which "has been working for many years now for the integration of immigrants into the social context, and intensifying its welcoming initiatives in this period . . . starting from the most basic needs—such as the collection of

[37] Pope Francis, Homily at Lampedusa, July 8, 2013, http://w2.vatican.va.

[38] Timothy Scott, CSB, "Pope Francis and the Periphery," *CRC Bulletin* 11, no. 1 (Winter 2014): 2, https://www.crc-canada.org.

[39] Ibid.

[40] Pope Francis, Address to the 66th General Assembly of the Italian Episcopal Conference, May 19, 2014, http://w2.vatican.va.

[41] See Permanent Observer Mission of the Holy See to the United Nations: "Responding to Refugees and Migrants: Twenty Action Points," https://holyseemission.org/contents/statements/5a2716362f88c.php.

food, clothing, furniture and other basic items, German lessons and looking for medical or legal aid," and in "concrete examples of daily life, like that of a couple from Munich":

> The evening before their departure for a weekend excursion outside the city, they received a phone call asking for their willingness to host for the weekend, a young Syrian mother with three small children, while waiting to continue her journey to Karlsruhe. Though they hoped that the four would leave soon so they could at least spend a part of the weekend in the mountains, the couple—despite their internal conflict—accepted; but "the moment we took the hand of our little five-year-old princess, the ice was immediately broken," they wrote. The weekend with the unexpected guests passed with the games played with the children, sharing their breakfast where "we renounced hotdogs out of respect for our Muslim guests who highly appreciated the yogurt and flatbread we bought for them," and a Syrian supper prepared together. And when we had to say goodbye on Sunday morning, "we all had tears in our eyes, and were happy and mutually grateful"—wrote the couple. "What a gift the Divine director of this unexpected programme had in store for us!"[42]

Youth, vowed members, and families in the Focolare movement have all participated in some way in living their charism call of unity in the world today.

In 2003, the US Conference of Catholic Bishops and the Episcopal Conference of Mexico wrote a pastoral letter about migrants, *Strangers No Longer: Together on the Journey of Hope*. In it they echo tenets of Catholic Social Teaching and basic human rights:

> The human dignity and human rights of undocumented migrants should be respected. Regardless of their legal status, migrants, like all persons, possess inherent human dignity that should be respected. Often they are subject to punitive laws and harsh treatment from enforcement officers from both receiving and transit countries. Government policies that respect the basic human rights of the undocumented are necessary.[43]

As asylum seekers and refugees continue to come to the United States border, women religious have also been coming to the border to assist in whatever way possible. Coming from a number of congregations, they find where the places of need are and offer days, weeks, or even months of volunteer work. This is also a moment when the Social Mission Office of the Leadership Conference of Women

---

[42]   Focolare Movement, "Germany: Initiatives for the Refugees," October 8, 2015, https://www.focolare.org.

[43]   USCCB-Episcopal Conference of Mexico, *Strangers No Longer: Together on the Journey of Hope*, January 22, 2003, 38, http://www.usccb.org.

Religious (LCWR) is connecting with women religious and with those working with the Justice Conference of Women Religious (JCWR) in disseminating information. The Conference of Major Superiors of Men (CMSM) in the United States is also moving on initiatives and inviting participation.[44] This is simply a beginning.

Across decades, relationships have brought together many groups in justice advocacy, and groups assist one another in responding, planning, and advocating. Collaboration is moving and growing. In addition, these efforts are becoming more public, allowing people to witness examples of mercy and solidarity. This has led to nonviolent protests in Washington, DC, where some women and men religious, among others, allowed themselves to be arrested in order to draw public attention to the cries they were hearing.[45]

Human Trafficking

Talitha Kum,[46] also known as the International Network of Consecrated Life against Trafficking in Persons, is another example of standing with people at the periphery. Started by women religious in 2009, the work of the organization is to galvanize efforts around the world to stop human trafficking. The group partners with various groups on this common cause project, which is a collaboration of the Union of International Superiors General (UISG) and the Union of Superiors General (USG).

In the United States, efforts are being made by religious and other interested organizations who sponsor conferences to make the training of employees about the trafficking of persons a requirement for the hotels with which they contract. One example is Nix Conference and Meeting Management, a group that works with many religious organizations planning conferences. Realizing that they offered a connected knowledge of the hotel industry, Nix started two efforts that have already led to saving the lives of persons caught in the sex trafficking industry:

> In 2014, we created the social action organization *Exchange Initiative* and presented the IGNITE: Sparking Action against Sex Trafficking conference. Two years later, we launched the incredibly popular free mobile app TraffickCam, which empowers travelers to photograph their hotel rooms and upload them to a national law enforcement database.
>
> We inform management of every hotel where they do business about the issue of trafficking and empower our clients with simple ways they can make a difference when they do business. We invite you to download the

---

[44]   See, for example, "Men Religious Participate in Catholic Day of Action on Immigration," September 5, 2019, https://cmsm.org.

[45]   Rhina Guidos, "Bishops Back Catholics Arrested at Capitol for Protesting Treatment of Immigrant Children," *America*, July 19, 2019, https://www.americamagazine.org.

[46]   Information on Talitha Kum can be found on the Union of International Superiors General (UISG) site at http://www.internationalunionsuperiorsgeneral.org.

free *TraffickCam* app and visit *Exchange Initiative* and learn how you can make a real difference in the fight against sex trafficking.[47]

Learning about human trafficking from women religious opened up both their knowledge and recognition that they had the skills to counter this violence at the peripheries. Bringing together needs, information, and opportunity for collaboration and initiatives across groups encourages creative efforts and multiplies the possibilities for good.

Earth, Our Common Home

Pope Francis's much anticipated encyclical *Laudato Si'* begins with praise to God for creation and calls earth our common home. Francis, with stark realism based on scientific evidence, speaks to the many-faceted ways we are harming our common home. The harm is not irreversible, though there are choices humans have made already that have long-term harmful consequences. We can, as faith-based people and with all people of good will, change the trajectory of our actions. This, however, requires a conversion. At a general audience on January 17, 2001, Pope John Paul II called us to an ecological conversion so as to avoid an ecological catastrophe:

> Man is no longer the Creator's "steward," but an autonomous despot, who is finally beginning to understand that he must stop at the edge of the abyss. . . . At stake, then, is not only a "physical" ecology that is concerned to safeguard the habitat of the various living beings, but also a "human" ecology which makes the existence of creatures more dignified, by protecting the fundamental good of life in all its manifestations and by preparing for future generations an environment more in conformity with the Creator's plan.[48]

Pope Benedict XVI, in the homily at his inaugural Mass in 2005, spoke of the many kinds of deserts we have created:

> There is the desert of poverty, the desert of hunger and thirst, the desert of abandonment, of loneliness, of destroyed love. There is the desert of God's darkness, the emptiness of souls no longer aware of their dignity or the goal of human life. The external deserts in the world are growing, because the internal deserts have become so vast. Therefore the earth's treasures no longer serve to build God's garden for all to live in, but they have been made to serve the powers of exploitation and destruction. The Church as

---

47   See https://nixassoc.com.

48   Pope John Paul II, General Audience, January 17, 2001, 4, https://w2.vatican.va.

a whole and all her Pastors, like Christ, must set out to lead people out of the desert, towards the place of life, towards friendship with the Son of God, towards the One who gives us life, and life in abundance.[49]

Pope Francis also calls for a conversion. In *Laudato Si'*, he writes: "The emptier a person's heart is, the more he or she needs things to buy, own and consume. It becomes almost impossible to accept the limits imposed by reality. In this horizon, a genuine sense of the common good also disappears."[50] Francis reminds us that ecological conversion is inextricable from all other areas of life. The cries of the people and cries of the earth are thus interconnected: "We are not faced with two separate crises, one environmental and the other social, but rather one complex crisis which is both social and environmental. Strategies for a solution demand an integrated approach to combating poverty, restoring dignity to the underprivileged, and at the same time protecting nature."[51]

To this end, in 2016 Pope Francis proposed adding to the seven traditional spiritual and corporal works of mercy an eighth: "care for our common home."[52] Francis calls us to live *integral ecology*. He notes: "Since everything is closely inter-related, and today's problems call for a vision capable of taking into account every aspect of the global crisis, I suggest that we now consider some elements of an *integral ecology*, one which clearly respects its human and social dimensions."[53] Integral ecology combines environmental, economic, social, and cultural ecologies.[54] It calls us to a way of life that engages all of creation as sacred and looks at the root causes of current challenges. What are the economic, political, cultural, social, environmental, and other systems that have created or contributed to our crises? The participation of every person is needed to address these problems. The global ecological crisis has many human-made causes, and it is humans who must shape life-changing responses. And the challenges presented by the ecological crisis hit the vulnerable the hardest. Pope Francis offers some reality checks from the peripheries:

> For example, the depletion of fishing reserves especially hurts small fishing communities without the means to replace those resources; water pollution particularly affects the poor who cannot buy bottled water; and rises in the sea level mainly affect impoverished coastal populations who have

---

[49]   Pope Benedict XVI, Homily at Mass for imposition of the pallium and conferral of the fisherman's ring for the beginnings of the Petrine ministry of the Bishop of Rome, April 24, 2005, https://w2.vatican.va.

[50]   Pope Francis, *Laudato Si,* 204. Hereinafter *LS*.

[51]   *LS* 139.

[52]   Pope Francis, "The Eighth Work of Mercy," Message of His Holiness for the Celebration of the World Day of Prayer for the Care of Creation, *L'Osservatore Romano*, Eng. ed., September 2, 2016, 7.

[53]   *LS* 137.

[54]   *LS* 138–55.

nowhere else to go. The impact of the present imbalances is also seen in the premature death of many of the poor, in conflicts sparked by the shortage of resources, and in any number of other problems which are insufficiently represented on global agendas.[55]

Future generations are also affected by the actions and inactions of today—thus, care for our common home is an intergenerational justice issue. Because it will take all generations to make needed changes, it is imperative that all, including the youngest generations, participate in all areas of integral ecology. This brings us again to the call to communal discernment and to engaging across generations and cultures.

We can respond to and live this call because our encounter with Jesus Christ affects our relationship with the world. Consecrated life can move communally, institutionally, and globally so that all areas are engaged and no relationship is untended. We know that "living our vocation to be protectors of God's handiwork is essential to a life of virtue; it is not an optional or a secondary aspect of our Christian experience."[56] Every place is a place to begin.

This is an immense task that requires ongoing conversion. The grace of the call continually leads us to work together with all people caring for our common home.

I now offer three examples of living into the conversion called forth by integral ecology and integral religious life, highlighting congregational, institutional, and personal/communal areas.

Medical Mission Sisters

A congregational example of communal discernment in action within a charism can be found with the Medical Mission Sisters. Their charism is to heal in the manner of Jesus of Nazareth. Their mission statement delineates this: "In our broken, wounded world, Medical Mission Sisters are called to live as a healing presence. We try to bring about a world where all live in harmony and where no one is in want. We try to live as Jesus lived, with care and compassion for all."[57]

Since their founding in 1925 they have served as doctors and nurses in hospitals, as community health workers, and as trainers for community health workers. Their ministries also include justice and peace work. It was during a General Chapter in 1997 that their discernment moved them to see that healing the earth had to be part of their healing ministry. They saw that the Spirit's gift of the charism to heal incorporated healing the earth. One of the ministry results of that Chapter is HEAL: Haven for Ecological and Alternative Living,[58] an ecological

---

55   *LS* 48.

56   *LS* 217.

57   Medical Mission Sisters and Associates website, https://www.medicalmissionsisters.org.

58   See https://mmsheal.wordpress.com.

education project begun in 2006 that links with efforts all over the world to heal earth and all on the earth. They describe their evolution as a healing presence in this way:

> Over the past 94 years, Medical Mission Sisters have offered care and compassion to millions of individuals in our world. As the times and the needs have evolved, so too has our focus in mission—from the curative, to preventative, to promotive, to community-based, to holistic health care. We also advocate and work for the health of our Earth and for a just sharing of our world's limited resources. In every ministry, each of our Sisters strives to be a healing presence in the community of life.[59]

This sentiment is mirrored in theologian Douglas Christie's writings. In *Blue Sapphire of the Mind: Notes for a Contemplative Ecology* he invites us to this vision: "One could learn to live in the world as a healing presence, attentive and responsible to the lives of other beings and capable of helping to reknit the torn fabric of existence."[60]

Loyola University of Chicago

Laudato Si' reminds us that "social problems must be addressed by community networks and not simply by the sum of individual good deeds. . . . The ecological conversion needed to bring about lasting change is also a community conversion."[61] The role of each person is also essential: "By developing our individual, God-given capacities, an ecological conversion can inspire us to greater creativity and enthusiasm in resolving the world's problems and in offering ourselves to God 'as a living sacrifice, holy and acceptable' (Rom 12:1)."[62]

A university is a perfect place for community and individual gifts to be used to engage the cries of the earth and the cries of the poor. In addressing climate change, President Jo Ann Rooney of Loyola University Chicago (a Jesuit school) writes:

> As Jesuits and as educators we seek both scientific and moral solutions. We invest in research and education that enable our students and faculty to work nationally and internationally to protect the environment. Our solidarity drives the innovative work of our Institute of Environmental Sustainability and departments across our campuses. It shapes the way we build our campuses and the way we educate students. . . .

---

[59]   https://www.medicalmissionsisters.org.

[60]   Douglas Christie, *The Blue Sapphire of the Mind: Notes for a Contemplative Ecology* (New York: Oxford University Press, 2013), 7.

[61]   *LS* 219.

[62]   *LS* 220.

We work diligently to link sustainability across disciplines—science and health, policy and economics, business and humanities. More than 1,300 courses at Loyola incorporate aspects of sustainability.[63]

Nancy Tuchman, ecologist and founding dean of Loyola's Institute of Environmental Sustainability, offers examples of education and research in healing efforts for the Earth community. She writes that she and her co-workers

spend much of their time researching ways we can help the planet repair itself: Which species of plants are best at pulling lead out of contaminated urban soils? Which evolutionary traits in plants can help us devise more sustainable agricultural practices? Can we use algae to remove chemicals from our biodiesel waste water? Can we make our own renewable methane gas, to replace the natural gas we use for heating campus hot water?[64]

These are important healing and renewing tasks. In addition, new systems must be created. To create them also requires conversion and conscious alternative choices. Tuchman writes:

In our current economic system, nature is depleted, natural resources have dwindled, and trash and toxins pile up. We've been operating under the premise that consumption and disposal mean economic growth. Yet, we are stealing the future, selling it in the present, and calling it gross domestic product. We must work to develop an economy that is based on healing and restoring the future instead of stealing and exploiting it. . . .

At Loyola, we know that every action, decision and purchase we make has a ripple effect both upstream in the supply chain, and downstream in the waste stream. *Laudato Si'* challenges us to recognize the urgent need to become integral ecologists, people who dare to imagine a healed Earth and are willing to put their hands, hearts, and minds to the task.[65]

Lifestyle Change

Our common home is calling for humans to make lifestyle changes for the sake of our relationship with one another and with the earth. In order to change at our core, we need a conversion that flows from our relationship with God. Our ability to see the world as a whole also flows from that relationship. Samuel Canilang writes:

---

[63]   Jo Ann Rooney, JD, LLM, EdD, "From the President," *Loyola: The Magazine of Loyola University Chicago* (Summer 2018): 3.

[64]   Nancy Tuchman, "Where Faith Meets Science," *Loyola: The Magazine of Loyola University Chicago* (Summer 2018): 26.

[65]   Ibid., 27.

Another name for consciousness of the whole is contemplative conscious-ness. It is also ecological consciousness understood as awareness of and sensitivity to the interconnectedness of all beings and things on earth. Here we see the connection between ecology and contemplation: they both involved consciousness of the whole. Contemplation is a manner of seeing: holistic seeing. Ecology is a manner of thinking and acting: holistic thinking and acting.[66]

Consecrated life must steep itself in these contemplative depths. This is part of what I call *integral religious life.* We are called to incorporate our ways of being and seeing in the way we pray, live community, and serve in ministry. The prophetic call requires a mysticism of open eyes and, as Cardinal Walter Kasper says, a mysticism of "helping hands."[67] This brings us again to the mystical-prophetic call,[68] a call to personal conversion, internal transformation, and external revitalization.

In these examples we see how the abundance of God, coupled with an under-standing of the realities of the people and earth, affect the evolution of our charisms. This unitive sentiment is also found in Pope Francis's 2018 World Day of Peace Prayer: "The wisdom of faith fosters a contemplative gaze that recognizes that all of us belong to one family, migrants and the local populations that welcome them, and all have the same right to enjoy the goods of the earth, whose destination is universal, as the social doctrine of the Church teaches. It is here that solidarity and sharing are founded."[69]

It is clear that the Earth community needs a change of attitude and action that stems from our depths. Nothing else can withstand the urge around us to consume, waste, and live for today. Our common home requires a depth of conversion that will change our attitude and actions from the inside out. This can come from external events that pull our interior lives into a new place, or it can come from interior movements that change how we see and do everything.

Religious life is first and foremost a call to see as God sees—in our prayer, community, and ministry. This is the conversion we are called to, for we all belong to one another.

Reconciliation and Peacebuilding

Peacebuilding is often confused with peacemaking and peacekeeping. There are key differences between these words we often use interchangeably. Sulak Sivaraksa offers helpful distinctions as she looks at the practices of peace:

---

[66]   Samuel H. Canilang, CMF, "Mercy, Care for the Earth, and Religious Life: A Biblio-Theological Study and Reflection," *Institute for Consecrated Life in Asia* 19, nos. 2–3 (September 2017): 57.

[67]   Walter Kasper, *Pope Francis' Revolution of Tenderness and Love: Theological and Pastoral Perspectives* (Mahwah, NJ: Paulist Press, 2015), 46.

[68]   Canilang, "Mercy, Care for the Earth, and Religious Life," 53.

[69]   Pope Francis, 2018 World Day of Peace Prayer (3). Pope Francis quotes here from Pope Benedict XVI's 2011 Message for the World Day of Peace, https://w2.vatican.va.

Peacemaking means keeping people from attacking each other. It is the process of forging a settlement between belligerent sides. *Peace building* refers to the entire range of long-term approaches to developing peaceful communities and societies based on principles of coexistence, tolerance, justice, and equal opportunity. *Peacekeeping* diminishes the most acute conflagrations of violence, and seems to attract the most attention but is a bit like fire-fighting. It's necessary to put out the fire of violence by keeping the peace, but it is much better if we can prevent the fire from starting. This is where peace building comes in.[70]

Most religious will not be involved in either peacemaking or peacekeeping. Peacebuilding, however, is absolutely within the call of religious life. In fact, how we build community within our congregations and among the people of God can either build or erode peace. Our ministries build peace to the extent that we engage difference with dignity and as part of the expected building up of the Reign of God. This is more than coexistence and tolerance. Peacebuilding is community building into a new creation. Peacebuilding is about integral religious life; all areas are included. So many economic, political, environmental, and social conditions are making it clear that something is being asked of us. We must also work with present realities, and peacebuilding is essential in this effort.

Many of the infrastructures religious created over the past centuries contributed to peacebuilding, such as education, health care, social services, and spiritual accompaniment. Done well and with the intention to build communion, these ministries have served a long-term presence for good. Today we must look to see if we are where the Spirit's gift of charism calls us to go. We must be where God longs to build peace through us. We must always look at how our institutions participate in sin, resist social sin, and how they, too, can become a new creation. Peacebuilding also requires creating spaces for reconciliation. As people of faith, one of the realities calling to us is the woundedness we find in our brothers and sisters everywhere. Aware that God is the healer, we can put ourselves in place to assist. The call is to all of us: "All of this is from God, who has reconciled us to God through Christ, and has given us the ministry of reconciliation; that is, in Christ God was reconciling the world to himself."[71]

How are we to do this? Through relationships built over time through our prayer, community, and ministry. We must distinguish forgiveness from reconciliation. To forgive someone for an offense means that you have let go of the wrong done to you.[72] To forgive someone does not mean the same thing as to

---

[70]   Sulak Sivaraksa, *Conflict, Culture, Change: Engaged Buddhism in a Globalizing World* (Boston: Wisdom, 2005), 9.

[71]   2 Cor 5:18.

[72]   Jesus taught much about forgiveness: We regularly pray in the Lord's Prayer, that Jesus taught his disciples: "and forgive us our debts, as we also have forgiven our debtors" (Mt 6:12). Jesus also went on to explain: "For if you forgive others their trespasses, your heavenly Father will forgive your trespasses," (Mt 6:14–15). And in Mark 11:25: "When-

reconcile with someone. When two people are reconciled, a new relationship begins, an estrangement is healed. Sometimes we forgive the wrong done to us, but for any number of reasons do not or cannot begin again. In our communities, congregations, and world we are called to be ministers of reconciliation, walking with persons and groups on the road to Emmaus, a space of new understanding and peace. We can do so when we are aware of our own journey to Emmaus and have known the Risen Christ listening to us, sitting with us, asking us questions, helping us reframe our narratives or create a new narrative. In the breaking of the bread with the stranger the disciples recognized the Risen Christ. We are invited to see all within Paschal Mystery. Then we are able to respond to the Risen Christ's question, "Do you love me?" with a "Yes" to feeding lambs, tending sheep, and loving neighbor and all of creation. This is what reconciliation offers.

I rely here on the work of Robert Schreiter, who has the theoretical, spiritual, and practical insights and experience to lead us in discovering reconciliation's distinctive elements and some resources for creating new reconciliation. Reconciliation is more about a spirituality than a strategy, as Schreiter asserts. The deepest work is spiritual and is thus necessarily assisted by our contemplative practices.

There are two kinds of reconciliation: vertical and horizontal.[73] Vertical reconciliation is concerned with being reconciled to God. God reaches out to wounded humanity and our graced yet sinful, wounded world in order to bring us, in Schreiter's words, "back into communion with God's very self through the action of Christ in the world. This action of Christ—especially in his suffering, death and resurrection—is definitive, even if not yet complete. It will only be complete when all things have been reconciled in Christ at the end of time, when 'God will be all in all'" (1 Cor 15:28).[74] It is vertical reconciliation that makes horizontal reconciliation possible.

Horizontal reconciliation takes place between persons, groups, and even with the earth. Schreiter offers five distinctive elements of Christian reconciliation.[75] In the next section, I use each as a stepping-off point for developing calls to religious life. As we look at this essential area of reconciliation, the mystical-prophetic dimensions become quite visible.

---

ever you stand praying, forgive, if you have anything against anyone, so that your Father in heaven may also forgive you your trespasses." See also Luke 11:2–4. From the cross, Jesus prayed for the soldiers who were crucifying him: "Father, forgive them; for they know not what they are doing" (Lk 23:34).

[73]   Robert Schreiter, CPPS, "Consecrated Life as a Reconciling Presence in the World," Archdiocesan Celebration of Consecrated Life Day, Chicago, February 19, 2011, 3, http://legacy.archchicago.org.

[74]   Ibid.

[75]   Ibid., 7–20.

Distinctive Elements of Christian Reconciliation

1. God initiates and brings about reconciliation.
2. God begins with the survivor.
3. God makes of both survivor and wrongdoer "a new creation" (2 Cor 5:17).
4. Christians pattern their suffering on the suffering, death, and resurrection of Jesus Christ.
5. Reconciliation is only complete when God has reconciled the whole world in Christ.[76]

1. We are reminded again and again that only God can bring about reconciliation.

The call to reconciliation and the ministry of reconciliation constitute an active call, which requires hard work. The wounds created by violence (physical, verbal, systemic, or personal) are often multifaceted and require a variety of responses. The pain cannot simply be willed away. Healing is needed, and this takes time. This process cannot even begin until the violence has stopped for a person, for a community, or for a country. Healing from genocide or a war cannot happen while the genocide or war continues. And even after the direct violence has ceased, people often need time to begin to live into another reality. Healing happens on each person's time. If we push too quickly, we can violate the person's healing process.

On some levels it is a bit easier working with individuals to discern where the person might be, rather than trying to get the pulse of a nation or even a congregation. Being attuned to the movements of God and open to the movements in individual persons as well as groups is essential.

One call of consecrated life in both personal and broader settings is to create and offer some safe, welcoming spaces. We can only do this as we ask to be attuned to God. We see again that our practices of prayer and contemplation must be part of the very fabric of our lives. If they are not, we may participate in re-wounding.

I personally came to understand this need for God to do the moving when my congregation experienced a traumatic loss. On July 17, 2014, Philomena (Phil) Tiernen, RSCJ, was on Malaysian Flight 17 from Europe en route to Australia when a Russian missile shot in the Ukraine brought down the jet, killing all aboard. I had only met Phil a few weeks earlier, at an international conference in England. She was amazing. Her piercing blue eyes were attentive and engaged from the moment we met. We had great conversations on religious life and on the Society of the Sacred Heart. At one point she told me I must come to Australia, for my energy and interests would be welcome. I said "of course," enthusiastically. When I later read an email explaining that Phil was on the Malaysian flight that had gone down, I was stunned. How could this be? I didn't know what to do, but Mass at the Passionist community down the street was at 7:30 that morning and I went there.

---

[76] Ibid.

I sought ritual, places of consolation and solace, and perhaps places where suffering is known.

For the next ten days, and before my retreat began, I wrote. I am not one to post a lot on Facebook, but I needed some way to respond to what was happening and to resist the evil that had happened. Almost every day I used one photo I had taken and offered a brief reflection that came from my own depths.[77] It was my way of working through the unimaginable toward the unknown next.[78] It cannot be emphasized too strongly that this entire process requires the virtue of contemplation.

I often think of reconciliation and peacebuilding work as very active, and it is. Yet Schreiter, my colleague at Catholic Theological Union who has decades of experience in forgiveness and reconciliation work, continually reminds us that the key to any such work is the practice of meditation. This work takes great patience, and Bob regularly tells students in his courses on forgiveness and reconciliation that if they want quick results, this is not the ministry for them.

> Contemplative prayer is particularly suited to the spirituality of reconciliation because it trains us to wait on God, to listen to God. It is a bit of a paradox that the most important part of our action for justice, peace and reconciliation is the one that is most non-active on our part. In learning this non-action we discover an important part of what being a "presence" is all about. Contemplative prayer and some of its near neighbors—such as recollection and centering prayer—are essential to being a reconciling presence.[79]

Peacebuilding requires the same contemplative stance.

2.   In reconciliation, God's healing begins with the survivor.

The concern is for the persons surviving—and for each person involved, including persons who perpetrated the crimes and their families. This is a call to consecrated life. We often think that the perpetrator must be present and repentant for reconciliation to happen. It is helpful when this is so. However, there are many times when the perpetrator is absent, dead, or unrepentant. The survivor must be the first focus. Healing means that the wrong done does not control the survivor, that the survivor can be freed from the poison of the trauma and not be continually under the thumb of the pain. This may be a process of years or even a lifetime. The journey may include looking periodically at areas that still need healing.

---

[77]   An edited version of these posts was later published as "Prayer in the Face of Incomprehensible Violence," in *Seeking the One Whom We Love: How RSCJ Pray*, ed. Kathleen Hughes, RSCJ, and Therese Fink Meyerhoff (St. Louis: Society of the Sacred Heart, 2016), 19–22.

[78]   It was years earlier that I experienced two other violent deaths, and so I think something deep within me must have known of the need to name and ritualize.

[79]   Schreiter, "Consecrated Life as a Reconciling Presence in the World," 9.

After the Rwandan genocide, work was begun with the families who lost loved ones and survived. There was also work with the persons who committed crimes and the families of perpetrators of crimes. If this work with perpetrators is not done, conditions will again surface for further atrocities. The women of Liberia knew this as they brought child soldiers back into the community after war.[80] The very same youth who had maimed and killed had nowhere to go after the war. Over time, and through a ritual the women created, the young men were brought back into the village.

As religious we can create spaces for the survivors to speak, to share their stories. Community as a door and destination is a sacred space. This means that as communities we also have to do our work within ourselves and with one another if we are to offer a space for healing. We must know ourselves, wounds and all.

3. God can make of both victim and wrongdoer "a new
    creation" (2 Cor 5:17).

God can change both survivors and wrongdoers. The process of reconciliation does not erase the past, but it helps one live differently in the present. The Resurrection stories are powerful in helping us see what new creation looks like. Peter cannot undo his denial of Jesus, yet in offering him breakfast, the Risen Christ begins the relationship again. His conversation with Peter also changes the relationship.

> When they had finished breakfast, Jesus said to Simon Peter, "Simon son of John, do you love me more than these?" He said to him, "Yes, Lord; you know that I love you." Jesus said to him, "Feed my lambs." A second time he said to him, "Simon son of John, do you love me?" He said to him, "Yes, Lord; you know that I love you." Jesus said to him, "Tend my sheep." He said to him the third time, "Simon son of John, do you love me?" Peter felt hurt because he said to him the third time, "Do you love me?" And he said to him, "Lord, you know everything; you know that I love you." Jesus said to him, "Feed my sheep."[81]

Biblical scholars point out that when Jesus asks Peter "Do you love me?" three times, this mirrors Peter's three denials of Jesus. With the lens of reconciliation, what we see here is Jesus asking a very fundamental, vulnerable, and tender question: "Do you love me?" We might imagine the deep pain in Peter as he answers that question again and again and yet again. The question is that of someone who loves and wants to know where the other is now on the other side of trauma. The

---

80 John Paul Lederach and Angela Jill Lederach, *When Blood and Bones Cry Out: Journeys through the Soundscape of Healing and Reconciliation* (New York: Oxford University Press, 2010), 147–69.

81 Jn 21:15–18.

past is not erased, but the present allows for sufficient love and relationship for Peter to go forth.

This passage also can speak to the survivor of a trauma. To hear from the one who also suffered and died, "Do you love me?" is an invitation to love again. Some survivors may have felt abandonment or God's absence in the midst of their suffering. That is normal, understandable, and quite painful. At some point this passage may serve as an invitation outward toward relationship again. The call to feed and tend sheep moves one outward again, out of one's own pain. It can be an invitation to care for others and engage in the world to prevent harm and build peace. We see here a connection between reconciliation and peacebuilding.

When people share stories of the moment they could let go of what held them bound, it is powerful. Often telling the story results in a different way of being in the world. And sometimes this experience has moved in them as a call. The experience becomes a lens through which someone serves, directly or indirectly.

Religious communities can assist in the process of healing by creating spaces for people who walk this journey. Religious life can hold such spaces. Churches can also offer this, though when the institution or those who represent it are responsible for trauma, they are not safe spaces. If a congregation includes members who have abused or traumatized others, those spaces may not serve. Sometimes when members of congregations have themselves suffered trauma, these can be healing spaces for all. Sensitivity is needed in all these spaces. Finding or offering spaces in our ministries can be a great service.

4.   Christians pattern their suffering on the suffering, death, and resurrection of Jesus.

Narratives are important. How we tell the story of our lives makes a difference. Suffering can easily isolate us and disconnect us from others who are not suffering. Suffering can also make us feel that no one else could understand. The Paschal Mystery of Jesus offers another possibility. The post-Resurrection appearances offer us hope. The disciples on the way to Emmaus had a narrative that was painful and left them with questions and grief. The stranger walking with them began to reframe the narrative, not with any denial of what happened, but with a wider view. The larger story of who Jesus was and is, and the reports from the women to whom Jesus appeared, could then begin to make some sense. When the stranger broke and blessed the bread that evening, the ritual sparked the memory, and the larger picture was revealed. It was then that they could return to Jerusalem, the place of suffering and death. One could imagine the scene after the Risen Christ disappeared—chairs strewn, food and drink left on the table—showing what a difference this new narrative made. They returned to the community, even back to the place of crucifixion, because the crucifixion was neither the end nor the whole of the story.

As religious we can create and be spaces where the survivors' narratives can be heard, reheard, and transformed.

5. Reconciliation will only be truly complete when
    all is reconciled in Christ.

Reconciliation is a long process. It takes time. And even when we think we have reconciled and "moved on," there are moments or triggers that can take us back to that space of woundedness. This is another opportunity for healing one more place in us. We do know from experience and survivors' narratives that healing can happen and that reconciliation is possible. This is why it is absolutely essential to share narratives of reconciliation. That sharing opens us up to more than we realize when we are close to trauma, our own or that of others. We need hope, ever mindful that this is a result of openness on the part of another person to be present to our pain, and we also need God's grace.

Reconciliation is about creating new relationships—with oneself, with others, and with God. Let us look a bit further into how we in consecrated life can participate in this process. We will look at: (1) imagination and creativity, (2) attending to wounds, (3) enlarging the community of participants, (4) yeasting, (5) ritual, and (6) the role of the arts.

Calling upon Consecrated Life

Imagination and Creativity

The work of Mennonite John Paul Lederach is particularly helpful. He tells us that if we are to see what new things are possible, we must cultivate a moral imagination, which allows us to see possibilities in what exists at the present.[82] According to Lederach, this includes cultivating, through practice, the following capacities:[83]

- *The capacity to imagine ourselves in a web of relationships that includes our enemies.* What we can even begin to imagine has a better chance of happening than what is impossible. This is God's work, helping us go from impossible to imaginable. Still, we need to pray for openness here. How we pray and for whom we pray (including enemies) is important. I must admit that often I pray for those with whom I am in conflict. When I can do so, I can imagine more peace between us. So it is with healing.

- *The ability to sustain a paradoxical curiosity that embraces complexity without reliance on dualistic polarity.* To be curious about someone's actions or responses means there is room for the other to offer me something I do not have, e.g., an understanding that eludes me. I can even refrain from saying "I'm right and you're wrong," and try instead to see wisdom from another perspective. This is different than dismissing a topic

---

[82] John Paul Lederach, *The Moral Imagination: The Art and Soul of Building Peace* (New York: Oxford University Press, 2005), ix.

[83] Ibid., 5. I am using and engaging these categories in the light of consecrated life.

with the oft-used refrain, "It's complicated," and instead looking into the complexity for the strains of truth. If I can see something from another's perspective, I can communicate my ideas toward a goal we may actually have in common. For example, if people can see that all parties want a better future for their children, all might be able to see ways forward differently.

- *The fundamental belief in and pursuit of the creative act.* Reconciliation must believe that something new (beyond the conflict) can emerge. Reconciliation work seeks what cannot yet be imagined: a way through. When Queen Elizabeth II visited Ireland in 2011, it created a new way forward between the Irish and English. The visit was replete with symbolic gestures that pointed to possibilities. As religious, the call to us is also to "find ways to create spaces and processes pregnant with the moral imagination."[84] Sometimes creating spaces and times for silence as well as sharing can open up ideas from our consciousness waiting to be born. This is also what it means to "Wake up the world!" with new ways of being and relating.

- *Acceptance of the inherent risk of stepping into the mystery of the unknown that lies beyond the far-too-familiar landscape of violence.*[85] Anytime we try to find another way, we risk failure. We also risk success. If there is no risk, there is no reason to think that the violence will change. There is always a risk in reaching out for the new, but its beauty may take us beyond the boundaries of what we have experienced. This is also the work of peacebuilding.

Tending to Wounds

Reconciliation and peacebuilding require acknowledging that we are a wounded people and that attending to our woundedness is a process. Nothing about this is short-term. The better we know ourselves, the better we can serve church and community. Wounds, whether from relationships, loss, violence, systemic injustice, or other pain and suffering, need acknowledgment and healing.

Within the Christian tradition we have ways to move through woundedness. Stories abound about Jesus healing in the Gospels. Jesus's desire is to point our healing toward faith, toward God. We have a God who also knew wounds of an extreme kind: torture and crucifixion. In the post-Resurrection appearances Jesus's wounds are visible. Wounds can heal, but the scars do not disappear.

Schreiter offers an interesting lens from which to view Jesus's own processing of his wounds and his own healing, as seen in the post-Resurrection passages.[86] In John, the first post-Resurrection appearance is to Mary and the women. Jesus

---

[84]   Ibid., 61.

[85]   Ibid., 5, 39, 62–63.

[86]   This was offered by Schreiter during a lecture in one of his classes on Forgiveness and Reconciliation at Catholic Theological Union.

appears, but says, "Do not touch me."[87] What if Jesus could not yet bear to be touched so close to the time of his torture and crucifixion? In the second appearance Jesus shows his wounds, the episode bookended by saying "Peace be with you."[88] One might wonder if the Risen Christ is trying to give the apostles courage by showing his own wounds—not simply so they recognize him, but also to convey that there is life after such suffering. Finally, Jesus appears to Thomas and invites him to put his hand in Jesus's side. Schreiter suggests this is the point at which Jesus acknowledged what happened to him and used it to help another believe in a future.

Many of our congregations have a response to woundedness or suffering as part of their mission. In my own Sacred Heart tradition, the pierced heart is both an image of suffering and life-giving love poured out to the end. The call is found in our Constitution, which states that: "The pierced Heart of Jesus opens our being to the depths of God and to the anguish of humankind" (Const. §8). The pierced heart of Jesus frames our spirituality and engagement with the wounded world.

Scripture scholar Barbara Bowe, RSCJ, beautifully describes this process of responding to woundedness from the depths of one's spirituality:

> At the depths of our spirituality we are compelled to respond to suffering in any and every way we can, both by trying to alleviate human pain and by working to change the sinful structures that deprive so many of the basic necessities of life. At the moment of Jesus' death in the gospel of John, when the soldier pierced Jesus' side, John tells us that "blood and water flowed out" (John 19:34). The multiple layers of symbolism in this text speak first of the total outpouring of Jesus' life given in love. But this scene also holds deep and resonant allusions to the life-giving waters that flowed out of the new temple envisioned by the prophet Ezekiel (Ezek 47:1–12). Those waters, remember, began as a trickle, grew to a river, and finally became a raging torrent of life-giving water. The blood and water flowing from Jesus' side also conjure up the waters flowing out of the Heavenly City in the book of Revelation (Rev 22:1–2), the waters that bring life and nourishment to the barren desert. And, finally, this scene in John's passion story suggests images of birth, of the outpouring of sacramental life, and of the everlasting waters that cleanse and give new life. The pierced heart is both an image of suffering and life-giving love poured out to the end.

As such, it invites us into woundedness—our own and that of our world. The open heart of Christ invites us to come with our woundedness and find solace and rest. The pierced heart of Christ invites us to come with our woundedness, to be with it, to feel the piercing, invasion, betrayal, discouragement, deep pain of our lives—not in a masochistic way, not to remain there, but to know that in feeling the pain, it can be

---

[87] Jn 20:17.

[88] Ibid.

transformed through love, through grace, through healing waters—of friends, of tears, of inner sources of life—into life.

And many of us discover that the precise place of our woundedness (abandonment—emotional or physical; abuse—emotional or physical; isolation—emotional or physical; dependency or co-dependency, etc.) becomes the place of our call—of our mission, the place not only for our own healing, but the source of our reaching out to others—not to convert the world, but because we have been there, we have been healed and those healing waters flow through us of their own power to others. Yes, blood and water flow out.[89]

You can see what a rich resource woundedness is to find in one's spirituality, in Scripture, and in the Constitutions grounding and moving us. The resources of spirituality, Scripture, and Constitutions strengthen us and give us courage to take on the realities in our midst.

This is happening in my province of the Religious of the Sacred Heart of Jesus as we are confronting a history of slavery. This began as we prepared for a bicentennial to celebrate the women who came in 1818 and made the Religious of the Sacred Heart an international congregation in the United States. It has become an impetus to acknowledge the enslavement of peoples that was part of the early history of the sisters here. One hope in the midst of encountering this difficult part of our story is that it may contribute in some small way to opening up and healing the wound of historical and persistent racism in the United States. This wound is deep, but if such efforts can open up spaces for the conversion needed, we must answer the call to make these efforts.

Including All

In the work of peacemaking in our world, women's roles are still underrecognized. As theologian Jeannine Hill Fletcher writes:

Many religious communities[90] continue to prioritize male leadership, to the exclusion of women in the most public interfaith roles, including interreligious dialogues and peacemaking. By looking at diverse models of interfaith work, this article highlights the alternative spaces in which women have been agents of peacemaking and peacebuilding. If "interreligious peacemaking" is conceptualized as complex actors embedded in localized material, social and political realities struggling across religious

---

[89] Barbara Bowe, RSCJ, "Sacred Heart Spirituality Today," meeting with RSCJ and associates, April 1–3, 2005 (unpublished talk).

[90] Hill Fletcher is speaking here not of religious life but of faith communities in general.

lines in the promotion of human well-being, then we might see more clearly women already at work.[91]

Women are in local areas among the people. Women are involved in the societal and political structures and realities in need of transformation. Women work for human well-being in areas that encompass child care, education, legislation, public service, and more.

Hill Fletcher's words remind us that all are needed in all areas of building peace, keeping peace, making peace, and in the work of reconciliation. The gender gap here is another opportunity for men and women religious to work together and to model another way of furthering the Reign of God. Our work at valuing difference of cultures must include valuing the gifts that women bring, including all areas of service toward reconciliation and peacebuilding. All are needed for the building of the Reign of God today. Church and government institutions need this conversion and transformation in structures.

Critical Yeast and Transformation

Peacebuilding and reconciliation require time and space. At times, members of religious orders may look at the great needs around them and wonder if they have the capacity to do what is needed. While I cover widening of our charisms in the next chapter, John Paul Lederach offers some wisdom on transformation and critical yeast. He reminds us that like yeast in bread making, it is not large numbers of people but rather a small critical mass that is essential. Lederach speaks of the transformative power of "critical yeast." He reminds us that "a few strategically connected people have greater potential for creating the social growth of an idea or process than large numbers of people who think alike."[92]

He describes some of characteristics of yeast, which religious life also has the capacity to offer:

- Yeast has to move and mingle with others to have an impact.
- Yeast needs a warm, inviting, and safe environment.
- Yeast is kneaded and mixed into the mass and has the "capacity to generate growth."
- Yeast is not static or stationary but "constantly moves across a range of different processes and connections."[93]

---

[91]   Jeannine Hill Fletcher, "Who Speaks for Peace? Women and Interreligious Peacemaking," *Interreligious Studies and Intercultural Theology* 1, no. 1 (2017): 11.

[92]   Lederach, *Moral Imagination*, 92.

[93]   Ibid., 91–93.

These are all practices and dispositions that are part of consecrated life. Religious connect with others. We must be intentional with whom we connect and widen the circle. Our communities can offer hospitality and a safe space for persons to speak their truths, remember the dangerous memories of our Paschal Mystery, lament and hope, and risk anew. Intentionality in our ministries and skill-building, along with a contemplative presence, can, with God's grace and time, generate growth. This is what we believe, that our lives, given in love, can and do offer the Good News. Just as our vows are public, our lives are a public way of being present where healing is needed. Religious life can, and does, link across people, cultures, and geographies. Religious have traditionally been present both among those without resources and those with resources, those with power and those without power. These connections can serve as bridges, as invitations.

Our lives and ways of being with people, with intention, can engage the moral imagination into action for reconciliation and peacebuilding. We must be intentional about our ministries.

Rituals for Reconciliation and Peacebuilding

When great harm has been done, there must be a way to acknowledge what happened and that it was wrong, as well as to signal a new way forward. This is what scripture calls lament. We lament because we hope—we hope for more than what happened because we know we are more than what happened. There needs to be a way to hope, to imagine a world beyond the present situation. The tensions between lament and hope, harm and peace, are often built into rituals. Sometimes the rituals are separate and sometimes they are joined.

In 1995, Sr. Joanne Marie Mascha, OSU, was raped and murdered in the woods of the suburban Ursuline College and motherhouse campus in Pepper Pike, Ohio. Not many weeks later, on Holy Saturday, the sisters in her congregation gathered for a ritual. During the ritual each was invited, as she wished, to take pieces of incense and offer aloud or in silence the feelings she held and then to place that, together with their piece of incense, into the fire. This was an offering to God, of sorrow, grief, anger, and more. It was during this time that memories of another sister murdered fifteen years before came forth.[94] Both losses and sorrows surfaced in this ritual of lament.[95]

Pilgrimage is another way of ritualizing. In August 2018, Joanne Doi, MM, led a group of Maryknoll men, women, and associates, and other religious on a pilgrimage that both educated about and acknowledged the painful history of the Japanese internment camp in Manzanar, California. These rituals are to both name

---

[94]   I refer here to Dorothy Kazel, OSU, one of the four church women raped and murdered on December 2, 1980, in El Salvador.

[95]   The actions that flowed from the murder of Mascha included a call to fight the prosecutor's desire for the death penalty—and the sisters succeeded!

the truth of these spaces and to beseech God for inspiration for another way in the present and future.

The Arts as Resources for Reconciliation and Peacebuilding

The arts are a powerful resource for both reconciliation and peacebuilding. All of the senses are part of healing—and through these senses, the arts help us discern realities in our present and past. Artists and poets also help us imagine what we can't yet see. I offer a couple of examples.

My heritage is Slovenian; and in Slovenia there were many years of oppression during and after World War II and the subsequent Communist occupation. In recent years, Slovenian mosaic artist Marco Rupnik, SJ, created a mosaic in a chapel built near the site of a mass grave.[96] His mosaic acknowledges pain on all sides, including the earth's pain. Perhaps the most powerful image is that of an empty chair—depicting that there is space at some moment, God's moment, for even the perpetrators. Rupnik helps his people begin to image what many still do not talk about easily.

I offer a second example, this one related to images of the moral imagination in Korea. In the first week of February 2018 I was in Korea presenting talks about religious life and also spending time visiting my RSCJ sisters in that country and meeting many amazing religious men and women from various congregations. One evening I came home to find my sisters glued to the television set. They were watching the first North Korean athletes land on South Korean soil. It was moving, and it was what they clearly longed for, a united people. For all the political challenges that would still have to be traversed, there was hope.

The years of effort and the Olympic Games themselves offered an opportunity to imagine a united future. Some weeks later the leaders of North Korea and South Korea were walking across one another's soil with smiles on their faces. These images awakened the imaginations and hopes of the people in these countries.

So much is possible in the midst of the needs in our world today, and consecrated life is called to do our part to "Wake Up the World" with possibility rooted in hope, grounded in action, reaching out to all. It is to this "all" that I go next.

Questions for Reflection and Discussion

1. Where is your congregation responding? Where are YOU?
2. Where/what do you sense are the growing edges for your congregation? For you?
3. What is some of the new wine that is being generated in your geographical region or congregation?

---

[96]   See article by Mateja Gomboc, "Poročilo o romanju v Kočevski Rog," and photo of the mosaic at https://katoliska-cerkev.si.

10

WIDENING CHARISMS FOR THE SAKE OF THE CHURCH AND WORLD

As noted in Chapter 3, all baptized persons are called to be missionary disciples. According to Pope Francis, "Every Christian is a missionary to the extent that he or she has encountered the love of God in Christ Jesus: we no longer say that we are 'disciples' and 'missionaries,' but rather that we are always 'missionary disciples.'" Francis concludes by asking, "So what are we waiting for?"[1]

The mission of God impels us to proclaim the Good News, calling us forth to be what Pope Francis calls "missionary disciples." As Pope Francis reminds us, in this call we find ourselves in wonderful company. We are *all* to be about God's mission together, even as we have different vocations and life commitments. Within the Vatican II understanding of the church as the people of God, more and more laity[2] have trained for ministry in the church. In some ministries such as education, married and single persons were already working together, while in parishes new ministries evolved. The changes within religious life have also led women religious to discern ministries that earlier were not possible. For example, congregations whose ministerial focus was on formal education now discerned service in social service areas. Often these new ministries were at the peripheries of unmet needs. Much of this came forth as Vatican II also called congregations to go to their founding charisms and explore the depth and breadth of all areas of their religious life.

Since Vatican II much more ministry is done in collaboration with laity, religious men and women, and clergy. In some ministries where members of religious orders were the dominant presence, lay collaborators in mission are in leadership and in greater numbers than vowed religious. Programs offering "formation to mission" from a particular charism and spirituality abound in institutions that name themselves as Mercy, Franciscan, Salesian, Dominican, and more. This is, in part, a recognition that whereas religious orders once thought their presence would facilitate an understanding of their charism, intentionality is now needed to inculcate

---

[1]   Pope Francis, *Evangelii Gaudium* (*The Joy of the Gospel*), 120, http://w2.vatican.va. Hereinafter *EG*.

[2]   I am aware that women religious are also laity. I am seeking to find language that will name the single and married sisters and brothers in mission, and partners or collaborators in mission.

the particular charism into an institution with fewer members of the order in a ministry.[3] As individual members as well as congregations looked to the signs of the times and the calls of the charism, some stayed in current ministries, but others joined new ministries or created new ministry opportunities. Congregations, particularly leadership, needed to look at current ministries as well as new ministry calls and discern where congregational members and resources were to go. It was a dynamic and challenging time, with change in all areas of religious life.

More than fifty years after Vatican II, religious life is again at an important moment in which to look more intentionally at charism and calls with a vision of being in mission with others. The call to renewal and revitalization is coming not only from within consecrated life, but also from Pope Francis and the Congregation for Institutes of Consecrated Life and Societies of Apostolic Life (CICLSAL). In November 2018, CICLSAL, in a style consistent with Pope Francis's call to "Wake Up the World," invited consecrated life to imagine, from their charisms, spiritual heritages, and the contexts and realities, the call of the Gospel to consecrated life in the world today:

> The Gospel message cannot be reduced to something purely sociological. Rather, it is a spiritual guideline that is always new. It requires the open-mindedness to imagine prophetic and charismatic ways to live the *sequela* of Christ through suitable, and possibly unprecedented, frameworks. There is a whole range of innovative *diaconia* experienced outside of the usual schemes that must also find a place in new institutional structures. These structures must be able to measure up to expectations and challenges. A renewal process that cannot affect and change the structures, in addition to the hearts, will not produce real and lasting change.[4]

This call to follow Christ in this time will, once again, invite consecrated life to both familiar and unfamiliar paths. Because religious life is in partnership with others on this journey, this discernment happens within a vision of being in mission with many others. Although each religious order/institute must take on the responsibility for discernment and decision-making, the gifts of those on the journey with religious orders have a significant call in this process. In different roles, we are all together in mission.

This chapter looks more widely at the call of consecrated life to partner or collaborate for mission. Grounded in the Spirit's call to our charisms, we first

---

[3]   There are problems with this idea, of course. One might presume that only members of religious orders embody a charism. That is not true. At the same time, it is important to be intentional about regularly naming the charism that was part of the founding of an institution and seeing how the charism is living (or not) in real time.

[4]   Congregation for Institutes of Consecrated Life and Societies of Apostolic Life (CICLSAL), *New Wine in New Wineskins: The Consecrated Life and Its Ongoing Challenges since Vatican II* (Nairobi, Kenya: Paulines Publications Africa, 2017), no. 3.

consider what collaboration is already happening and what calls us anew within the wider "family" in which a congregation's charism lives. Some implications and challenges of collaboration will also be discussed. Second, I explore current collaboration for mission across charisms and ask what calls now. Third, I look at areas that could be models for future possibility where consecrated life is in partnership across religious traditions and/or in civic/public sectors. I look to where some of the new has emerged and where more longs to emerge.

Three theological lenses ground and guide this exploration of partnering for mission: (1) the Spirit guides this process; (2) a Trinitarian lens offers a way to be in partnership; and (3) the Gospel call moves us to the peripheries of need. Although these have been discussed in earlier chapters, there are points in each that are particularly salient here.

The Spirit Grounds, Guides, and Calls

Kirsteen Kim reminds us that "biblically, the terms 'Holy Spirit' and 'Spirit of God' are ways of talking about God's presence and activity in the world."[5] The Holy Spirit is a messenger of Good News, which is not always easy to hear—at times, we struggle to know what to do with such news. Four attributes of the Spirit, which we identified earlier, can assist us. The Spirit is (1) prophetic, (2) creative, (3) focused on Jesus Christ, and (4) free.

As *prophetic*, the Spirit both denounces where we have lost our way and points to a new way. The Spirit comes at times of crisis and endows women and men with her prophetic energy. Charisms have come into the church and world to continue building the Reign of God. The Spirit at the source of our charisms is *creative* and transformative. Sometimes letting go and surrendering are called for in order to make space for the new. Creativity is part of the Spirit's very essence. The *focus on Jesus Christ* is the grounding of the Spirit's movements to us in the gift of our charisms. Our way is the way of Jesus Christ. We encounter Jesus who teaches us by his life about the Reign of God and who we are as God's beloved. We are taught *how* to be as we respond. The Spirit leads us to participate in the Reign of God in our time. The Spirit is also *free* and *freeing*. Although our way is the way of Jesus Christ, the Spirit leads us across religious traditions and to all places where she dwells. The Spirit goes where the Spirit will. The Spirit is not bound by any one religious tradition but goes anywhere and everywhere. Our call is to follow the lead of the befriending Spirit.[6]

---

[5]   Kirsteen Kim, *The Holy Spirit in the World: A Global Conversation* (Maryknoll, NY: Orbis Books, 2007), 2.

[6]   *Gaudium et Spes*, 4.

The Triune God Teaches Us How to Be in Relationship

Roberto Goizueta reminds us that in the Trinity we learn about the "intrinsically and constitutively communal character of God."[7] Mercy Oduyoye sees the unity in diversity of the Trinity as a helpful model for relationships among individuals and the community. She notes that "we find the Persons in constant and perfect mutual relationship and we are reminded of the need for properly adjusted relationships in our human families, institutions, and nations."[8] Each person of the Trinity is distinct and yet equal.

Recall that using Trinitarian imagery, Catherine Mowry LaCugna also offers us an image of community and how we are to live: "We were created for the purpose of glorifying God by living in right relationship as Jesus Christ did, by becoming holy through the power of the Spirit of God, by existing as persons in communion with God and every other creature."[9] The way we are to relate brings us into community with all. Nontando Hadebe further illumines the implications of such community and communion. She writes that "to be made in the image of the Trinity means that relatedness, difference, equality, interdependence, and community define what it means to be human."[10] These descriptions offer us ways to see ourselves in God and to imagine how we can collaborate in mission.

The Gospel Call to Follow Jesus Brings Us to the Peripheries

Jesus of Nazareth knew himself as beloved, called to bring good news to the poor, proclaim release to prisoners, heal the lame and sick, give sight to the blind, and show us the way to follow him. He preached and lived love, forgiveness, and peace. He reminded us that the Reign of God is at hand, so we are to repent and believe the good news.[11] Jesus preached a message of love to all and welcomed the outcast, sick, poor, those possessed by demons, and all those without hope. Though tempted, he did not use power over another, but rather used his power simply to love. He taught by example, showing his disciples that their call is to serve, to wash feet, rather than to be served. His message and actions led to his torture and death. He loved unto death and was raised to new life, returning and reminding all that Love prevails.

---

[7]   Roberto S. Goizueta, *Caminemos con Jesús: Toward a Hispanic/Latino Theology of Accompaniment* (Maryknoll, NY: Orbis Books, 1995), 66.

[8]   Mercy Amba Oduyoye, *Hearing and Knowing: Theological Reflections on Christianity in Africa* (Maryknoll, NY: Orbis Books, 1986), 140.

[9]   Catherine Mowry LaCugna, *God for Us: Trinity and the Christian Life* (New York: HarperCollins, 1991), 319.

[10]   Nontando Hadebe, "Toward an *Ubuntu* Trinitarian Prophetic Theology: A Social Critique of Blindness to the Other," in *Living With(Out) Borders: Catholic Theological Ethics on the Migrations of Peoples*, ed. Agnes M. Brazal and María Teresa Dávila (Maryknoll, NY: Orbis Books, 2016), 214.

[11]   Mk 1:15.

The call continues for us to bring a message of love, hope, and peace by our presence, proclamation, and actions, to those on the margins. The call is to all the people of God, and this is particularly so for consecrated life. In the introduction to the Guidelines in *New Wine and New Wineskins*, we hear:

> The present Guidelines are situated within the context of "an exercise in *evangelical discernment*, wherein we strive to recognize"—in the light of the Spirit—"a call which God causes to resound in the historical situation itself. In this situation, and also through it, God calls"[12] the consecrated men and women of our own time, because "all of us are asked to obey his call to go forth from our own comfort zone in order to reach all the 'peripheries' in need of the light of the Gospel."[13]

Our locations and contexts determine where the peripheries are. The call of consecrated life is to preach the Good News *there*. Amid the many needs and cries, the Spirit of God leads and accompanies us. Led by the Triune God who teaches us about relationship, we are also led by the Spirit to respond where the Gospel is to be lived. This is a particularly inviting call as we consider the calls of charisms within our "family," across charisms, and in connection with the wider world, with all people of good will with whom we find common cause.

As mentioned earlier, working together across various vocations is not new. In *Vita Consecrata*, Pope John Paul II encouraged consecrated life in all its forms to "communion and cooperation with the laity":

> In recent years, one of the fruits of the teaching on the Church as communion has been the growing awareness that her members can and must unite their efforts, with a view to cooperation and exchange of gifts, in order to participate more effectively in the Church's mission. This helps to give a clearer and more complete picture of the Church herself, while rendering more effective the response to the great challenges of our time, thanks to the combined contributions of the various gifts.[14]

He notes both the spiritual and apostolic dimensions possible for combined contributions, dependent on the form of consecrated life.[15] He mentions both lay volunteers and associate programs and their participation in the spirituality and ministry in some forms of consecrated life. Over the past twenty years this participation has continued to grow.

---

12   *EG* 54.

13   *EG* 20; CICLSAL, *New Wine in New Wineskins*, Introduction.

14   Pope John Paul II, *Vita Consecrata* (March 25, 1996), 54, http://w2.vatican.va.

15   Contemplative orders, for example, would have apostolates that are different from those of ministerial or apostolic groups. Both have ministries, though they are different.

More is calling us in all vocational forms. A Spirit-led creativity asks us to see how we may respond to the cries of the world. The cries of this time also ask for ways to be and work together in the world so as to unite rather than divide, to bind rather than wound, to include rather than to exclude, to share rather than to be selfish. This requires grounding both in the core of who we are in God and as community. This is a call to transformation, interiorly and exteriorly, asking us to engage our religious imagination. Mennonite scholar and peacebuilder John Paul Lederach describes the religious imagination as "the capacity to imagine something rooted in the challenge of the real world yet capable of giving birth to that which does not yet exist."[16] It is this that moves us from possibility to what the Latin American liberation theologians call "possibilitizing," making words into action. As religious after Vatican II were called to be open-minded, so are we called today to have that same open-mindedness to imagine prophetic and charismatic ways to follow Christ. How is this possible? This is only possible through relationships. We are called to create in our relationships a weave strong and resilient enough so that no one will fall into the cracks, and so that the earth has time to heal. We are called to create webs of relationship that will ultimately encompass all persons and all creation. Now I offer three ways to weave this fabric for our time and world, in three areas that call consecrated life today.

Linking and Connecting with Our Charism "Family"

The Spirit is inviting our congregations to deepen relationships with our charism family members, those with whom we are connected through our spirituality and, often, our baptismal call, but not necessarily in vowed religious life. Much is possible when we invite the family to the shared table of imagining responses to current calls. Family members may include members of different congregations who have the same charism even if not the same founder. There may be a common spirituality that brings people together—for example, a number of congregations claim Ignatian roots and spirituality. In addition, various ministries work out of a particular Ignatian framework of discernment. Jesuit schools teach out of an Ignatian framework, and some students and collaborators in mission find that this is also their spirituality. These can all be members of the same "family." The opportunity in this is to imagine together what and how the Spirit is calling forth out of this charism to respond to the needs today. What is possible? So much!

Common Projects

I offer an example from my Sacred Heart charism. There are Sacred Heart schools all over the world, at every level from preschool to university. What if

---

[16] John Paul Lederach, *The Moral Imagination: The Art and Soul of Building Peace* (Oxford: Oxford University Press, 2005), ix.

members of the RSCJ family, through a discernment process coordinated by the international Justice, Peace, and Integrity of Creation (JPIC) Commission, discerned a call to insert ourselves in all areas relevant to water issues?

Imagine what could be possible with schools in different cities, countries, and continents, with students, faculty, and staff who would focus on this area for even five years. Imagine if parents, alums, associates, and boards of trustees were part of this effort? What if everyone in the family was asked to imagine and "possibilitize" and to communicate and share what groups are doing around the globe? The efforts would weave a network stretching around the world, omitting no part of the world.

This is a means of deepening local impacts in areas of need while engaging global efforts. The local areas could report, ask for, and offer assistance to other areas. Creative ventures could begin on a local level, and experimenting could yield results that would affect other areas. Learning about each area's social locations and looking at the analysis surrounding each issue could create abundant and fruitful links.

The projects could involve members of religious orders, but not necessarily. Leadership would be local even if there would need to be resources at the national and international level to communicate information and facilitate linking. What is possible would be beyond any one group and would likely flow over into the next two areas of linking: across charisms and with all in common cause.

Spiritual Life

Although consecrated life does not own a charism, it does have a responsibility to articulate it as well as to nurture the spiritual life of its family members. As families connect, the responsibility will be to continue to nurture the spiritual life of its members. In some families the religious orders will offer means for this to happen (i.e., via retreats and days of renewal). Increasingly, spiritual leadership will also come from collaborators in mission who are steeped and trained in the spiritual tradition. The Franciscan family, for example, has many women and men in all forms of life who are experienced in the Franciscan spiritual tradition.

Radical Availability

As mentioned in an earlier chapter, one of the markers of apostolic religious life is radical availability for the needs of the mission. Once that meant that people could be sent anywhere, regardless of whether the person had any skills or affinity for the particular ministry. This happens much less frequently in many congregations today. Today what is urgently needed are persons and congregations who are willing to go where the unmet needs exist, provided there is resonance with the charism. One of the challenges is that congregations may already have ministries and locations where they have a significant history and relationship. Some ministries that were once begun out of an urgent need have become institutionalized in the congregation. This in one way is understandable and often represents a personnel and fiscal commitment. The question is always whether there is still room in the congregation for the emerging needs and cries of God and God's creation.

A way to engage emerging needs may be to look at the wider family and ask whether our current ministries require the continued involvement of congregational members or even whether the family can or should continue the ministry.[17] If there is no freedom to respond to emergent needs, the congregation must ask why. At the same time, the urgent need could also be considered from the family lens to see what is possible. *New Wine in New Wineskins* reminds us that "new poverties question the conscience of many consecrated persons and press traditional charisms to respond in new and generous ways to these new situations and the new rejects of history. Out of this reality new forms of presence and ministries in many existential peripheries have blossomed."[18]

An old saying in the Maryknoll family about the time frame of ministry is: *"We went where we were needed but not wanted and we left when we were wanted but not needed."* The question today is whether where we are still serves an urgent need or whether we are called "in new and generous ways to these new situations and the new rejects of history."[19] This calls us to let go of comfort zones for the sake of others. We do not need to go alone, nor should we, for we have a family and an even wider set of communities.

Interculturality

When a family brings together the diversity of all the members, something new can emerge. Interculturality has roots in groups honoring and engaging their differences in order to see anew what is calling. Whether it is a new way of praying, communicating, celebrating, or ministering, these are the growing edges and potentialities that can enrich us and the world around us. We each bring gifts to the table of encounter. This brings us to the edges of newness, where the Spirit thrives.

Massive Unrealized Potential

Much is happening in consecrated life today, yet I sense there is still massive unrealized potential[20] in partnering and collaboration between religious and members of the wider family. Families need to find ways to share what each hears from the Spirit. Sometimes those not in vowed religious life are a bit reticent to

---

[17]   This does not eliminate the need for regular discernment on ministries as to whether the unmet need has been met. If yes, does the ministry continue? If yes, who will continue it?

[18]   CICLSAL, *New Wine*, no. 7.

[19]   Ibid.

[20]   Ann Marie Sanders, IHM, "Solidarity with African Women Religious," *Review for Religious* 62, no. 1 (2003): 90–95.

speak, yet this is to the detriment of the whole. When collaboration is sought, religious congregations must publicly ask for dialogue and have courageous conversations for the sake of God's mission. Each group in the family will have to determine how to live out a call.

Religious orders must discern their congregational calls, but they do so far more integrally when there are opportunities to hear from the wider community. The call is not for associates to take on all the commitments of religious congregations. Associates must live their charism call in their particular vocation. Yet more is possible when the individual and collective wisdom can be shared in processes that model mutuality and equality. Prophetic dialogue can happen in a safe atmosphere that allows for respectful, nuanced conversation that can move people to action for the common good. More is possible with encounter and dialogue on areas of challenge and need. There are roles and responsibilities within each call, but much more is possible together.

Risks

There are inherent risks. To open consecrated life to the wider family members means that the gifts offered can be in the form of challenges and invitations to engage in ways not recognized by members in consecrated life. Our lives, from vows to community and to ministry, can be offered as a mirror and invitation to greater depths. Years ago, a friend read a congregation's mission statement and challenged the sponsored university's social justice work. At another Catholic university students called into question the investment portfolios of the school based on both the catholicity of the institution and the mission of the sponsoring institution's religious order. If we truly desire to model collaboration and partnership, this means that the partners in the conversation must have a voice and a seat at the table. This does not mean that the religious order cedes its responsibility for living the charism as a congregation. It does mean that we can be moved, influenced, and fully engaged for the sake of promoting the Reign of God. If this is the telos, we are called to be obedient, listening for the Spirit who can work anywhere and anytime. We risk wonderful transformation!

But we also risk that perspectives at the table may not be in the majority in our forms of consecrated life. When women are at the table of a men's congregation, or the reverse, and respectfully engage one another, it is an incredible witness for the church and world. Generations that are not part of the majority group can offer helpful lenses on external calls and internal cries for depth of living and responding for today.

The risk is a gift. Discernment can be transformed, and all may learn more about how to engage the Spirit's calls as a community. Bringing in voices from diverse backgrounds who stretch and challenge us beyond our imaginings is risking new life. These efforts, intentionally communicated with the wider communities, affect our efforts and witness to needed hope in our world.

Linking across Charisms Locally and Globally

We must find ways to connect with one another across charisms from our common charism of religious life. Many congregations began their own particular ministries and lived a way of life they called their own (e.g., Sisters of Notre Dame, Companions of Jesus, Sisters of the Holy Names of Jesus and Mary, Clerics of St. Viator, Passionists), even as others may participate in the ministries.[21] This didn't mean that the congregations had no connections. There was a practice, for example, of congregations offering hospitality to religious newcomers when they began a new foundation (e.g., Ursuline Sisters in New Orleans welcomed the Religious of the Sacred Heart in 1818). For the most part religious orders worked in their separate ministries in addition to living and praying separately. This was the dominant model for many religious orders until the time of Vatican II.

There were some exceptions, though, which began networks that would grow in the years to come. In the United States in 1954 the Sisters Formation Conference (now known as the Religious Formation Conference) began in order to address needs for initial and ongoing formation in religious life.[22] The bulletins that came out before, during, and after Vatican II included articles by key figures from the council, including Yves Congar, OP, and Bernard Häring, CSsR. This situated women religious well to begin the renewal called for by Vatican II.

There has been greater collaboration among religious congregations in the years since Vatican II, though more among women than among men. In the United States, women religious began some collaborative ventures in educational and justice projects. Some congregations of women religious with NGO status at the United Nations joined together as one NGO to utilize their members' resources and to galvanize the possibilities together as one. A number also have representatives from the wider family on staff or as representatives.

The time we currently live in asks us to do more creating and ministering together. Some impressive examples are already happening. Cristo Rey, an educational initiative for high school students from families from underserved, low-income communities, was begun by Jesuits in 1996. The classroom education is college preparatory, and students also spend five days a month working at a local business; this in turn helps to defray the students' tuition costs. Two years later, at an International Christian Brothers meeting, members were challenged

---

[21] There are, of course, always exceptions, such as the Marianists, which began under the leadership of their founder, Fr. William Joseph Chaminade, with the formation of sodalities, lay faith communities of men and women, and then added brothers and priests, followed by sisters. Within a few years the Sisters of Mary Immaculate (Marianist Sisters) and the men's apostolic community, the Society of Mary, were founded. See the Marianist website at https://www.marianist.com.

[22] See Dawn Cherie Araujo, "Religious Formation Conference Marks 60 Years of Dramatic Change," *Global Sisters Report*, September 24, 2014. Print issue headline: "A Passion for Formation," September 26–October 9, 2014.

to find creative ways to educate and otherwise serve students from low-income backgrounds. The example of the Cristo Rey program was considered, and then an initiative of the Christian Brothers was begun to serve the needs of students in their areas. In 2000 the Cristo Rey Network[23] was begun. Over the course of more than twenty years, various congregations replicated the model and brought in their own charisms. St. Martin de Porres High School[24] in Cleveland, Ohio, was created as a joint project of two congregations who serve as endorsing communities: the Midwest Province of the Society of Jesus, a congregation of men, and the Sisters of the Humility of Mary. The administration is lay-led. Cristo Rey St. Martin College Prep[25] in Waukegan, Illinois, is another example, endorsed by the Clerics of St. Viator and the Sinsinawa Dominican Sisters. Congregations are working across charisms for the sake of mission.

Some congregations creatively and collaboratively respond to a need in a way no one group alone could do. Guadalupe Regional Middle School[26] in Brownsville, Texas, close to the US–Mexico border, is an example. Sponsored by the Congregation of Christian Brothers, the Marist Brothers of the Schools, and the Sisters of the Incarnate Word and Blessed Sacrament, this tuition-free Catholic middle school is part of the Nativity Miguel Network of Schools modeled on the Nativity model of education begun by the Jesuits.[27]

There are international examples as well. The Solidarity with South Sudan project was created in 2008. Their mission statement explains:

> Solidarity with South Sudan aims to create self-sustainable educational, health and pastoral institutions and programs that will help to empower South Sudanese people to build a just and peaceful society. Solidarity is a collaborative commitment of religious institutes of men and women, members of the Union of Superiors General and the Church in South Sudan working in partnership with the Sudan Catholic Bishops' Conference.[28]

Over 260 congregations have participated since it began. Talitha Kum is another international and intercongregational project. Begun in 2009, it is an international network of women and men religious working against human trafficking.[29] Talitha Kum is a project of the International Union of Superiors General (UISG) in collaboration with the Union of Superiors General.

---

[23]   See https://www.cristoreynetwork.org.

[24]   See https://www.saintmartincleveland.org.

[25]   See https://www.cristoreystmartin.org.

[26]   See http://www.guadalupeprep.org.

[27]   Gary Long, "Guadalupe Regional Middle School Celebrates 10 Years of Providing Catholic Education," *Brownsville Herald*, August 23, 2011, https://www.brownsvilleherald.com.

[28]   Further information may be found at www.solidarityssudan.org.

[29]   Further information may be found at www.talithakum.info.

On the southern border of Italy, UISG also coordinated an effort called Migrant Project/Sicily. The evolution and configuration are described in this way:

> The Migrant Project/Sicily was born from a question asked by two women religious, JPIC coordinators in their respective communities: after the massacre of Lampedusa, what can we, Consecrated Women, do to respond to the urgent cry of the migrants? This question found an immediate echo among the members of the Executive Committee of the UISG who were asking themselves what sort of concrete solidarity project could be launched on the occasion of the celebration of the Jubilee of UISG (1965–2015).
>
> Upon receiving this proposal, many Superiors General responded enthusiastically: some sent sisters to be a part of the project, others offered economic resources.
>
> The project, on the invitation of Bishop Franco Montenegro of the Archdiocese of Agrigento and with the support of Bishop Calogero Peri, bishop of Caltagirone, provides for the establishment of an intercongregational, international and intercultural community, residing in three houses, one in Ramacca (diocese of Caltagirone), one in Caltanissetta and another in Agrigento where they will "be a bridge between the migrants who come ashore in Sicily and the people of the area, in order to build a true integration." The sisters involved represent different congregations, different charisms making themselves available to the dioceses of Agrigento, Caltanissetta and Caltagirone, at the service of migrants.[30]

It is important to note how much this is a collaborative project, linking migrants, sisters, local churches, and the people of the area. This is crucial, particularly the linking between the migrants and the local people, for it serves as a form of bridge-building. Sr. Elisabetta Flick, SA, who is responsible for the project, offers a bit more detail on the role of the sisters:

> We go on tip-toe, respecting the richness of listening to the needs in order to then build, together with our local partners, an ad-hoc project that respects the rights and dignity of those arriving in our country. We wish to be a credible witness that it is possible for different cultures, nationalities and languages to live together, if we are united by a common mission and moved by the one Spirit who acts and is present in each of us and in the world.[31]

These models serve well as examples for engaging efforts across religious traditions and among all people of good will. This does not mean this model is the end result. This is the role of religious life today—to listen, see, reflect, engage,

---

[30]   See http://www.internationalunionsuperiorsgeneral.org. After a period of formation that took place in Rome in October and November 2015, the sisters arrived in Sicily on December 14, 2015.

[31]   See http://www.internationalunionsuperiorsgeneral.org.

collaborate, and continue creatively. This is also about creating relationships among congregations and people in need of refuge, very much in tune with Pope Francis's call to "welcome, protect, promote and integrate" migrants and refugees.[32]

Role of Leadership

Congregational leadership is crucial to efforts to engage what is calling. If leaders are not innovative thinkers, they must be connected to those who are, whether by relationship, membership, or access to information. The time we currently live in calls for agility, and leadership must know how to balance planning efforts with emergent processing. Agility asks for more conversations and connections across all groups, as well as quicker response times. The principle of subsidiarity needs room to work even as communication among all groups needs to increase for responsive efforts to happen as needs emerge.

When the different groups that represent consecrated life work together, so much is possible even amid transition, risk-taking, and new ventures. We hear this on more than one level in CICLSAL's *New Wine in New Wineskins*: "It has become increasingly necessary to have a ministry of leadership that can promote a true synodality that nourishes dynamic synergy. Only through this communion of intention will it be possible to manage transitions with patience, wisdom and foresight."[33]

There is a vibrancy in places where the gifts of different charisms and of the wider community can be offered. Religious in various regions are also increasingly working in ministries with multiple charisms, offering their gift for the whole. Catholic Theological Union, the graduate school of theology where I minister, was begun in 1968 as an effort among several congregations of male religious to join charisms in theological education. Soon laity were welcomed, and the table of learning now includes married and single women and men, religious brothers, and women religious. Today the institution has as its gift a concert of charisms in which all come together as a model of what is possible.

How do we do this? Together. In today's world we must publicly witness to this kind of collaboration and solidarity. While for some in society the focus is on divisiveness and competition, our Gospel mandate is to proclaim another way. This moves us to a discussion about joining our charisms to common cause efforts in society and among religious traditions.

Joining Our Charisms to Widen Global and Local Efforts in the World Today

We know that the work of consecrated life is one effort among many. The call today is to find ways to work together with all people of good will. The church reminds us of the many ways that consecrated life has and continues to benefit

---

[32]   See Pope Francis's Message for the 104th World Day of Migrants and Refugees 2018, http://w2.vatican.va.

[33]   CICLSAL, *New Wine in New Wineskins*, no. 8.

greatly when in collaboration with the wider church and the world. Again, from *New Wine in New Wineskins*:

> Not to be forgotten are the proliferation of volunteer initiatives in which laity and religious, men and women, are involved in a rich synergy of "renewed apostolic dynamism,"[34] thus "rendering more effective the response to the great challenges of our time, thanks to the combined contribution of the various gifts."[35] A similar symphony is based on the rediscovery of the common baptism shared by the disciples of Christ who are called to unite their strengths and imagination to make this world more beautiful and liveable for all.[36]

A powerful example of such an initiative began in anticipation of the so-called "caravan" of migrants coming to the United States–Mexico border in late 2018. On the US side there were calls to religious congregations for volunteers and donations. Volunteers were needed to welcome persons who came into the United States, and who were then detained, and later released. Volunteers were needed to translate, serve food, connect migrants with family members in the United States, and transport persons to buses. The notice went to religious congregations. A few congregations had ministries at the border, but many did not. Connections were made not only with religious orders but with social service organizations run by different ecumenical and secular groups. As a few at a time came from different religious orders, so did associate members of religious orders and other persons from faith-based organizations. Many people came for a short time; others stayed longer. Organizing happened at the local level and was communicated to LCWR (Leadership Conference of Women Religious) and to social media outlets such as *National Catholic Reporter* and *Global Sisters Report*. The intention was to share accurate accounts of what was happening on the ground so that the truth was told.

This is an example of what response looks like today: agile, smaller groups linked together at the peripheries, supported by congregations and social media, and in collaboration with the wider justice communities. Small groups are effective because they are linked. In some ways consecrated life can serve as yeast: as a necessary ingredient linking to common cause efforts in the world. Pope Francis, using the image of yeast, reminds us that our role is not to be massive but intentional: "Our congregations were not born to be the mass, but a bit of salt and yeast which would have given their own contribution so that the mass grows; so that the People of God have that 'condiment' they were missing."[37] The pope goes

---

[34]   Pope John Paul II, *Vita Consecrata*, 55.

[35]   Ibid., 54.

[36]   CICLSAL, *New Wine in New Wineskins*, no. 7.

[37]   During his trip to Milan in March 2017, Pope Francis told the diocese's priests and religious not to fear the challenges that come with their ministry nor the increasing number of empty convents, urging them instead to focus on the core of their mission:

on to encourage creativity that can move people toward the Reign of God.

All of this reminds us of what peacebuilder John Paul Lederach spoke of in the preceding chapter—the transformative power of critical yeast. Yeast is an image that resonates with the calls for consecrated life today and our collaboration with others.[38]

Indeed a call to religious life today is for us to form partnerships with those in common cause. We can be mobile. We can create spaces where people are able to be silent, speak, heal, feel acceptance, care, and be cared for. Community can indeed become a doorway and a destination. The focus is not on ourselves but on advancing the Reign of God. Creativity and agility are critical for us to respond to the needs of ministry and community.

It remains to be seen whether consecrated life was yeast in response to migrants or whether we added a particular faith-life ingredient to what was being created. Sometimes others are the yeast and religious life offers another ingredient. All ingredients are necessary. Examples of both abound. I offer a few more to galvanize our imaginations.

The International Union of Superiors General (UISG) consists of the congregational leaders of women's religious congregations. UISG is based in Rome and is developing an international network to connect and support religious working in the field of migration. This effort is impressive in its integrative approach—the project will ultimately be able to not only connect religious but also to connect all people working in migration. This is a fine example of leadership[39] that can organize resources and then free groups and persons to develop further connections. The goals of this UISG effort to reach out to efforts around the world with support, education, and linking are instructive. UISG clearly states that it is working to establish an international network connecting congregations that work in the field of migration:

- To share information about migrants, refugees, displaced peoples;
- To develop reflection processes on the phenomenon of migration and to explore the implication for formation and education within religious congregations;
- To discover and to get to know what is already in place: the responses already implemented by congregations;
- To listen to people working directly with migrants, to learn from them especially from their experiences in the field; to work hand in hand with them and to offer mutual support;

---

bringing Christ to his people. See Elise Harris's article, "Don't Fret about Numbers, But Your Mission, Pope Tells Milan Religious," March 25, 2017, Catholic News Agency: https://www.catholicnewsagency.com.

38   Lederach, *Moral Imagination*, 93.

39   Sr. Patricia Murray, IBVM, is Secretary General of UISG for this and other innovative projects. It is interesting to note is that she also created the Solidarity with South Sudan program and was its first director.

- To link sisters working in sending countries with those involved in countries of arrival;
- To pool and offer resources;
- To start a small platform in order to offer formation and advice through resource persons already identified;
- To raise awareness among congregations and their institutions, about the need to take the growing multicultural dimension of our contemporary globalized world into account;
- To encourage and coordinate reflection on these new challenges and responses;
- To stimulate the creation of new intercongregational projects in different parts of the world at the service of migrants;
- To strengthen cooperation with international, civil, and religious organizations and educational institutions working in the field of migration.[40]

The UISG website notes that this project "aims to provide mutual support for religious at an international level," that it will "be at the service of the congregations that wish to avail themselves of it," and that it will "help to answer the new challenges of migration in the twenty-first century."[41] Ultimately this will serve as a network for all who are working with migrants and all who would hear a call to this ministry. It serves as both an organizing set of strands and at the same time as yeast that can bring together all those working with a group on the margins.

The following are a few additional examples.

The Healing Earth Project

The Healing Earth Project is a free online textbook for secondary school students, college students, and adult learners. It is a global online community of ethical analysis, spiritual reflection, and action for attending to all the areas that Pope Francis names in *Laudato Si'*. It is an interactive space, with articles from all over the world. It is a joint global venture. Unlike any other environmental science textbook, *Healing Earth* presents an integrated, global, and living approach to the ecological challenges we face on our extraordinary planet.[42] A Jesuit initiative, it is meant to launch a new process and project that is a response to a deep need. The scholars and teachers from around the globe are all committed to the tenets of *Laudato Si'*. This is the kind of collaborative initiative needed today. Although one group or institution is needed to create a space to begin this project, it can

---

[40]   See http://www.internationalunionsuperiorsgeneral.org.

[41]   Ibid.

[42]   See https://healingearth.ijep.net. The website notes: "We invite teachers around the world to use this resource in their classrooms and share their experience with us. *Healing Earth* is an ongoing project, so we hope that everyone—teachers, young students, adult learners—will join us in using and improving *Healing Earth*."

only work at an international level. Connections need to be made not only among Jesuits but among all people in common cause responding to the cries of the earth. Nothing like this can be done alone; it is always a group effort, even as leaders are needed to begin and to maintain open spaces for creativity. Fiscal resources are certainly necessary, and it is equally essential to bring together key people who can move toward what is needed. People with skills to meet a need and people of creativity are both essential, and building relationships is key. There are many areas of need and communities must always discern among those needs.

The PREDA Foundation

The PREDA Foundation begins in the Philippines but stretches beyond its borders. Columbans, formally known as the Missionary Society of St. Columban, are drawn by the call to be pilgrims for Christ and engage the mission of Jesus in the world around them. Columban priest Shay Cullen, SSC, is an example of someone who embodies engaging one's charism for the needs of his time and whose efforts spark and point to hope where there was little. I met him in the Philippines in January 2018. The challenges of the world in which he found himself led Cullen to create the PREDA Foundation[43] in 1975. The ministry is described as follows:

> The People's Recovery Empowerment and Development Assistance (PREDA) Foundation Inc. is an active social development organization today with 63 professional Filipino employees implementing projects that save children from sexual abusers, and from life in the brothels and sex bars frequented by Filipino men and foreigners of all nationalities. It saves children from jails and detention centers and gives them a new life of dignity and self-esteem. It advocates for human rights and educates the communities.[44]

In many ways this is a modern day rendering of the story of Jesus's mission in the Gospel of Luke: "The Spirit of the Lord is upon me, because he has anointed me to bring good news to the poor. He has sent me to proclaim release to the captives and recovery of sight to the blind, to let the oppressed go free, to proclaim the year of the Lord's favor."[45]

PREDA has international volunteers serving and learning about the systems and structures that create such pain as well as engaging the young people seeking to heal from trauma. PREDA is yeast, activating justice work around the globe, including new generations skilled and motivated to serve those on the margins and creating just structures for living with human dignity. Cullen has a regular newsletter and is working with other countries to eliminate the trafficking of young

---

[43]   See http://www.preda.org.

[44]   Ibid.

[45]   Lk 4:18–19.

people. He was a key person responsible for closing down brothels in the town near where he ministers.

The response to needs is less important than who leads. We can and must take turns leading, accompanying, and following. While speaking of the role of bishop, Pope Francis makes an apt analogy to leadership for consecrated life today. In *The Joy of the Gospel* he writes:

> The bishop must always foster this missionary communion in his diocesan Church, following the ideal of the first Christian communities, in which the believers were of one heart and one soul (cf. *Acts* 4:32). To do so, he will sometimes go before his people, pointing the way and keeping their hope vibrant. At other times, he will simply be in their midst with his unassuming and merciful presence. At yet other times, he will have to walk after them, helping those who lag behind and—above all—allowing the flock to strike out on new paths.[46]

Engaging Systems

I offer one more example that combines direct engagement with systemically addressing unmet needs. The call to risk, to be creative, is bearing fruit and we can see what is possible in linking with others.

The common desire to transform society and systems can bring together a wide international higher education community together in economics. Understanding the truth in *Laudato Si'* that "we are faced with not two separate crises, one environmental and the other social, but rather one complex crisis which is both social and environmental,"[47] a group of international Jesuit scholars and colleagues wrote a report titled *Justice in the Global Economy: Building Sustainable and Inclusive Communities* (2016).[48] Scholar Gerry O'Hanlon, SJ, writes that the report "urges us to pool our resources in order to retrieve a vision of the common good, in which solidarity is a defining characteristic."[49] O'Hanlon describes the Spirit-led prophetic call to name what is wrong with the system and work to change it. The challenge is *how*. O'Hanlon offers three ideas. The first step is engaging in communal discernment, asking for the freedom to discern well. Second, he suggests a "harnessing of our Jesuit resources at an institutional (primarily university) level, in coopera-

---

[46] I'm grateful to Steve Bevans for noting this example! Pope Francis, *Joy of the Gospel*, 31.

[47] Pope Francis, *Laudato Si' (On Care for Our Common Home)* (2015), 139, http://w2.vatican.va.

[48] Social Justice and Ecology Secretariat, Task Force on Economy, *Justice in the Global Economy: Building Sustainable and Inclusive Communities* 1, no. 121 (2016), http://www.sjweb.info.

[49] Gerry O'Hanlon, SJ, "The Winter of Our Discontent: A View from Europe," *Conversations on Jesuit Higher Education* 52 (Fall 2017): 42.

tion with others, believers and non-believers, so as to think through the causes of our present crisis and to begin to imagine an alternative economic and social paradigm."[50] Finally, O'Hanlon tells us that we must resist "the temptation to hopelessness, helplessness and apathy."[51]

To collaborate with others, including those outside of our faith traditions, with groups with whom we share common cause and values is imperative. The way in which we collaborate shall model the respectful dialogue indicative of the inherent dignity of each person.

Collaboration and Partnering

These are all ambitious projects, and they must be, for much is at stake. What makes this type of project possible is the collaboration and partnering among groups of people within religious life, within their particular charism families, and intentionally partnering with those whose projects have a Gospel vision. God's creation is good. Partnering with goodness leaves us hopeful.

Questions for Reflection and Discussion

1. How might an unmet need be met in your "family"?
2. In your context, where do you see some further possibilities for inter-congregational efforts?
3. Where have you seen efforts between interfaith or ecumenical religious groups?
4. What would be some further areas of engagement with all people of good will in common cause? Between religious congregations and secular society?
5. Where have you seen emerging areas, growing and inviting edges?
6. How might the Good News in these areas be better communicated?

---

50   Ibid., 43.
51   Ibid.

Index